First published 1931
Reprinted 1966

CRITICISM

AND OTHER ADDRESSES

By

SIR JOSIAH STAMP, G.B.E.

Fellow of the British Academy

Essay Index Reprint Series

BOOKS FOR LIBRARIES PRESS, IN

FREEPORT, NEW YORK

CONTENTS

8   *Contents*

PREFACE

This volume mainly comprises the chief addresses I have given on general and non-technical subjects during the past two years. Their acceptability depended, I imagine, less upon any intrinsic qualities than upon the spirit of the occasion, and I realise, with some apprehension, that, as reproduced here, they may have lost their main support. In the case of those that were not prepared in detail beforehand, I have relied upon the verbatim reports and have not attempted to modify the form of free and conversational address that is often the only medium in which speaker and hearers are comfortable on many topics in this day. From a number of speeches and addresses prior to 1929, devoted to current problems, I have also taken several where the interest was not entirely ephemeral, and where some principle of general public value was specially illustrated by the facts of the day. But I have excluded from this collection speeches and articles of a statistical and definitely financial character, and those dealing with the popular presentation of facts and principles connected with the social consequences of changes in prices and the gold standard; and to my correspondents who ask for references to these over the past ten years, and for reasons for modifications of view, I can only promise that an attempt will be made, when opportunity offers, to put forward a similar collection dealing with these subjects.

In the nature of the case, I have been unable to avoid some overlapping and some repetition, while, in at least one instance, the inclusion of an address has been entirely on account of my American friends and their appreciation.

I could not have attempted this compilation but for the generous assistance of my daughter-in-law, Mrs. Wilfrid Stamp, B.A., in seeing the matter through the press, and also for the characteristic courage of Sir Ernest Benn.

J. C. STAMP.

I

CRITICISM AND SCHOLARSHIP[1]

The motto of University College, Aberystwyth, is "Nid byd byd heb Wybodaeth" (The world is nothing but knowledge). Certainly there is no world for us, in a pragmatic sense, but the world that affects our senses and minds and that we ourselves can consciously affect – the real world for us is the world of which we have knowledge. And all knowledge is some view of the world as it has been and now is. The growth of knowledge in each of us is the growth of our world. A small and poverty-stricken knowledge is a small and poor world, and a small and poor life. Rival philosophies turn upon the implications of this outlook, but they are not our thought to-night. Those who think of scholarship and the acquisition of learning as merely a preparation for life miss half the truth – it is life itself, because it is a view of the world and a relation to it. Those who think of scholarship as a mental training for something which is not scholarship, a series of relatively useless exercises for mental analysis which have afterwards to be applied to tasks of real significance, certainly go very far astray. College life may be fitting us for life's work, but it is certainly also fitting us for life's leisure. In some ways that work is only a means to an end – incomes are to be secured in order that they may be spent. True, no man will do his main business well unless he treats it as an end in itself and enjoys it. But, however he succeeds, he will fail in life if, in the leisure he has won, he has

[1] Commemoration Oration at King's College, London University, December 12th, 1929.

no command of the world, in art, music, literature, languages, and spiritual ideals. There are two acid tests of education. The first is: Does it fit us for leisure as well as for work? Does it pervade idleness as well as activity? And the second is: Does it grow by what it feeds on? Is it a state or a process?

The essentials of such a high scholarship are, I think, the power to acquire facts and to classify them; the power to appreciate principles, and to apply them for ourselves; the nice perception of differences, understanding the nature of evidence and proof in the different fields of thought; the judgment of rival issues compounded of facts and principles in conflict, and of incomplete evidential supports. The process of acquiring scholarship is a blend of receptivity and activity. Activity of mind is of two kinds, critical and constructive. The constructive outlook asks new questions, finds new facts, classifies them in a hundred ways to find new principles, puts principles to many new tests, and achieves a positive theory or scheme of action. The critical outlook takes some interpretation and construction of the world as presented to it, checks the facts involved, brings up other facts it has ignored, reapplies the principles in different connections, and shows that a general assertion may have only a particular application. It sifts the evidence. In particular it applies certain canons of rightness or goodness and determines how far there is conformity with them. My subject is *Criticism and Scholarship*.

When we say that such a one has a critical mind, we imply that he has much better mental powers of criticism than of construction – that he can pull to pieces, but cannot build up. When we say that such a one is very critical, we often suggest that he is censorious, and better at finding fault with things than occasions for praise and appreciation; so much so that, if a good opinion is wrung from him, we call it "praise indeed," as though it were some superior test or examination that had been passed. But we do him undue honour. The fact that a man can be habitually churlish in his mind is no reason for getting excited when he praises. There are those with minds just as discriminating, whose appreciation is just as well worth having, but who are not so parsimonious with it.

Criticism is a vital factor in our attitude to knowledge. It may be said that power to see what others are doing wrong is an essential preliminary to setting out ourselves to do right. But, unfortunately, so many stop at that preliminary, and never bother to "set out." The undiscerning, seeing great skill in the analysis of wrong, impute or infer great ability to be right. Because a man can cleverly tumble down a hero, he may get a reputation, for a time, as a likely successor.

We have all known those who have had great skill in answering such questions in English examination papers as: "Point out any error in the following sentences," or "Comment upon the style of the following passages." But we know that they have not always been the ones to produce a blameless and beautiful essay on "One of the following subjects." As the French proverb says, "Criticism is easy, and art is difficult." In marking papers on economics and political science, how often have I seen that the merest tyro can tell you what Ricardo did wrong, or recount a foolish heresy of John Stuart Mill! If, however, the question is not directed to defects, but runs "What was the constructive contribution of Ricardo or Mill to economic thought?" the answer is meagre indeed. Many people think they have satisfactorily dealt with a problem and *done* something when they have found out *who is to blame*. They exert much more energy on this quest than in taking the situation as it is and seeking the remedy. So many students get their whole initial interest

in a subject in quickly absorbing all the wrong
theories that have been held, and feeling very
superior to, and even sorry for, the poor intellects,
deceiving an earlier age, that had entertained such
notions. Often those students get no further. I have
known teachers in literature, history and economics,
philosophy, and even in geology and natural science,
who do not see the value of building up a genuine
hero-worship for great names in the minds of their
younger students as the first process of enthusiasm
for a subject. These views can be judiciously qualified
as time goes on, and a critical discrimination exercised. They prefer to show their own superiority
by displaying the feet of clay and pointing out the
warts. Their lectures are cynical, spirited, and attractive; but they are ill-adapted to create the feeling
that the subject is a high vocation for a life purpose.
If I had to place a young and unformed mind into
its new university environment, I would let its first
years be those of warm and hardly discriminating
enthusiasms and intellectual generosities – an outlook to life that is positive and absorbing. I should
dread the lecture-rooms that are like baths of corro-
sive acid. I dread the false note of destruction and
disillusionment and hero-murder to the eager seeker
after knowledge.

Isaac D'Israeli said "the defects of great men are
the consolation of the dunces." The naughtiness of
saints and the fallibilities of greatness always have an
appeal to raw intelligences and lazy spirits. I suppose
they flatter our own weaknesses and for a moment we
feel kin. But the loftiness of main purpose and the
weight of main achievement should prevail, and, if
criticism fails to keep inspiration and enthuse new
effort, it is no friend of scholarship.

Speaking to students who seek the verdict of ex-
aminers in literature, in history, in the moral and
mental sciences, I may say that several distinctions
clearly exist in mental calibre, which often find

objective reality in the lists. It may be said that, other things being equal, a competent knowledge of facts must command a third class; a critical knowledge of facts, with an ability to compare and select and to move freely among them, is a definite second class; the constructive ability to evolve original ideas and build upon the facts demands a first. But these are built one upon the other and are not alternatives. Criticism involves knowledge. It is no substitute for it. It is well that the student should be acquainted quite early with Macaulay's faults as an historian, but that is no reason why he should know nothing more about the greatness of his work, and sneer at his purple patches as though they were something an undergraduate could do quite well himself if he wished, but to which he has the grace and wisdom to rise superior. If you resolve to steep yourself in Carlyle's virtues before you swallow all the nonsense about his personal character, then some of that rubbish will choke you.

The words "criticism" and "critic" have had many meanings, and we still shift almost unconsciously from one to the other. To Shakespeare, the critic was inimical to love. "A very beadle to a humorous sigh – A critic, nay, a night-watch constable." You know that unnecessary criticism in the home circle is not always the best way to be loved as a companion. Yet Dr. Johnson was flattered when Miss Cholmondely told him he was the best critic in the world. He gallantly rejoined that nobody in the world could judge like her of the merit of a critic (Letter to Mrs. Thrale, 1780). We must glance at some of these suggestions and learn as we go.

In the latest "best seller," *The Art of Thinking*, Dimnet says:

Criticising is only another aspect of the effort to comprehend. The word in its etymology means "to judge," and, in fact, we think of a critic as a competent, not a carping, judge. The capacity to resist oral or printed affirmations, to have one's own opinion about an idea, a poem, a doctrine, or a work of art, and to see it clearly enough to give it forcible expression is an exception. Most people suspend their judgment till somebody else has expressed his own, and then repeat it.

In the first instance, according to Dryden, who was called by Johnson, "The Father of English criticism," criticism has a definite bias in favour of praise: "Criticism, as it was first instituted by Aristotle, meant a standard of judging well; the *chiefest* part of which is to observe those excellencies which should delight a reasonable reader." But a contemporary of Dryden's exclaims: "How strangely some words lose their primitive sense! By critick was originally understood a good judge; with us, nowadays, it signifies no more than a fault-finder." A real effort at some restoration of the higher connotation came nearer to our own times. Matthew Arnold says, "I am bound by my own definition of criticism, a disinterested endeavour to learn and propagate the best that is known and thought in the world," and Dowden, in his *Literary Studies*, "The effort of criticism in our time has been to see things as they are, *without partiality*, without obtrusion of personal liking or disliking." The nice balance of opinion is put even more pointedly by Arthur Symons, who gave no place to the positive duties of appreciation: "The aim of criticism is to distinguish what is essential in the work of a writer. It is the delight of a critic to praise, but praise is scarcely part of his duty. . . . What we ask of him is that he should find out for us more than we can find out for ourselves."

These repeated recoveries of meaning in the word "criticism" are not paralleled when we come to the *critic*. As popularly understood, he is not an admirer. When you meet your critics face to face, you do not expect a love feast. When you need comfort and a little wholesome self-deception to carry you through a rainy day, you do not seek him out. In character the critic varies, from an ill-natured fellow, revelling in giving pain, to a regrettable necessity like quinine. Let us look at the charges against him. He is a creature who delights to hurt (according to the *Oxford Dictionary*). Said Dekker in 1606, in *Newes from Hell*: "Take heed of critics; they bite like fish at anything, especially at bookes." And the literary folk are those who, perhaps, have suffered from spite for spite's sake more than any other. Certainly they are themselves given to full criticism of the critic. Peter Pindar refers to them as "proud to find faults and raptured with defect!" The critic does his job with disquieting gusto—"Each line shall stab, shall blast, like daggers and like fire" (Johnson). Then he is one who has himself made a mess of the things he professes to judge so skilfully. Disraeli knew something about the class when he said, "You know who the critics are? The men who have failed in literature and art." But the commoner gibe is that the critic has not even attempted to do anything at the trade himself – as the proverb says, "he is a mere brusher of other men's clothes." Byron's complaint was that

> A man must serve his time to every trade,
> Save censurers – critics all are ready made.

Concerning the very general idea that a man has no right to criticise unless he can himself perform, I might say much. The measure of truth in it is overborne completely by the practical disadvantages that would follow.

> Let such teach others who themselves excel,
> And censure freely who have written well,

said Pope; and it is a very healthy reaction to the

characteristic lack of humility in the fault-finders and the critical that, whether they do ill or do nothing, we should occasionally demand something from them. If music pleases us, we resent, a little, the complaisance of the companion who says so often, "I may not be able to play myself, but I *do* know what is good." Pliny rebuked the blacksmith criticising music, "Do you not perceive that you are speaking beyond your hammer?"

> If four play whist,
>   And one look on,
> They make blunders,
>   He makes none.

It is, perhaps, this instinct that gives rise to the present vogue for having newspaper criticisms by first-hand experts—the retired Rugby international or Test-match hero to write of the doings of his successors. It is fortunate if the supreme performer is also a supreme exponent. But often genius or great talent hardly knows its own processes; it conquers in spite of its defects, and has no gift of analysis and little of presentation. More than once a great and original scientist has been a poor lecturer, and the knack of making things simple to the unlearned has not been an attribute of the most creative minds. Exposition is a separate gift, and may be separately cultivated. The great truth-seeker is most concerned with truth as it leaves his own brain; the great teacher or critic with the truth as it reaches the minds of others. It does not follow, therefore, that a man who has been a fine performer will be a fine critic, but no fine critic is the worse for having some experience of performance – indeed, he must continually challenge his own competence. The born critic who can dispense with all personal experience is no doubt a fact, so far as criticism is an art, but his natural skill is limited to one field, and in all others he is as frail as the rest of us, and has no more peculiar rights. To know where the difficulties are, and from personal experience, is to appreciate the skill of others in avoiding or overcoming them. Our sprightly little friend, in *Gentlemen Prefer Blondes*, uttered a great truth when she said, "I thought a girl was really more reformed if she knew what it was to be unreformed than if she was born reformed and never really knew that was the matter with her." I do not see how I could really appraise the work of our local philharmonic society in their rendering of the *Messiah* or the *Dream of Gerontius* if I had not myself, a dozen times, been rescued from missing or messing a difficult lead only by the superior skill or alertness of my neighbour. Hazlitt declared: "We do not say that a man, to be a critic, must necessarily be a poet. But, to be a good critic, he ought not to be a bad poet." Have you not observed that the onlooker at the football-match who is shouting most vociferously, "Shoot, you fool, shoot," or who groans and cat-calls when a pass is missed, is seldom a fine athletic type? He is usually a white-faced, unhealthy-looking specimen who never shot a goal or took a pass in his life. Condemnation is mitigated by the reflection that he is at least as vociferous in hero-worship as abuse.

As to the right to criticise where we cannot perform, much depends on the reason for criticism. If it is to inform and clarify our own minds, and if we are not so unduly vocal as to provoke the criticism "armchair critic," then we are the gainers and no one is damaged. If we have to be outspoken when we cannot ourselves execute, it is the nicest test of the gentlemanly instinct. I do not mean that we must "wreathe the rod of criticism with roses" or praise with faint damns, but a modest sincerity will meet the case. An adverse judgment can be given more in sorrow than in triumph.

The importance of public criticism is so great, and

many of you will soon be teachers, preachers, or writers called upon to play your part, that I would not pass it by in silence.

In reviewing published work, different canons apply to style and to matter, for one is largely a matter of personality, of taste and fashion, whereas the other is truth or falsehood, misunderstanding or vision, careful and faithful workmanship or slipshod and shoddy.

The commonest feature of bad reviewing is the trick of imputing to the author a purpose or plan which he never intended, and then showing triumphantly that he has not achieved it. The first aim of just criticism is as Pope said:

> In every work regard the writer's end,
> Since none can compass more than they intend;
> And if the means be just, the conduct true,
> Applause, in spite of trivial faults, is due.

You may fairly say the author ought to have aimed at a different object—that he is misguided in spending time on what does not matter, but you may not misrepresent his intentions in order to score off a failure you have manufactured. So many people who have cultivated a taste for sermons only like one kind —some idealised form that they have invented— and they will condemn what does not touch that model. They forget that each preacher does his best in his own medium, of simple, popular exposition, of weighty learning, of personal experience, of logical analysis, of humour and irony. They forget he has to appeal to many different types of mind, and what is one man's meat is another man's poison, and that he has to deal with many subjects and problems, each with its most appropriate medium. Old Herbert pleases me much when he says:

> Judge not the preacher. . . . Do not grudge

> To pick out treasures from an earthern pot.
> The worst speak something good; if all want sense,
> God takes a text, and preacheth patience.

The second vice of criticism is to lack proportion; to be more offended by transgression of rules or conventions than pleased by constructive contribution to pleasure and wisdom. What do you think of a man, reading a work of great force and beauty, who proceeds, angrily and because of a split infinitive, to bang down the book in disgust? Hazlitt calls "ultra-crepidarian critics" those who find faults with small and insignificant details.

One of the worst charges against the critic is that he is a foe to genius and gives the constructive and creative life so much a fit of the nerves that it falls short of its best work. The critic is, therefore, said to be a bromide, and even a spoiler.

Dr. Johnson wrote: "There is a certain race of men that either imagine it their duty, or make it their amusement, to hinder the reception of every work of learning or genius, who stand as *sentinels in the avenues of fame*, and value themselves upon giving ignorance and envy the first notice of a prey." And Byron seems to have had the echo of this in his mind in the line: "Those cut-throat bandits in the paths of fame."

The history of literature is full of the bad effect of inhibition, of the "peculiar sensitiveness technically called 'criticophobia'" which has possessed the mind of nearly every great author. Some, indeed, of the sterner sort, or in the sterner moment, have bid defiance to his wiles and his gibes, and, like Scott, "Count not the critic's smile nor dread his frown." In Miss Browning's prayer to the good God to pardon all good men, she includes the

> Good critics who have stamped out poet's hope.

The risks of unjust criticism or ignorant criticism

are twofold: first, in this effect upon the mind of the producer, in damming up the flow of his creative spirit, and depriving the world of new conception; and, second, in spoiling the currency and purpose of what he has already done. The Romans did not cultivate the pseudo-Christian virtue of enheartenment of authors, but they had this practical outlook. Quintillian, the Roman critic, said: "Judgment on men of such eminence should, however, be pronounced with diffidence and consideration, lest, as happens to many, the critics should condemn what they do not understand."

It has happened, however, that work that might have fallen into oblivion has been preserved for ever by the eminence of the critic. I doubt if any but the curious in literature would know to-day of Robert Montgomery's poem, "Omnipresence of the Deity," if Macaulay had not immortalised it by tearing it to pieces. We may have a worse fate than attracting the notice of a great critic, as with the man who used to boast that he had been kicked by George the Third.

But my main preoccupation is with the function of criticism as an exercise or faculty of your own minds in the acquisition of scholarship and of mental power. First, as regards the work of others, criticism, not for publication, but for your own good, and criticism of criticism itself. Second, as regards your own work, the criticism by others, and, most valuable of all, criticism by yourself.

The best constructive and creative work is done under emotion, enthusiasm, penetration, and freedom from restraint. You should not think of negatives while you are at work. Your subconscious mind may do a good deal for you in keeping you right, but never do your work under the influence of negatives; never think you are producing good work when you are avoiding mistakes. Such an attitude of mind will cramp the best style. Your work might avoid every solecism, every mistake, and might even achieve certain positive and manufactured excellencies which criticism demands, and yet finish up flat, stale, and unprofitable. You will remember that Lord Oxford told the story of the American girl who was scoffing at the Ten Commandments and said, "They don't tell you what you ought to do, and only put ideas into your head." No enthusiastic lover ever stopped to unsplit an infinitive! We have a certain admiration for Barrie's Sentimental Tommy, who lost the prize for the essay and dashed the hopes of his friends when he sat waiting for the inspiration of the single missing word that should exactly meet his artistic need. But I think that in practical life we should finish the essay with the best word we know, and come back to it later.

The work that has been done in this way should never be left there, but criticism should follow hard after – in the cold light of the next day, if you like – and then, without reducing the temperature too much or taking out contrasts of colour, unwarranted exaggerations can be removed, concessions can be made to the exceptions, the argument can be clarified, and the point of view of the other man can be met. Then, without having spoilt your creative faculties, when your critical ability has done its work with whatever detachment you are capable of, then comes the candid friend, the tutor, the fellow student, or, most exacting of all upon human graces, some member of your own family! At this stage it is nice to get praise, but if you look for it you have not learned the secret of the contribution that criticism can make towards scholarship. Do not forget Blake's words: "Damn braces, praise relaxes." As to how much you accept of the criticism given will depend, further, on its equity and judgment as distinguished from bias. Your critic may not be worthy of you; he may not have your inspiration; he may have

his own axe to grind! If you are really in doubt as to
whether he has made out his case and you are likely
to be unjust to your own intellect, surely you can try
the criticism of another. It will be said that this is
going to a lot of work for no particular end if the
matter under discussion is not for public use or
publication. Not at all. You are forming your own
mental equipment or stock in trade, as a scholar,
and you are forming your own *power* as a scholar,
and ability to use it. Both of these are in the making;
and, in both, criticism is a vital factor. If I may be
personally reminiscent, I recall that for some years,
from the age of seventeen upwards, I wrote a critique
or review for my personal use, or for one or two
friends to see, of nearly every book I read. I did it
partly because I was appalled at the ephemeral nature
of one's recollections if they were not fixed by active
effort, but more because I desired to clarify my own
standards of judgment, and to force myself to see
wherein excellence consisted, and to re-think the
subject matter with the author's mind. It is extraordinary that in this private intellectual exercise one
says fewer cutting and unwarrantable things than if,
in the light of day, the dangerous rewards of intellectual smartness are to ensnare.

The constructive or creative must always be of
greater value to the world than the critical, not
merely because it is rarer, but also because the world
marches on by it. Nor does it much matter that
creative genius has little power to criticise either its
own work or that of others. What there may be
useless or impracticable about it will quickly be
exposed and cleared out by the army of critics. The
critics thus do most valuable work, but the value
depends on how it is done. Without its thoroughness
the genuine creator may discredit good work with
his admixture of bad, and even the good would not
survive. On the other hand, if it is too drastic, the
good may be discredited. It may even be inhibited.

Criticism is often the more pungent if it is indirect. In Bernard Shaw's political extravanganza, *The Apple Cart*, his picture of future political life is a caustic comment upon the present.

In some fields, constructive suggestion is faint or implied criticism of the *status quo*. When H. G. Wells writes on Utopia he criticises the present State and the present mentality. It is often suspected, however, that construction of Utopias, though clever, is safe, because there is no chance of a critical test. A simpler piece of original machinery actually made to work here and now is more convincing.

Finally, I may refer to the value which a critical habit of mind may have, not merely for scholarship itself, but also for the practical affairs of business life. The man who can look through things as they are, and see their defects and the possibility of amendment, in a business organisation is worth a high place. The remedy is then so obvious, when once the diagnosis is made, that constructive improvement follows without difficulty. But, for every four who think they can see, only one has really seized on improvement, for change often means a new set of defects or short-comings of a different kind, and "it may be better to suffer the ills we have, than fly to those we know not of." One hundred per cent. may be unattainable, and there may be several ways of making up ninety-five per cent. The choice between centralisation and decentralisation; between division of tasks by function and by locality; between the production of the mass and of the specialty; between cultivating freedom and initiative in subordinates and the safeties and public expectation of uniformities; between pleasing the old and attracting the new; between diffusion and concentration, – these are all nice discriminations in which something is always given up for something that is gained. And business life meets these choices every day, and a hundred others. Oftentimes the mind that can really look at familiar objects until they seem strange, as Mr. Chesterton advises, until those objects are actually seen instead of being suggested, is a mind of real critical power. It may also be constructive so far as revision of the existing scheme is concerned. But, presented with an entirely new problem, for which a scheme or plan is required, that same mind may be singularly ineffective and unproductive. Criticism is an essential feature of scholarship, both in scholarship itself and scholarship for life's activities. To evolve new principles from the data given, the data must be continually passed under review and criticised from new angles. To choose between rival theories, and especially rival programmes, the function of just criticism is of greatest value. Above all, out of the immense output of human minds, the choice of what is to be handed on, and what is to go into oblivion, is a real responsibility. It must be done with as much circumspection as the packing of a trunk for a long journey. As Santayana says, "Criticism is a serious and public function; it shows the race assimilating the individual, dividing the immortal from the mortal part of a soul." No man has done justice to the knowledge he absorbs unless he has taken something unimportant or unworthy out of it, or fitted it all into a new setting, and made a new relation. Criticism is a dynamic process – the good of one age is only the moderate of the next. " As the arts advance towards their perfection, the science of criticism advances with equal pace," said Burke. The new and the old have to live together, and the new becomes old in the flux of things, world without end. For I do not picture heaven as stagnation, and, if it is progressive, criticism must be the agency of change. Indeed, Christ himself taught what scholarship would then be. "Have ye understood all these things?" When they said "Yes," he replied: "Therefore every scribe " – that is, every university graduate – "which is instructed unto the Kingdom of Heaven is like unto a man that is a householder, which bringeth forth out of his treasure things *new and old*." Innovation and preservation are the two parents of the world of vital knowledge.

II

The college of a great university is one of the most striking groups produced by modern social life; its members may differ in practically everything – race, religion, politics, class, and age – but they are united intensively in one common purpose. That purpose is the acquisition of knowledge or definite outward indications of that acquisition – its certificates, diplomas, and degrees. But the moment one goes behind their common purpose there is again great diversity of motive, and they are seeking knowledge and its signs for many different reasons. Some frankly want a passport to a profession or a calling, either the ticket of entry at the lowest possible price, as one who is quite happy to scrape through a qualifying examination, or else they desire to be expert in that profession, as one who seeks, not merely the ticket of entry, but the skill and equipment to shine in his profession afterwards. Then there are those who have a desire for general prestige and distinction, which knowledge or its signs may confer. A third class present this aspect rather negatively, and a scholastic course is a by-product of the main object of distinction in sport. It may be the price of getting a Blue in the Rugger team that a course of study should be taken and a pass degree secured. Or it may be that in a certain social creed the absence of this particular scholastic achievement is a detriment. There is a fourth class, seeking knowledge because they have a thirst for it in detail – they are

[1] Foundation Oration at Birkbeck College, London University, December 11th, 1930.

born engineers, geologists, linguists, musicians, and they are sufficiently impelled by the love of the subject, and are relatively indifferent to the other motives. There is, perhaps, a fifth class, who are animated by the desire for general culture. They wish to make the best of their time, opportunities, and talents, though they are not stimulated by any inner *flair* or passion for a particular subject. In many these various motives are mixed ; in many they change from time to time. Quite clearly some motives are more utilitarian than others, but they are not less worthy for that.

This great institution, whose foundation we are commemorating to-day, must surely have an unusual proportion of students who have been pursuing knowledge not along its easiest paths. It is a more serious business to them. Knowledge is won by self-denial and hardship, and, therefore, is highly prized or valued, if not for its own sake, at any rate for the passports it may give.

This institution must have a smaller proportion than most, of the casual and careless, of those who pursue knowledge as a by-product of social life or of sport. Our college, therefore, ought to be relied upon to take knowledge seriously, and I should be the last to assert that, because knowledge may have a utilitarian aspect, this sense of responsibility does not bring about also a love of knowledge for its own sake, or for its higher use.

The Knower's Influence upon the Known

I should like to analyse a little what the sense of responsibility really involves, and to develop thoughts in your minds that perhaps have been lying dormant and unexplored. In every one of the five classes of students, or groups of motives, that I have referred to there is a common question: "*What will knowledge do for me?* What effect will it have upon my life and character?" It is my desire to turn this question round entirely, and to ask: "*What will my possession of knowledge do for the knowledge itself? Will* the fact that I acquired it make any difference to it?" *Ought* it to make any difference?

Knowledge as an Asset

Now, knowledge is, of course, an asset. We may take that as common ground. The acquisition of any asset in life connotes a responsibility in its use.

First, that one should not be either a nuisance or a danger. The possession of a piano or a violin, or a parrot, illustrates the first kind of responsibility in the possession of an asset. The possession of a motor-car or a bulldog is an illustration of the second.

There is another obvious duty in the possession of any asset – not to waste what others might use better; not to monopolise or exclude. There is nothing we hate more than a "dog in the manger"!

The third duty towards any asset that has been painfully built up by the efforts of many before us is to preserve it from damage, to make good its wear and tear, to pass it on in as good a condition at least as we found it, and, if possible, a better.

The fourth duty follows from the modern ethical view that the justification of personal property is a sense of stewardship, so that every asset we have shall be put to its highest use for ourselves and for society. This asset of knowledge is fast becoming a liability !

Now, if I have truly stated the fourfold doctrine about the possession of assets, substitute "knowledge" particularly for the general term "asset" and see how important these four tests are. They go to the very roots of the purpose of life itself. Knowledge is either lumber in your mind or else it does something to you, and it is the something it does to you that is your asset. First, it sets the mind free, and, second, it influences action. Just look at this freedom and see what it implies. One of the greatest words of the New Testament is this: "*And ye shall know the truth, and the truth shall make you free.*" If you are a slave, and under elaborate rules and inhibitions, you are living a determined or fatalistic life, you are an automaton ; you have hardly any responsibility. Knowledge is not doing very much for you if it is not giving you freedom, and therefore added knowledge means added responsibility. The great value of a university life is not that it piles fact on fact, or rule on rule, in your mental equipment – though that may have its place and advantage – but that you gain liberation of mind, a power of true discrimination, a sense of rightness and the quality of proof appropriate to each type of thinking. You are gaining insight, and a larger outlook for the one in the many, mental poise and calm, and you are making your own the gateway, you have a "life-pass," to the the accumulated treasures of all time – you know the tangled path to the hill of vision. You know why and how men have got to the greater secrets of life, and you begin to realise your own deep centres of mental reserve. You are being given the freedom of your own city. Your private certificate that you know how to get the best from contact with men's minds in book, and speech, and art, and travel, and common worship, is the supreme diploma that the university can offer. It is the greater freedom and the greater responsibility. For while it is your responsibility to select as far as you can that environment of book, and speech, and art, and travel, and common worship, you yourself are part of the contact of the millions around you. Either you will write books, for better or worse, or you will make them popular and known or obscure, for better or worse, by your praise or neglect. *Others* will hear your speech and disputation, charity, or shoddy thought. You will be something that a traveller observes as part of an environment that will make common worship, for him, either an impossible or else an ennobling exercise.

So much for freedom. Now knowledge – translated into action, or preventing wrong or violent action – knowledge is both a dynamo and a brake.

Knowledge influences action, or it should do so perhaps far more than it does. But often we find people know so much they are afraid to move, afraid to trust their instincts, because they will not act unless everything is perfectly clear and logical. They are like the centipede that floundered in the ditch, because it could not work out in its mind which of its legs it ought to move first. And so many think that they must wait until their knowledge shows a perfect way before they move, or their knowledge keeps the imperfections and risks so clearly in view that they cannot act. So long as they do nothing, they think responsibility does not arise. The idea that responsibility only applies to positive action and not to negative decision is instinctive. Amiel in his *Journal*, said that he could bear with some strength of mind all that was unimputable or providential; but "responsibility mortally envenoms grief, and as an act is essentially voluntary, therefore I act as little as possible." In other words, he thought he escaped the perils of responsibility by doing as little as possible. He dreaded responsibility; but this was the whole point of Christ's condemnation of the one-talented man.

The battle against multitudinous ignorance in all directions is so difficult and doubtful that every laggard or coward with the weapon of knowledge, rusty, damp, or unused, has the responsibility for inaction, just as much as every hothead for his particular excesses.

The Custody of Knowledge

The responsibility of knowledge is first to your own knowledge itself. You have chosen a particular subject as your own, and you are one of its custodians for this age; your teachers will die off; those to whom you will pass it are not yet ready to take it; for a time its welfare will depend upon you. We have the responsibility for its purity and clarity, for its progress and development, for its vitality, and its appeal. If it loses its place in the ranks of humane studies, it may be our fault. Our responsibility to our subject should make us zealous and jealous, conservative and progressive, pure in spirit. It is a house we dwell in, and others are to follow us. We must see that our subject does not become pretentious and specious, parasitic upon its past heroes, cocksure and snobbish. You have heard of such and such a period being the golden age of chemistry or geology or art; or perhaps of the barren period, when nothing bright and vigorous was added, and when a subject was choken by its own unpruned growths and rankness. You think of imposing tomes, with pages two-thirds full of laborious and tedious footnotes, masquerading as knowledge and rolling forward its erudition into succeeding works like a snowball. Then compare some sprightly invigorating, fresh-minded, speculative, broad-principled treatment of the soul of the subject, having new facts experimentally verified and vitally related, and ask which represents the true age of knowledge. What we call Teutonic thoroughness may be very pedestrian indeed, and carry knowledge forward only in the sense of reprinting past thinking on new leaves, and more of them. The erudition of the Schoolmen had much of this quality. "Close examination of the works of the commentators . . . and the encyclopædists has shown in a surprising way that they repeat each other indefinitely," says Emile Mâle.[1] "The apparently immense library of the Middle Ages consists, after all, of a very few works. Ten well-chosen books might almost literally be said to take the place of all others."

[1] *Religious Art in France, Thirteenth Century.*

So your responsibility to the knowledge of which you are the custodian is for its purity, that it be free from corruption and speciousness; for the additions that your age makes to it, its growth and strength; for its vitality and power to evolve and emerge; and for its power to appeal and convince.

In the company to which you belong, responsible for history or economics or physics, or almost any branch, there is a fourfold task, and you may specialise in one of the four. There is the research-worker delving into the unknown, to conquer new truth, perhaps a lonesome, baffling task. It is like cutting coal "at the face." Then there are those who work upon the discoveries or supposed discoveries, relate them to the work of other specialists, test their implications in other studies, translate them to the rank and file of the exponents of the subject. These work in the mine, but bring the coal to the light of day. Then there are the rank and file themselves, the teachers and popular writers that carry the knowledge over to the general public whose thought has to be influenced by it, and who make up the society which is to be benefited by it. These often rank to the public as the real "authorities" on the subject. They are the distributors who take it to people's homes and teach them its qualities and its power to satisfy human needs. There is, perhaps, a fourth class, which studies the application of theory and discovery to practical arts, and modifies the machinery of life to give objective reality for the wider good. Wherever, in your subject, you elect to be, your responsibility stands.

By carelessness in your own statement, by succumbing to the picturesque, by helping to popularise the wrong book, and by not searching out and supporting the right one, you may help to give a twist to historical interpretation that is equally hurtful to truth whether you do it with a class of children or in the debating-room. By careless analysis or conscious choice of facts and figures, you may be specious in economic argument, and, with the weight of your authority and the pressure of your personality, you may carry the day and lose the cause. It is yours, if you wish, to join in the general debasement of choice and distinctive words till they become merely fashionable intensives and expletives, and are lost for ever from their place of power and honour in their rare and often their moving usage. Thus the dinner you went to last night may have been "awful" or "weird" or "uncanny" or even "terribly nice"; at any rate, you were positively thrilled by the ices, which were "hyper-super," and the band was "priceless" or "putrid." Small wonder that we must look to the West for a new supply of apt, if less elegant, helps to distinctive conversation, and make it "snappy" with "come-backs" from "go-getters."

What I mean by being responsible for purity, for growth, for vitality, and for appeal may, perhaps, now be sufficiently clear.

The Subjectivity of Knowledge

It is a rather curious thought that knowledge itself may be altered or conditioned by the *way* we know it and our attitude toward it. What there is to know changes in character by the very act of knowing it, because knowledge feeds upon itself, quite as much as upon a set of unalterable objective facts. In the field of economics, for example, the overmastering problem is the credit cycle – the cycle of trade prosperity and depression. Many objective causes are at work, such as the initial impulse given from agriculture by good and bad harvests. But it is widely agreed that psychological causes are most important in amplifying what would be mere ripples into large, disturbing waves. The mass suggestion and collective half-knowledge of the whole truth by the business community, the aggregate excess of separate

optimisms in good times, and the aggregate excess
of separate pessimisms in bad times, produce the
extreme swings of the pendulum. If natural causes
of harvests, spurts of invention, variations in monetary supplies, etc., were alone at work, they would
tend to cancel each other out, and no large cycle
would be produced. I, therefore, assert that if we
thoroughly ascertained and widely understood the
credit cycle, it would, *ipso facto*, cease to exist.
In history we cannot pretend that a mere record
of objective events – however accurate – gives us
"knowledge"; it would be a mere medley of statements about people dying in hundreds by violence
at a particular spot, and a hundred other coeval
incidents, such as the sending of a piece of paper
from one person who lived in a big house to another
a long way away; or a certain quantity of goods being
carried by sea from one country to another, or people
working in a place fewer in numbers than before –
all incidents that might be objectively recorded for
the "knowledge" of an intelligently trained simian.
But we desire to call that event a battle, and we seek
a causal nexus with the event. It may have had a
connection with that piece of paper, or some other,
one of which contained a reference to royal ambition
and dynastic power, and the other to a religious
belief; or it may have issued out of economic rivalry
in lost markets, or it may have followed social dislocation and civil strife through the visitation of a
microbe in the Black Death. On the other hand, what
look like causes may have been effects. History is not
the knowledge of objective facts, but of those facts
as causally connected, and knowledge can only use
the causes it recognises or knows about, and so it will
make different causal connections and write a different history about the same events, from time to time.
At one time, when it knows nothing about microbes,
it will employ eclipses for reasons; at another, when
it knows nothing of the effects of gold supplies upon

prices and wages, it will attribute happenings to over-production, tariffs, capitalist cupidity, labour stupidity, and a hundred local or temporary causes. History may be seen with a dynastic, religious, an economic, a biological perspective, and events significant in one become unimportant in others. It must be rewritten with each new knowledge of general causes. We can now discern that a different popular philosophy of heaven and hell may be as profound an historical solvent as Napoleon. Napoleon and all his like may someday be explained in terms of glands or special twists in the ether. So history, economics, medicine, psychology, as branches of human knowledge, change with the quality of knowing itself. No language remains the same whether it is well or badly known by its conveyors; it becomes different knowledge, better or worse adapted for human use, by the quality of their knowledge. Books, of course, may be a great preservative of the best quality, despite a generation of bad students, but, even there, if we have a whole generation of careless and lazy students of a subject, then the shoddy and pretentious books may be boomed and survive, and the good ones may come stillborn from the press, and in a future age some diligent excavators in the British Museum may rediscover them as gems unnoticed in their day. Since the objective reality has not much relevance for knowledge except as it is made by knowledge, irresponsible knowledge destroys its own basis, fouls its own nest. Knowledge progresses in the ratio of the square of its own sense of responsibility.

I can imagine that those of you who do not deal with the humanities, and moral sciences and ideas, but with the hard objective facts of the natural world, are congratulating yourselves that nothing you may do can spoil the material of your knowledge. That material seems proof against our abuse and bad handling. It "abides our question." Be as flippant or as careless as you will, but an electron, it seems, must remain an electron, and oxygen defies your mood. But are you sure? Science is now full of problems in which the temper and mood of the scientist matters. Niels Bohr said recently: "We cannot obtain any knowledge concerning natural phenomena without influencing them by our observation." And all workers in the sub-material or ultra-physical world are insisting on the subjective character of new knowledge in physics. Dr. Donnan says: "It is a dead world, and is only animated by our consciousness." Mr. Gerald Heard said the other day on the wireless: "We have reached a point when just because what is being dealt with is no longer anything that can be produced and pointed to, just because we are dealing so largely with deductions, it becomes for the first time so important that the scientist should realise exactly what his own position is. If he does not, he may fail to give full weight to every possible explanation, and to the suggestions of all other workers. A subconscious prejudice to-day may do as much harm to the advance of truth as a deliberate falsification of scientific facts fifty years ago." In his *Mysterious Universe*, Sir James Jeans says: "Heisenberg and Bohr have suggested that electron waves must be regarded merely as a sort of symbolic representation of our knowledge as to the probable state and position of an electron. If so, *they change as our knowledge changes, and so become largely subjective.*" In fact, "the personal equation" in experimental work has taken on a new and more subtle significance. It is no longer a physical error of measurement, or even the taking of a delicate reading through a telescope so that the presence of the body of the observer shall not itself change the reading. It is a new mental awareness and sense of responsibility.

The Responsibility of Division of Labour

Your next responsibility is to your co-workers in your own subject. The range is vast, and only by allocation of the field of research or of teaching, only by division of labour, can it be successfully covered, and the advance across the whole field kept in line. It may be that, in some piece of research-work, one worker has, by consent, a practical monopoly ; no one desires to dispute its possession with him, and it is often a matter of professional etiquette to keep off his ground and not to duplicate the subject of his research. He finds himself examining some difficult and abstruse material, ancient records, or files of old journals or original correspondence, with the knowledge that when that material has once been gone over the task ought to have been performed for ever; at any rate, it is very unlikely that another worker will pass that way for many, many years. Here is the temptation to sleep at the post, to sacrifice strict veracity for picturesque presentation, to ignore or hide the ugly fact that would kill the beautiful theory, to generalise too easily, to take short cuts and tendentious routes. By the lack of the sense of responsibility, or by being too much the artist when scientific care is more in keeping with the task, the whole trend of subsequent opinion upon the topic may be wrongly influenced. Froude was the cause of a quite unnecessary revulsion of feeling after Carlyle's death, and this was due to suppression, manipulation, and wrong rendering of documents to match Froude's preconceived intention, and body forth a theory of his own. Professor Eliot Norton found one hundred and thirty-six corrections necessary in the first five pages of the *Reminiscences*, but even these may not equal in their effect a single violent twist of language. It is an irony that this should have happened to Carlyle, who, however tendentious in spirit, spent infinite trouble to verify a fact that perhaps figures only as one of a torrent of adjectives in the result. Everyone writing in the historical, biographical, statistical, and even geographical field, must have known the temptation to be graphic and impressive by quoting an extreme case, at the risk of that case being taken by the reader as a type. Honesty or responsibility in selection and in generalisation is the great test of the isolated worker, and he ought to have over him the favourite framed text of a puritan Victorian boyhood, "*Thou, God, seest me,*" with a large, searching eye to enhance its effect. Workers in the field of physics and chemistry may congratulate themselves that these temptations do not come to them, for they cannot be slack or irresponsible without being immediately found out by the next experimenter, or the facts themselves, on the next application of their results. Examples of knowledge being put on the wrong track through irresponsible work are very rare. It is true that a too casual treatment of residuals or observational error may hold back discovery for a long time, but I do not think that anyone could regard Cavendish, for example, as in any sense falling short of his opportunities when, out of what he had left aside, Lord Rayleigh discovered argon. Indeed, Cavendish is praised by the Rayleighs, father and son, for the sharpness of his questions and the quality of his work, considering the appliances he had. There were several workers who must have been within an ace of discovering X-rays some years before they were actually recognised, but no experimenter can look for everything at once; if he did, he would probably find nothing; for research, after all, is getting a definite answer to a carefully planned question, and half the trouble is in asking the right question. But clearly the subdivision of labour in knowledge connotes a special responsibility in each of us.

The Responsibility for the Institution

As an exponent of knowledge, you owe a responsibility to your institution, to your university, and to your degree or diploma. If their reputation is already high, your responsibility is the greater, for you cannot long enjoy their prestige undeserved without helping to destroy that prestige. Here, obviously, I leave you with an unspoken sermon. But a great tradition ought to key us up to our best moments and make them our standard. I have examined for various degrees in different universities, and, when I have been in genuine doubt about a border-line pass or failure, I have been attacked by sentiment and had visions of a white-haired mother and a family distraught with anxiety over a pass-list, and there seemed then only one decent thing to do. At that point, I have put to myself the responsible question: Is it a good thing for this university that this young man (or woman) should be allowed to go out to the world, and very possibly let the university down in the eyes of the scholars and discerning people? Will it be fair to Bachelors of Science that one who was capable of giving such and such an answer may easily publicly degrade the hall-mark? That is the check upon pure humanitarianism in scholarship – a rather painful thought for the candidate, I fear.

These are utilitarian responsibilities to the institutions. But there are also sentimental ones that have a moral claim upon us, even if only negatively, to be worthy of those who, by vision and self-sacrifice, made and endowed the institution, upon which otherwise we are mere parasites.

Dr. Isaac Barrow, in 1693, in his five discourses on "Industry," treated finally of the calling of scholars, and, after dealing sententiously with the joys that must follow the industrious exercise of the mind in reading, in tongues, in rhetoric, in history, natural and moral philosophy, and theology, concluded by shaming the scholars before the memory of pious founders –

How, being slothful in our business, can we answer for our violating the wills, for abusing the goodness, for perverting the

charity and bounty, of our worthy Founders and Benefactors
who gave us the good things we enjoy, not to maintain us in
idleness, but for supports and encouragement of our industry.
Let every scholar, when he mispendeth an hour, or sluggeth on
his bed, but imagine that he heareth the voice of those glorious
Kings or worthy Gentlemen complaining thus and rating him:
Why sluggard dost thou against my will possess my estate? Why
dost thou presume to occupy the place due to an industrious
person? Why dost thou forget or despise thy obligations to my
kindness? Thou art an usurper, a robber or a purloiner of my
goods, which I never intended for such as thee! . . . If to be a
dunce or a bungler in any profession be shamefull, how much
more ignominious and infamous to a scholar to be such? From
whom all men expect that he should excell in intellectual abilities,
and be able to help others by his instructions and advice.

Reception as Important as Transmission

Now comes a new and difficult type of responsibility
– not of faithful production, but of transmission – a
responsibility for studying form as well as substance.
The object of teaching, or speaking or writing, is to
convey some truth to another mind. However exact
words and ideas may be as they leave your mind,
their exactness is wasted if the words and ideas are
not well adapted to get into the receiving mind.
Effective truth is that which reaches the other intelligence, and you have not done enough if you have
merely shaped it to please your own fancy; you must
study the form which is best adapted to be understood. Study the capacity of the "receiving sets" as
well as the quality of "transmission." You may have
to sacrifice something of artistry or even exactness to
achieve it. In the *Dolly Dialogues* we learnt that
"telling the truth to people who misunderstand you
is equivalent to promoting falsehood." Your responsibility as a transmitter of knowledge goes beyond
satisfying your own sense of rightness, and you must
judge it also by the accuracy of grasp in the recipient,
and the pleasure or ease of reception.

Men of knowledge in business, in religion, in law, in politics, in diplomacy, are sometimes satisfied if their words will bear the strict scrutiny of others like themselves, and pass muster as truth, and yet convey far less, or even suggest something pleasanter, to those less well-endowed or ignorant of the context. I always remember a fine passage in a judgment by Lord Blackburn[1] which puts the issue very bluntly: "If, with intent to lead the plaintiff to act upon it, they put forth a statement which they know may bear two meanings, one of which is false to their knowledge, and thereby the plaintiff, putting that meaning on it, is misled, I do not think they can escape by saying he ought to have put the other. If they palter with him in a double sense, it may be they lie like truth, but I think they lie, and it is a fraud. Indeed, as a question of casuistry, I am inclined to think the fraud is aggravated by a shabby attempt to get the benefit of a fraud without incurring the responsibility." It is not enough to issue the truth from your factory; you must deliver it clean and wholesome at the door of your customer.

Illegitimate Extension of Authority

Students who have a college education and a university degree often find themselves living amongst people who are impressed by such attainments, and have no discriminating knowledge of what they really cover. Someone who has taken a classical degree is referred to in the most touching way as an authority upon history or physics; and, generally, we have a most serious responsibility not to abuse the standard we have secured through work in one field by imposing our views, or – more subtle temptation – accepting the deference of others in fields of knowledge in which we have had no discipline or training. People who have won renown for

[1] Smith *v.* Chadwick (9 App Case, 1807).

some particular study are often encouraged to become pontifical or oracular in other subjects, especially in economics, theology and philosophy, and political science. Mrs. Sidney Webb once went to Sir Victor Horsley, at a time when she was engaged upon one of her great studies in Local Government, and received from him a great homily on the principles of government and a general "put-the-world-right" oration. She asked him, with gentle point, how he would like her to give him a discourse on surgery!

Of course, results of the very greatest value can come from a vigorous intellect going from its own field into adjoining territory, and, with a fresh mind, and threads of analogy, it may discern weaknesses and points of view which those brought up in the work have failed to appreciate under their noses. Especially is the border-line territory between two well-explored domains of knowledge worthy of close examination by one who knows both. But there is no good reason why an eminent physicist, or a prominent money-making business-man, without going through any discipline in economics, should immediately jump into print as an authority on economics, showing what fools all the regular exponents and fully equipped students of the subject really are. We have a responsibility, then, not to pretend to a wider field of knowledge than we have actually tilled, and not to think, because we have paid for a ticket from London to Birmingham, the ticket-collector will pass us over the whole L.M.S. Railway. But, all the same, the freedom of knowledge, which in lateral fields must be carefully guarded from licence, is a real freedom of movement, vertically, through all the strata of social life. "Is it not that the love and pursuit of culture lead each of us out of his class, and that class views of any kind, whether of the aristocracy or of the middle class or of the people, inevitably narrow the mind and hinder it from receiving pure

truth; have you ever known any person who lived
habitually in the notions of a caste, high or low, without incapacitating himself in a greater or less degree
for breadth and delicacy of perception?"[1]

But, even within the exposition of our *own* subject,
we may abuse our position. For long enough in the
series of positive, comparative and superlative, "lies,
damned lies, and statistics," the last has been
rivalled by the "expert witness." His knowledge has
been abused, in both senses of the word, in every
court. For it is so hard for him to be called in
evidence without being under pressure to stress an
aspect, and his money often depends upon his maintenance of a position where he becomes, not an
exponent of esoteric knowledge, but an advocate.
He has to make clear matters which the judge cannot
be expected to know personally, and if in the process
he directs the judge wrongly by statements which
are true but partial, he prostitutes his knowledge for
gain, and is rightly resented.

The Unity of Knowledge

My final plea for responsibility is upon the integ-
rity·of all knowledge, and the interdependence of
knowledge and righteousness. "Veracity is the heart
of morality," said Huxley – the importance of
honesty. "When a man's knowledge is not in order,
the more of it he has the greater will be his confusion," said Herbert Spencer – the vice of sloppi-
ness. "There is no source of deception in the investigation of nature which can compare with a fixed belief
that certain kinds of phenomenon are impossible,"
said William James – the imperial value of open-
mindedness. "Irrationally held truths may be more
harmful than reasoned errors," said Huxley, again –
the importance of the intellectual basis of knowledge. Truly the responsibility for honesty, clarity,

[1] Philip Hamerton, *The Intellectual Life.*

receptivity, and rationality in our knowledge is as far reaching as life itself.

Our responsibility does not end with doing good or bad work in our own particular field. Knowledge is too much like an organism with sensitive interconnections of an unexpected kind for that to be true. As Eucken has very well said –

> The worth of the individual is measured, not by his direct achievement, but first and foremost by its value for the whole; the individual piece of knowledge by its significance for the search after truth. . . . Science is not a mere juxtaposition of individual opinions, but the worker who puts forth effort at any particular spot is conscious that his effort is girt about and sustained by an effort of the whole to which he willingly yields his contribution. . . . Truth won at any particular point is valid and binding throughout.

It must be equally true that ignorance or falsity at any one point affects the whole. The most recent writer on psychology and religion[1] makes the point clear, when he is putting side by side truth of two qualities, or orders or dimensions: "All this does not mean that one sort of truth can contradict another sort; on the contrary, laziness or hypocrisy in one region of our efforts after truth will react on the others, and we daie not neglect or violate our intellect in religion." What a chain of ideas, resting on relevant and interrelated facts, we get wherever we start our minds! Moral ideas on sex – social institutions, population, food supplies, and agriculture – finance – nationalism – armaments, conscription, freedom. Any false facts or bad logic at any point can alter the whole chain. A similar interdependence in the whole field of physics, mathematics, chemistry, astronomy, meteorology, shows the oneness and intervalidity of knowledge.

[1] Dr. Yellowlees, *Psychology's Defence of the Faith.*

Responsibility for Action

"The great end of life is not knowledge, but action," said Huxley (and, before him, Vincent of Beauvais, in *Speculum majus*), and you can never be quite the same in your responsibility for action after you have learned a new fact as you were before it. One of his biographers says that Abraham Lincoln had "never remembered the time when he did not believe slavery to be wrong." But one item of knowledge turned passive belief into active conviction. "From the time that he saw slaves chained and sold in the New Orleans market, he had felt some measure of moral accountability for a system which prevailed in his country and which his conscience condemned."

Robert Bridges[1] says:

> And since we see how man's judgment of Right and Wrong
> varieth with education – and that without effect
> to strengthen or weaken Duty – we conclude therefrom
> that education shapeneth our moralities.

A life of reflection with no action is not the best soil for knowledge. Several of our greatest critics, who are called in, or who come in themselves, to pontificate on every human affair under the sun, would have been far more use to us if they had ever taken on a single responsible task of organisation and direction. Ernest Dimnet says, of Balzac the printer:

> Perhaps the effort he made as a business man kept his will power up to the mark as an artist. Everybody will be benefited by going into some enterprise, charitable or other, in which responsibility of a more definite character than literary responsibility will be involved; by being in some fight for a real ideal, and by speaking in public about it.

*   *   *   *

Of all the responsibility attaching to knowledge, there is none so great as I have assumed to-night. I

[1] *Testament of Beauty*, iv. 155.

presume to add to your knowledge something which another twenty or thirty years of life have given me, and the presumption of advice drawn from superior experience calls for all the precautions I have mentioned already – for veracity, open-mindedness, and the humility of the everlasting learner, to whom every one of you is a piece of new knowledge which gives new responsibility.

To what end is all this, in a life so short and brutish? I conclude by quoting Philip Hamerton's words (in *The Intellectual Life*):

> The intellectual light of Europe in this century is not only due to great luminaries whom everyone can name, but to millions of thoughtful persons, now utterly forgotten, who in their time loved the light, and guarded it, and increased it, and carried it into many lands, and bequeathed it as a sacred trust.

These are my key-words: to love, to guard, to increase, to carry, to bequeath. Hamerton goes on to point out the effect of this view of our responsibility upon our view of the brevity and uncertainty of life.

> Whoever has fully realised the grand continuity of intellectual tradition, and taken his own place in it between the future and the past, will work till he can work no more, and then gaze hopefully on the world's great future, like Geoffroy Saint Hiliare, when his blind eyes beheld the future of zoology.

> "We live by the light of a thousand years,
> And the knowledge of millions of men."

III

Except the Lord build the house, they labour in vain that build
it: except the Lord keep the city, the watchman waketh but in
vain. – Ps. cxxvii. 1, Authorised Version.

> Unless the Eternal builds the house,
> Workmen build in vain.
> Unless the Eternal guards the town,
> Sentries are on guard in vain.—
>
> MOFFAT'S translation.

The visits of the British Association for the Advancement of Science, over a period of one hundred years,
to different parts of the Kingdom and the Empire,
have, it is believed, been a most important means of
quickening public and popular interest, not only in
scientific attainments and progress, but also in
scientific methods and scientific men. The meetings
bring together scientists who have been in contact
only through their writings, and heighten, by personal intercourse, the community of aim and interest.
In a score of ways, they advance the cause of science
amongst its exponents, but these advances are not my
theme to-day, for they might come about equally
well if the meetings took place always in one centre,
and the general public had no lot or part in them. But
what difference does it make that different places and
different publics should be brought into close contact
with these gatherings of experts? What difference,
that is, not to the scientists themselves, but to the

[1] At the Central Hall, Bristol, on the occasion of the meeting of the
British Association for the Advancement of Science, September 1930.

successive different publics and localities? It may
well be hoped that the importance of scientific knowledge is more strikingly brought home to the average
man, that the vastness and variety of human effort
and study make an impressive background to many
everyday human lives, and that the nobility of the
search for truth, and its impassive and serene temper,
enter into character, shame littleness, annihilate
provincialism both of aim and place and time. This
influence the plain man may *receive*. But receiving
can never stand alone, for long, satisfactorily. What
can the plain man *give*? Can he have any share in
scientific progress? Can he, in the popular phrase,
"do anything about it"? Ought he to? Or is science
something of which he can only receive the material
benefits and sometimes drawbacks, and which may
have also indirect beneficial influences on his moral
character?

What is every man's share in scientific progress?
By this, of course, I mean, not his share in benefits,
but his share in responsibility or in contribution to it.
By progress, I do not so much mean progress in the
laboratory or in the study, as that part of progress
in civilisation and society which is brought about
through scientific method and application of principles, and by emancipation from muddled thinking,
haphazard and superstitious beliefs. A strange subject
for a sermon, you say! Time was when the meetings
of the British Association were felt by religious bodies
to be almost an attack within the citadel of religious
truth itself. The man in the street scented a pretty
scrap between bishops and physicists, and science
versus religion was staged, so to speak, as a mild
entertainment. For a time, then, the local pulpits
resounded with defence and counter-attack, warning
and defiance. Later on, when it was seen that these
two were complementary ways of approaching truth
in two separate aspects, the pulpit took milder
courses – the familiar ones of reminding the man in

the street that he must not be led away by the
apparent finality of the biologist and physicist, that
there are more things, in heaven particularly, than
were dreamed of in his philosophy; in general a
toning down of the direct exclusive effects of scientific attack upon the mind. Nowadays, I gather, we
welcome the scientist himself into sermon-making,
not that he may expound his subject as he has been
already doing in erudite address and popular lectures, but that he may tell us what contribution he
has to make to our moral nature, and to our spiritual
destiny, that he may criticise our standards in the
light of his own. It has been well said of the scientist
as the truth-seeker that the value of his work can
only be determined by its significance in the whole
of knowledge, and the final aims of life, which are
essentially moral. "Truth won at any particular
point," said Eucken, "is valid and binding throughout." It does science good to be asked to lift its head
from its microscope and differentials, and take its
bearings in all experience and all knowledge, of
which the loves and hates, the ambitions and passions
and purposes of a never-ceasing stream of human
life are not the lesser part. It may well happen that
what appears to be a truth in its little local setting
may be of doubtful validity when these bearings are
taken, and it may well be re-examined with profit
to itself.

I know that many of my hearers at a Sunday service
will feel happier, and a little less unconventional, if
I have a text. And, if that is a foible – and for my own
part I don't think it is – then I believe in humouring
every foible and meeting every harmless require-
ment that will relieve me from the risk of antagon-
ising my hearers' minds at the outset, so that I may
get the better chance on the main issue. For how
often have I seen a speaker, with a difficult proposition to deliver, lose his ground in the first sentence
with some heedlessness in studying his hearers'

feelings on some quite unessential feature. But here
is my text, and it needs no apology. It is a sermon in
itself. It has stood, for example, as a motto for an
ancient Yorkshire borough for over a thousand years,
and who can estimate what unconscious influence it
may have had upon a succession of inhabitants in
their ruminating moments over those centuries?
Science will tell you that, unless you study building-
construction, public health, ventilation, stresses and
strains, voltages, and material qualities, you will
make a thorough mess of house-building. Science
will tell you that, in your commercial life, eternal
vigilance is the price of liberty, and no city can with-
stand its innumerable enemies and general disinte-
gration unless ignorance gives way to enlightenment,
and clamour to educated leadership. But the Psalmist
says something else is wanted. What is it that can thus
complete the work of science, and without which
science cannot attain its real function in human
advancement?

You all have views about the world as you live in
it, and as to the direction in which you want it to go.
You all have ideas as to what constitutes progress.
A form of government – a better weekly wage – less
misery, more comfort – fewer taxes – less spite, less
crime, less human frailty, less unhappiness through
evil – the material or economic, and the moral or
"character" parts of life. But you know that progress
does not just "happen." The world is to be made
better or worse by the opinions and knowledge which
build it. These opinions need force, and they become
convictions. This knowledge needs application, and
it becomes skill. So the minds and souls of men are
the plan and dynamic of human betterment. But,
you may say, does not *evolution* just *bring about*
progress by eliminating the unfit, and choosing the
survivor best able to use his environment ? May be.
But this enabled man to proceed from using eoliths –
flints with edges so roughly chipped that we doubt

whether they are not the results of natural accidents – down to the use of paleoliths, where the stones are more closely adapted to human purposes of cutting and scraping and boring, over a period of tens, or even hundreds, of thousands of years. Every time I go along the Kentish Weald, I look up at the hills where the village grocer, Harrison, spent a lifetime of scanty leisure in unearthing that great scientific secret of the past, one of the romances of scientific method and attainment, by the natural passion for truth. One is always bound to reflect upon the vast spaces of time that were necessary to secure what seems to us the tiniest advance in human power. But it was not by this chance evolutionary process that the standard of life of these crowded islands was raised fourfold in one hundred years in the nineteenth century, and the moral tone lifted for all child life and employment. Make no mistake, hardly a fraction of either of these was achieved directly by betterment in work and ideas among the great mass of our dwellers, for child employment, and its abuses, was abolished almost in spite of popular sentiment and against the common notion of what was worth while – the workers had to be protected against themselves, and shown their own best interests against their inclination. While man was developing a moral sense and an intellectual grasp of the forces of nature and of the organisation of society, over hundreds of years, successive civilisations rose and fell. Recently, in the war, we have had a narrow escape from continuing this sequence in a similar catastrophe, due even less to radical defects in individual moral character than to defects in national control of our great social forces, and particularly to the absence of a check upon an anti-moral element securing the key positions in a complicated international situation. It is certainly not the teaching of science that natural selection must necessarily lead to a better world – using "better" in the only sense in which it has a decent meaning for us – and that it is the scientific way of progress. As Canon Streeter says, "Natural selection no more brings into existence instincts or qualities which have a 'survival value' than a scholarship examination brings into existence clever or well-taught boys."[1] Even Mr. C. E. M. Joad admits:

> The inference is irresistible, that the achievement by life of mere adaptation is not enough, but that living beings are evolved at more complicated and therefore more dangerous levels, in the endeavour to attain *higher* forms of life. The amœba, in short, is superseded by the man, not because the man is better-adapted life, but because he is better-quality life. In making this inference, however, we are admitting the suggestion that evolution is not a haphazard but a purposive process – an admission which is incompatible with materialism.[2]

We cannot wholly defeat the force of automatic selection that has been so potent in the past, but we can now retard it or accelerate it by conscious human purpose. The remainder of the way of human progress is to be mapped and worked out by the mind and soul of man in unison, and not by blind chance, or crowd forces and un-co-ordinated mob minds, led anywhither by unmoral or immoral personal ambitions.

In this, for each of us, our own opinions and alertness of character are an important and twofold ingredient. First we must, where we have to act ourselves, *know* enough to act wisely in taking the more sensible course, and be *good* enough to act rightly in taking the more virtuous course. Secondly, as we have to depute to others the right to choose and act for us, we need to know enough ourselves to discern the able man from the quack with the oily tongue, and be keen-witted enough in our moral senses to choose the righteous man instead of the rogue.

---

[1] *Reality.*   [2] *The Meaning of Life.*

This applies to local and central government (to choice by area); to trade union and group activity and directors of business (to choice by trade or function); to the newspapers we read, and authors and preachers we encourage by our attention and favour (in the collection of facts and presentation of ideas). We ought to be *good soil* for the sound in fact and principle, and we ought to be *bad soil* for the charlatan and the plausible and shallow. So progress will be *jointly the product of our power to act wisely and to choose wisely*, using "wise" in both its moral and intellectual senses.

The choice of the expert, and the power to secure a right judgment upon a vast world of conflicting fact, count for more than any other single factors. But, you will say, how does a discovery in engineering or in the bacteriologist's laboratory affect society, within the plain man's scope? No single scientific discovery but what, quite soon in its incorporation into our social organism, creates new values or displaces old ones or alters man's relationships! The internal-combustion engines make new social problems of the rights of speed against those of rest and quiet. The moment Eli Whitney invented the cotton-gin he gave a "mighty impetus to slavery" (Barton, *Life of Abraham Lincoln*). Every discovery affecting health alters the facts of mortality, disturbs the age distribution, makes great new social problems. The advances in knowledge, prudential considerations, and public health have altered the age composition of our population. The war period introduced a new and special factor. The consequence is that the age distribution in the next ten years will have important effects upon industrial employment. We have been passing through a period when 150,000 more people have come up into the field of employment yearly than have passed out of it. Shortly, the entry and the exit will nearly balance, and the shortage of new labour will be very marked.

Not all the changes in society are brought about by scientific advance, but such important ones are so caused that continual alertness is required to preserve or reconstruct our social fabric. The plain man has task enough here, in all conscience.

I suppose most of us have confidence in our own judgment. We like to think we are right. We are predisposed to the view that we are right. Once having given an opinion, how difficult it is to see the other side, to accept a new fact, to own ourselves mistaken! (A great scientist once said the greatest tragedy was a theory slain by a fact.) But it is a healthy and sometimes humbling exercise to go back over the past – over the great issues that have divided men often for long periods of time, with bitterness and finality. See the cruelties and excesses of religious bigotry, often on points that now seem ludicrous to us, and that we should not injure a cat nor lower an eyebrow in anger about to-day! Think of saintly men holding their prayer meetings, and writing some of the great hymns you sing to-day, in a ship's cabin beneath which sweltering and suffering masses of African niggers, bound for the West Indian slave market, were penned under conditions that to-day we should blush to permit for swine. That was a great dividing issue, that of slavery, even within the lifetime of our old people now. Think of the treatment of children in industry. The question I ask myself is: "*Should I have been on the right side?*" The right side seems so obvious *now* – it must surely have been impossible for any sensible, any right-minded, person to have any doubt. But if you read the contemporary discussions, the *false emphasis in facts*, the refusal to *accept unpleasant ideas*, the reluctance to be disturbed, you begin to wonder. Of course, reading wise accounts afterwards is no test. The goodness of the reformers and the reactionary wickedness of the opponents are all made so obvious, and you are made by the author to feel how completely you would have been on the side of the angels. Take, for example, the famous contemporary debates between Lincoln and Douglas which really made Lincoln president afterwards, and see how Lincoln's gold was heavily mixed with dross, and Douglas's dross was often streaked with gold. You would need a very forward view, a very idealised conscience, a very patient scientific mind, and strong patient moral sense, to find your way out. *"Should I have been on the right side?"* If you have any doubts, you will then say: "Am I equipped to take the right side to-day, in subjects of great contention? Am I pulling towards betterment, or acting as a brake?"

We approach these matters, most of us, inevitably, from one of two standpoints. We either have an intellectual solution or a moral solution. We either say: *"Men* have got to build this house, anyway, on human plans – the Lord building the house is mere sentiment or excellent stuff for those who feel that way," or else we say: "Let *the Lord* build the house – don't bother your head to study architecture, or engineering, or building-construction – I don't know that you need to bother even about fetching the bricks!"

Now, the intellectual solution always looks for a high degree of perfection and improvement in systems. Get the right kind of council here; get a better system of election there; make it impossible for A to do so and so unless B has been consulted. Give C a better training. Take taxes from D and spend them on providing an institution for E, F, and G. Make it illegal to do this, that, and the other. Above all, make everyone a check on everyone else. The great fallacy of the nineteenth century, in political thinking, was that, if you gave everyone a chance of getting his will and idea represented in the collective will and final decision, you would get wisdom and right action. It was not easily recognised

that democracy can go as fatally wrong in governing
itself as ever it can be led by an autocrat. It is not
even now realised that a thousand men with equal
rights will not make the progress that they can if
there is one good thinker and nine hundred and
ninety-nine "recognisers." If you cannot be an
original thinker, have you trained yourself to be a
good, honest, quick, reliable, unprejudiced "recog-
niser," aider and abetter of new truth when it has
been found, or can you be hoodwinked by cunning
or made obstinate by prejudice? It is different, of
course, in the moral element – the moral element
must be a common property – you will not make
the same moral progress if you have one saint and
nine hundred and ninety-nine people who admire
him but don't follow him. Even Christ is helpless to
save the world unless people become Christlike.
We say, then, about all our ills: "Take these present imperfect human beings and re-arrange them
properly in the right ways and you will get a more
perfect world." But you can't say about rancid butter
and old eggs, "Make a better recipe, get a new
cookery-book, apply more skill and art, and you will
make a better dish." It is true a bad recipe will spoil
good materials, and good materials may be made to
go further and do better with skill and a better
cookery-book. So some blame conditions for quality,
and others quality for conditions. To some drink is
the cause of poverty, to others poverty leads people
to drink. The interactions are subtle.
No one can deny the immense importance of right
and appropriate organisation for making the most of
human qualities, both of mind and heart. The difference between the good and the bad framework of
effort is the difference between aiding, or even
generating, good results and stifling and thwarting
them. It must always be our aim so to order society
that it is easier to do right, harder to do wrong. Now,
every scientific discovery alters the centre of gravity

of human life in some way, and makes necessary new adjustments and relationships. These can be made, either willingly or grudgingly, either wisely or foolishly, either safely or dangerously. But, until they are successfully made, the scientific discovery has not become progress, it is only disturbance. Society has to strike a new profit and loss account, so that the gross gain of the discovery is put at its highest point (for example, the boon of broadcasting), and the gross cost or price at its lowest point (for example, a loss of initiative in music, in thinking, in personal religious worship), and so that the net advantage, which alone constitutes progress, is therefore at its maximum. Perhaps a better example of a complicated new account, with pluses and minuses, before we can determine whether scientific advance is also progress, is given by the motor-car and its innumerable social reactions. These reactions and the organisation to meet them are essentially the plain man's contribution to progress, and he has to be zealous, indeed, that life does not become mechanised and unbalanced, that leisure does not become aimless or feeble and vapid as it becomes abundant and free, that the deep oasis of the spirit may be enjoyed undisturbed.

But those of us who do not fly to remedy the world's evils by re-arrangement of people in new organisation sometimes resort to a police-ridden or police-bidden world, and seek to make laws to keep people right. The two things are not identical, but they are closely related, for bitter experience shows that it is little use passing regulations unless we have inspectorial and inquisitorial machinery to check abuse and evasion. The truth is we can only successfully legislate, for permissive purposes, and without coercion, on the basis of the average or general moral force and acquiescence, or perhaps a little bit in advance of them.

Neither the organisational nor the police solutions

of progress are really satisfactory by themselves; there is something lacking.

I referred to the second group of approaches to the problem of progress as the "moral solution." "If only people were good all would be well." "We want better hearts." If there is anything wrong and requiring amendment, someone must be to blame. Indeed, the mentality of many people is limited to finding scapegoats. If there is not one, and they have to do a little real mental toil, their plight is pitiable. The stern moralist is, perhaps, not so bad as the sentimentalist in the poverty of his contribution.

> So many gods, so many creeds,
> So many paths that wind and wind,
> But just the art of being kind
> Is all the sad world needs.

A beautiful verse and a perfect sentiment, in its place! But what a weapon to face the cancer problem, or currency depreciation, or unemployment, in these days! Another aspect of the personal element is the reliance upon individual capacity and adroitness.

> For forms of government let fools contest
> Whate'er is best administered is best.

The fact is that the times are out of joint, not merely because individual men lack goodness and ability, but because continual toning up of the whole people and a continual choice of the right way of meeting change is necessary. In this case, individual blame is quite out of place. The sentimentalist, who refuses to do any intellectual or scientific work higher than blame, sees no difficulty or vice inherent in the conditions and natural circumstances – it is all personal and individual. As the hymn says,

> Every prospect pleases,
> And only man is vile.

You may have heard the old story of the Eastern king who had a famous philosopher living in his dominion of whom he became intensely jealous. It irked him exceedingly to think that any subject could be held in such popular esteem, and be so prominent in the public mind. Besides, the man seemed to have nothing about him, he was uncouth and wretched, and, moreover, cynical to authority. The king thought to impress him and perhaps humble him by an exhibition of his own power and glory. So the philosopher was summoned to the presence and taken round the Court and the palace, to be impressed by the richness of the marbles and furnishings, and the beauty of the king's surroundings. When the perambulation was nearly complete, the philosopher suddenly spat full in the king's face. You can imagine the consternation of the courtiers as they stood back aghast and thunderstruck, until someone had the presence of mind to ask him what he meant. "It's the only fit place to spit in," expostulated the philosopher. I don't defend his action, but, if the ancient story is true, he was a very effective exponent of the moral delinquency point of view.

My own view is that so many of the problems of to-day are fundamentally intellectual or mental, and not moral. I have instanced currency or price stability, unemployment, much sickness and infirmity, and poverty. The burning questions of "Free Trade" and nationalism, though full of sentiment, are mainly of this order. I am still very sceptical that the Christian spirit will actually alter the standard of living materially – if I had to choose between sentiment and cheap synthetic nitrogen, I should unhesitatingly choose the latter. But, if it comes to being happy and in the best sense contented with the improved standard when you get it, I should want Brotherhood, and no more nitrogen. *Nitrogen* may build the house, but, unless the Lord build it, it will be uninhabitable. Even the issues of peace and war cannot be solved merely by well meaning. The underlying irritants must be removed, and differences reconciled, and this needs hard passionless thinking, to which men of every stage of moral advance can contribute. Thinking is like swimming – we like to keep parallel to the shore, and, with one leg on the bottom, may put up all the appearance of it. But how few there are who will strike out into the deep, with only their own skill and endurance on which to rely!

All of this goes to show that the plain man cannot leave progress to science – the scientist will only show him new ways; it is for the plain man to adapt them, absorb them into the greater fullness of life and its possibilities. The plain man is very naturally tending to rely on science to find always the next step. He is becoming parasitic to science for happiness and the satisfaction of the next craving, even for the improvement of his standard of life. Anatole France once said: "The worst of science is it stops you thinking." How paradoxical, when we can do nothing in science without thinking! But, if we cease to ponder, and cease to wonder, science will be a snare. Even the scientist himself may be so absorbed in the quest and its technique as to lose sight of the glory of it. We can go so fast in a motor-car, and see so much, that we can see nothing well or satisfactorily. In the old days, with infinite planning and labour, an enthusiast could reach a chosen spot, and then live upon it, absorb it, make it his own for ever. To-day, we can, with no planning and no effort, see twenty times as much, and be no better for it. Nothing is ever our own till we have *made* it our own. Science is not progress until we possess it, instead of science possessing us. The plain man's contribution is, therefore, to prove all things and hold fast that which is good, to choose well his leaders and demand wise adjustment, to eschew the haphazard and look for cause and effect in the moral and political realm.

So long as the community is made up of the two classes which are both so essential to progress, but they remain in separate classes, true progress cannot be achieved as rapidly as might be possible, and it may even be thwarted altogether. A perfectly designed engine is essential to first-class mechanical progress. This design is science. But it must be perfectly constructed too, and of the right materials. This construction is organisation and society, but the right materials are the right-hearted and right-minded human beings. But no perfect engine will go without perfect combustion, and this is the spiritual element of power and motive; nor can it go in a right direction of use to mankind without a plan and a mind. This is the spiritual view of life and destiny. "Except the Lord build the house. . . ."

An American writer, Will Durant, in his *Mansions of Philosophy*, asks whether progress is a delusion. After a masterly summary of human advance upon every line from the earliest beginnings, speech, fire, conquest of the animals, agriculture, social organisations, tools, and science, all the factors of intelligence, he comes to morality, and concludes: "So far as character is concerned, we have probably retrogressed; subtlety of thought has grown at the expense of stability of the soul." But he urges that in the code of Christ we are kinder, gentler, and more generous. When dealing with man's mastery over matter, he says it has not been matched by any kindred victory over himself, for psychology has not controlled conduct.

I would fain allege that science is progressing faster than our power to absorb it into the full and rounded and purposive life, because we have not introduced, *into our spiritual feeling and thinking*, the study of cause and effect. As the preacher says, "Taste and see, that the Lord is good." The Bible is full of invitations to experiment, and directions for doing it. We can rid ourselves of superstition and haphazard

moral life by trying these ventures of faith and of
spiritual power.

The intellectual temper that I have set out as
essential on the part of the ordinary man to contribute
to science, requires a freedom from prejudice, from
haste, from immediate aims, from materialistic
motive, from human jealousy and passion, that mean
a demand upon a great source of spiritual power and
cleansing. "Except the Lord build the house. . . ."
The moral level that I have asserted is required to
make good soil for progress, is an individual task
that every soul must achieve for itself. But it cannot
achieve it by itself, and the soul that has no access to
a spiritual source must too often fail. In human
progress God *alone* seems to me nearly as helpless
as man. You will remember the pious old gardener,
who was taking rather easily to himself the con-
gratulations upon his work of turning a wilderness
into a joy, when he suddenly pulled himself up and
remembered the Master Gardener, so that he ejacu-
lated, "Yes, that is – God and me together have made
it what it is – but I'm bound to say He hadn't made
much of a job of it until I joined in."

All the advances of science in industry will turn
to ashes if we cannot achieve industrial peace, and
that is the plain man's contribution to it. But it is a
complex problem. We may well assume that people
have erred through want of thought or knowledge
and not want of heart – charity and calmness against
censure and fussation. It is compounded of psychology, politics, economics, scientific change, biological tendency, of hard statistical fact, of moral
sentiment. I see no way of securing it but a higher
moral temperature, and the power to choose the
better way. Guidance from our deepest reflections
and experiences means the over riding of the Master
Builder. In the fullest scientific spirit there is ample
scope for reading and prayer to tap the sources of
spiritual energy, to rid us of slavery to self-imposed

notions and ancient facts and outworn phrases. Consider the character and work of Lord Shaftesbury. He was calm, calculating, studious, and dispassionate, with infinite endurance and patience to achieve his end. He tried to perform no conjuring tricks – he knew that you could only get a pint from a pint pot. He worked in a scientific temper. Yet he had great visions, his moral indignation was red hot; he worked as one possessed, and with the fervour of a prophet and the patience of Job. These were the ideal combination of qualities.

The plain man's contribution to scientific progress is to be scientific in temper himself, to make the right adjustments of himself and society, that science be worth having. To do this he must work a great moral revolution in himself, and live on his worthiest level, to be the best citizen and largest and most unselfish soul. The price of liberty is eternal vigilance – science and the world must not enslave him, and the Lord must join in building his house and watching over his city.

If reality is "something that makes a difference" to man there are two ways by which it may be apprehended: the cool, calculating, self-controlled temper of scientific method, and the warm, unreckoning self-abandonment of religious experience, and, in the frailty of the natural man, both demand the co-operation of a Master Spirit.

IV

Man shall not live by bread alone, but by every word that proceedeth out of the mouth of God.—MATT. iv. 3, 4.

The mere announcement of a title of this kind raises in the minds of the majority a certain complex of ideas, and generally a sense of conflict between two realms of thought.

If it is not the speaker's desire to follow the subject on conventional lines, his first task is to break down these preconceived notions in confused or even harassed minds, for unless this is done no progress can be made. The title "Christianity and Science" brings forward to the consciousness the whole hinterland of conflicting views about the facts of man's past and his destiny. Christianity and physical science are supposed to put them in antithesis. The average man says "that is right" or "that is wrong." Similarly, "Christianity and Medical Science" stimulates thought about two rival methods of controlling matters of health, and "Christianity and Economic Science" leads everyone to think that the speaker will deal with the rival ideals in the realms of wealth-making and use, and intimate that Christian teaching and economic science are in conflict, and that a "choice" must be made. Each time the emphasis is upon rivalry and exclusion.

Now life is not quite so clean cut as this, and few things are either black or white. The truth is that we should much more often discuss co-operation

[1] Address at Birmingham, for Industrial Sunday, April 27th, 1930. (For a fuller treatment of the subject reference should be made to my book, *The Christian Ethic as an Economic Factor* – Epworth Press.)

than rivalry. There is in each case a great task to be performed, a great field of knowledge to be conquered; and there are two broad lines of approach, which are not mutually exclusive, for each can play a most important part. Our task really is to discover how best we can combine the two agencies, which are each excellent in themselves, but each of which may be made stronger by the assistance of the other. Co-operation, not rivalry, then, is my theme, and I desire to lay bare to you how best two great engines for truth and the good life, both "Christian," can be combined in operation.

This view is, of course, modern. Time was when religion and religious literature was supposed to hold the key to all knowledge and all human activity. Physical science is now a separate study, and medical science has also become free from religious implication. One after another branches of knowledge have earned their right to self-government, and become emancipated, but, for long enough, Christianity was supposed to teach us the whole duty of man in relation to wealth and economic activity. The view that there is any separation, either by way of rivalry or by way of co-operative effort, is only lately asserting itself. In the past the emphasis has been upon their identity, and that identity has been a perennial question in the history of thought. The breakaway came towards the end of the seventeenth century. Richard Baxter, the greatest theological figure of that age, was the last of the old theologians who judged that the Bible gave guidance in every economic problem. There was nothing too modern or too complex to be elucidated by direct reference to textual authority.

In my great folio volume, Baxter's *Christian Directory*, there is laid out in the form of question and answer every conceivable problem of human contact. Here you may learn what was regarded as the Christian doctrine of usury, and you will find

justification, in scholastic logic and great biblical
erudition, for many practices which would not be
tolerated to-day. It was not yet a Christian thing to
charge interest for the use of capital; but, under the
pressure of industrialisation and growing commerce
of widespread character, even good men were beginning to feel increasingly uncomfortable about the
rigidity of the doctrine, and were making concessions.
Baxter's concessions to modern practice are very
interesting in the light of to-day. Hard facts were
pushing him away from so-called scriptural theory,
and you can see that it must have caused him many
searchings of heart to make his concessions. Would
you like to know whether it is moral and Christian
to keep two shops in adjoining market-towns? Would
you like to learn what is your duty when you are either
buying or selling an article and happen to know, what
the other party to the bargain does not know, that
there is a ship in the offing, making for the port,
which contains a new supply? Are you worried about
whether it is a proper thing to send your grown-up
son on a commercial errand to a foreign country
where, perchance, infidels may congregate? Well,
Baxter will tell you to your complete satisfaction,
and the workings of this old man's mind remain here
for all time like a fly in amber. This state of affairs
was natural with them when the world was emerging
from simple and parochial outlooks, but to-day the
world is so complex that we should despair of guidance in any text-book of theology, however practical.
Yet there are people who still say of the Bible that
it is all-sufficient. So, in germ, it might be, but
nothing can gainsay the fact that two individuals
with equal zeal and confidence may work out the
principles in a complex series of circumstances to
different conclusions.

What do we mean by "economics" in my subject?
I should say, for brevity, the conditions in which
wealth is made and distributed. I do not use "wealth"

in any sense to which exception can really be taken. Since life is to be lived, we must all have sustenance and shelter – these conditions are physical, and naturally they are also human and physiological. The former will defy any ethical pressure; the latter may be susceptible to the extent to which the physiological shades off into the mental and psychological. There is nothing in ethics that you would regard as a guide to chemistry or mathematics or climate; and, although economics is naturally partly conduct, a large part of it is like chemistry or mathematics or climate. It is our task to determine where the division comes, and to which sections the problems in question really belong. A schoolboy's definition of political economy was: "The thing that tells you how to get the maximum you want, from the minimum honest effort." If he had said that economics is the field of knowledge in which people think they can have the maximum positive opinions, with the minimum honest effort, he would have been quite right. The people who hesitate to express themselves in any other science become, in economic questions, positive, outspoken, and confident. On the other hand at the opposite extreme are those who would regard economics as a science quite independent of and regardless of ethics. These people have reached in the past many cruel conclusions of economic inevitability through the working out of so-called "laws," using the idea of law in quite the wrong sense. So we get "the iron law of wages" and "the subsistence level." Can you wonder that, on seeing such conclusions, a good-hearted man spontaneously rebels, and exclaims, "Then so much the worse for economics." The truth is that many things that were economically inevitable once are not so any longer, for, where there is a general change of human habit and structure, economic necessity may change also. These changes have been brought about partly through growth in knowledge and science, partly in the realm of higher motive and mind. The possibilities of change are much greater to-day, owing to the immense changes by invention and transport. They are also greater because men have a different outlook towards many problems such as cruelty to children and to animals, and their attitude even towards the stranger met along the road is different from that of a hundred years ago.

Economic science occupies a position of peculiar importance to-day; it is of crucial significance to civilised life that we soon make great advances in it. There have been times past which we regard as the special age of chemistry, physics, and ethics; when it was worth almost anything to focus almost all our resources upon the immediate advance, but now it is the day of economics. There have been so many extraordinary changes in the world that they have quite outrun our economic control of it. "Man's control over science has outstripped his *moral* powers," it is said, but the economic failure ought to be recognised too.

The spread of economic knowledge and a radical change in the framework of government are the essentials of real advance, for there is fundamental difference between economics and the physical sciences. The labour of research by several gifted workers in chemistry or physics, some flash of genius, will in itself raise the standard of life of the whole community, without any correlative change in the mass of the people. But in economics it is not merely the creative and discovering progress that is needed – the receptive recognition of millions must be advanced at the same time. For the application of any discovery requiring any change in habit or position demands willingness; and willingness, in a democracy, is based upon understanding. Hence economic advance must be along both fronts: we need specialists, but we also need a higher level of education in such matters on the part of thousands. The

inclusion of elementary economics in the qualifying
curriculum of all the different professions – accountancy, banking, law, estate agency, engineering –
which has been a marked feature of recent years,
ought at least in time to make a solid nucleus of
instructed receptivity, to influence public opinion,
apart altogether from the advantage of its influence
upon the profession itself, and of the counter-
movement of realism which should affect economics
in turn. The best economic solution may fail because
in the classes and masses concerned there is no sense
of urgency and necessity – no realisation that isolated
individual advantage is not a test of the greater
individual advantage which comes from solidarity in
advancement. Again, the solution may fail because an
instructed minority can bring no effective pressure
on the legislative machinery. The economics of the
people are still far too much in the field of fancy, of
human volition, of chance, passion, and moral
suasion. You may remember the story of Dr. Pepper,
of ghost fame, when lecturing on chemistry before
Queen Victoria, in an age when adulation of royalty
was characterised rather by thoroughness than
discrimination. "We have now reached the critical
point, when the oxygen and hydrogen will have the
honour of combining before Your Majesty!" There
would have been nothing amusing about that in a
former age, an age of magic, when the elements were
supposed to answer freely to human direction. The
progress of knowledge has the continuous process of
taking sections from the sphere of loose thinking and
vague generalisation, and making a discipline of
them, more and more subject to measurement, to
ordered causation, and less and less to moral suasion
and caprice of passion. Someday, in judgments in
economics, the word "fair" will come to mean a
necessitated quantitative equality instead of an empirical moral judgment.

In many economic questions to-day, the moral issue

is exceedingly difficult to isolate, and to determine. Owen Young, speaking from a New York pulpit on "What is right in business," has a telling and true illustration from the bank rate.

"Now, I am not here to say that all is right with business. It is far from that. But I am here to say that, in the last quarter of a century, we have made great progress toward the right. Our difficulty does not come so much from bad men or bad principles as it does from the difficulty of applying right principles to increasingly complicated situations. . . .

"Let us take an example or two. What is right or wrong with the discount rate of the Federal Reserve Bank of New York, or with the bank rate, as they say in London when it is fixed by the Bank of England? Do you say there is no question of right or wrong in the moral sense of the bank rate – that is a financial matter? And yet I am here to tell you that I know of no act in business which bristles more with moral problems than the fixing of a bank rate. I do not mean problems in the sense that the men who fix that rate are likely to act in bad faith. Not at all. I mean in the sense that men may fail to apply correctly the sound moral principles which they recognise to a difficult and complicated business problem. Sometimes later, when the thing has been done, and, looking backward, it is found that a mistake was made, then it seems so clear what should have been done that men without experience or with little experience, or men who are looking for trouble, say something is wrong with business – 'Look how that bank rate was fixed.'

"Now the making of a bank rate affects the volume of currency and credit. It increases or diminishes the value of money. As a result of it a debtor pays more and a creditor receives less, or else the converse is true. Every wage earner is affected in the purchasing power of his earnings by the bank rate. Every aged person or invalid dependent upon the income of a trust fund may have more or less of the things he needs as a result of the bank rate. It is a high moral responsibility to fix a bank rate.

"When I was in Germany in February of 1924, working on the Dawes Plan, you will remember that the currency of Germany was depreciating so rapidly that the industries paid their wages daily, and sometimes indeed twice a day. Standing with the lines of employees was another line of wives and mothers waiting for the marks. The wife grabbed the paper from her husband's hand and rushed to the nearest provision store to spend it quickly before the rapid depreciation had cut its purchasing power in two. When the representatives of labour in Germany appeared before the Dawes Committee, I put to them this question: 'What can this committee do for German labour?' I expected the answer to be some of the slogans of labour, such as the eight-hour day, old age or disability pensions, insurance against unemployment, or something of that kind. Much to my surprise the answer came promptly: 'What your committee must do for German labour is to give us a stable currency.' 'Do you know,' the representatives of German labour said, 'that for many months it has been impossible for a wage earner in Germany to perform any of his moral obligations?' Knowing that a child was coming to the family at a certain time, there was no way by which the husband, through effort or sacrifice or savings, could guarantee his wife a doctor and a nurse when that event arrived. One knowing that his mother was stricken with a fatal disease could not by any extra effort or sacrifice or saving be in a position to ensure her a decent burial on her death. And so he said: 'Your committee must, just as a basic human thing, give us a stable currency, and thereby ensure to the worker that his wages will have the same purchasing power when he wants to spend them as they had when he earned them.' Ladies and gentlemen, prior to that

I had always thought of money and currency and credit as a mechanism of finance, impersonal in its operation. Not until then had I appreciated how closely it lies to life and the basic moral problems of every man and woman. Yes, indeed, here the traffic is heavy and the signals complicated."

There are certain typical "Christian" views of economics that must be passed in review. The first is the inability to see any economic fact as a scientific fact like those of chemistry. Every economic condition to such minds is either just or unjust. If it is unjust, then something is wrong, and therefore someone is to blame. Thus every economic problem becomes a moral problem, requiring only the resources of indignation and fervour to elucidate it. A wage is "fair" or a profit "reasonable" or a rent "unconscionable" or conditions "abominable," by reference to some subjective standard of judgment. Without a real statistical basis of comparison, and an economic principle of testing necessity and inevitability, such fulminations, while sometimes very comprehensible, have no economic value, and serve only to confuse the issue. Economics cannot be a thermometer of the comfortable. Yet many people think they have an interest in economics, because they have learned the trick of judgment by opprobrious adjectives. Beyond this point their mental resources are exhausted – they do not know the next move. They are invited to move on a different plane. At a meeting, say, of the Royal Statistical Society, if there is no scope for their particular talent of tub-thumping, some speakers on public questions seem to be "all dressed up with nowhere to go."

There is, however, a class that goes beyond this, with an intellectual apparatus in support of their opinion. But it is all obtained *in support*, and conclusions do not follow, they precede. As with Alice, "Sentence first," if you please, and trial, perhaps, afterwards.

Another class, while not judging on moral grounds, settle many of their economic problems on the basis of their likes, and yet consider they have been economists. "What *I* think is economics; what you think is politics." It has been the fate of schools of economic thought to become political schools too, and here all the reservations and half-tones must be given up in the exigencies of the game. The politician can rarely afford to admit exceptions, or any "bear" points, in his case. No. A patient and suspended examination, with many issues in suspense and unproven, is inconvenient in any field of practical politics, and yet it is the only base on which economic science can maintain itself as such with self-respect. If results of the examination are unwelcome, or uncomfortable and disappointing, then say these people, there must be something wrong with the economics, and their view is that economic science is necessarily dismal and inhuman, materialistic, and on a lower level of truth than spiritual truth. At the time it got the title "dismal" it thoroughly deserved it, but the fact that it has stuck for wellnigh a hundred years is a case of giving a dog a bad name. At present there is nothing inhuman in its teaching, for it only bids us face facts and analyse until we have gone beyond mere appearance: it begs us to examine causal connection and aggregate effects. The charge of materialism is due to the supposition, quite erroneous, that the economist regards economic welfare as supreme, and belittles all other kinds of welfare. Because he necessarily isolates certain aspects for more definite study, he is supposed to have forgotten the true ends of life. He is indeed wrong if, upon reintroducing his conclusions into the real complex world of moral and spiritual values, he does not make allowances for the changes which altruism, self-sacrifice and spirituality may make in any scheme of things based on the hedonic postulate of personal advantage.

One of the one-sided, but typical, views of
Christian people about economics is due to their
preoccupation with one small field of economics as
though it were the whole – that is the subject of
distribution, meaning the distribution between rich
and poor, and inequalities of wealth, or the opposition of capital and labour. But even in the problem of
distribution there are other very important questions,
such as distribution between different kinds of labour
which is equally far-reaching, inasmuch as the price
of articles bought by one section of labour is largely
influenced by the wages of another section. Then
the distribution of the reward to capital in its different
applications, and the dates at which it has been
provided, gives rise to problems of great subtlety and
importance. The distribution of reward between
different industries, particularly between the extrac-
tive, the manufacturing, and the distributive, is
not wholly to be left to chance in a complex society.
Distribution between like classes of workers in
different countries is probably the real "economic
war" of the future.[1] Then the whole problem of
distribution is also bound up with the choice that has
to be made between the maximum change in the size
of the shares of individuals, as compared with something less in size accompanied by greater stability
and comfort and non-disturbance.

This view of the scope of economics also leaves out of
account the great subjects of production, involving
to-day the tangled question of rationalisation, and of
exchange, involving the over-mastering and almost
non-moral problem of the mechanics of the currency.

But the mistakes are not all on the side of the
attitude of Christianity to economics. Economists
often have a too limited conception of the part Christianity and moral teaching can play in gradually
modifying economic conditions and laws. Some have
said in the past, for example, "Because that particular

[1] *Vide* Hon. George Peel, *The Economic War*, 1930.

set of conditions is the effect of present forces it is
inevitable. The only motive we can really count upon
is a mercenary one of pure self-interest. The utmost
Christianity can give is only a few enthusiasts, and
these cannot affect the whole to any extent." Any
careful historical survey of the progress of moral
principle in public affairs – for example, in slavery –
ought to belie this. The lives of Shaftesbury and
Barnardo were powerful forces modifying economic
life, not so much for the direct changes they made in
their own time in social conditions, as for a new
general minimum standard of attitude of mind
which acts as an economic force to-day. But those
lives were in the direct tradition and under the
immediate influence of the movement of religious
thought started by John Wesley.[1]

Again, apart from the unalterability of motive, the
economist tends to assume too much the unchange-
ability of the conditions in which given motives may
work. If all the forces round a man have been against
the survival of his best and least selfish motives, then
the whole economic dynamic may be kept on the
lowest plane. If honesty is *not* the best policy, then,
making due allowance for the principle that some
things thrive best when their living is not made too
easy, honesty may not be in the survival of the fittest.
The conditions which react upon economic motive
include the more fruitful productivity of the soil,
more scientific control of disease, biological consciousness, and birth control, ease of transport, dissemination of knowledge of other peoples and their
lives by cinema and broadcast, and particularly those
features of rapid and general information about
quantities of production, or specifications of quality
in goods, which so alter the economic relations
between buyer and seller, and the whole ethics of
bargaining, secrecy, and the higgling of the market
which so worried Baxter and his kind. The economic

[1] *Vide* the two works on Shaftesbury and Barnardo by Dr. Bready.

conditions in which land is tenanted and owned and cultivated differ widely in different countries to-day, and in our own over a period of time, and these differences have important reactions upon the "cultivability" of certain Christian virtues, not, indeed, with particular chosen spirits who would exist, and even thrive, in any conditions, but with the mass of spiritually frail humanity.

The reactions of conditions of life, and especially of knowledge, upon production are subtle, but very real, and economists by now should be very chary of drawing generalisations for all time. The derivatives of the Malthusian school, largely true in their day, linking the birth rate with the standard of wage, have been wellnigh reversed in a century. A century ago we heard the screams of the millowner about the fencing of dangerous machinery, and the economist's wail about the last of the long daily hours of an industry being the difference between profit and loss, unemployment and employment; more recently we have seen that a sweated wage is the dearest, because the least productive, and the introduction of a minimum, when it has a reaction upon production, has provided the very means out of which it can be paid.

We are now beginning to appreciate the productive or economic reactions of changing incentive, and a sense of dignity. The Christian teacher needs the warning, however, that these reactions are the survival of a long series by trial and error, where appeals to sentiment and moral issues have had either none of the expected economic reactions or the reverse. Thus the shortening of hours proves not to be continuous in its improvement of production; the increase of wages has been known to lead to less effort; large expenditure on welfare has undermined self-help and may lead to a new type of social parasitism, for those things thrive best which are won with a little effort and personal interest.[1] But, with this reservation,

[1] *Vide* my Rede Lecture on "Stimulus in the Economic Life."

I am here reminding the economist that he does not think of life under the eternal stars, but here and now only, subject to a better to-morrow which, indeed, he can help to make better.

Another of the faults of emphasis in the economist is that he tends sometimes to overstate the economic case as a part of the whole. This is not a fault of ignorance, but the natural one of an expert's preoccupation with his subject, and a very just enthusiasm for its value in life. But he has suffered so much, and often so undeservedly, from the imitators of Carlyle and Ruskin who get a cheap reputation for breadth and moral elevation by sneering at the labours of economists, and treating moral indignation as an economic calculus, that the fault is now rarely found amongst economists, even of a severely academic type. There is no nobler writing in any books on the whole aims of life and the realm of ends than the opening chapters of the treatises by Marshall and Pigou. But still the economist of the platform does often talk as though, when an economic solution is found, that is necessarily the right solution, or the whole duty of man. But the Christian of to-day almost as often makes the same mistake of urging that an increased economic welfare means a better life.

The economist, by the same standard, is sometimes prepared to sacrifice too much of the beauty and antiquity of the land, too many of the real amenities of life, for economic advance, though, indeed, that is usually rather the fault of the moneymaker, whose habits and weaknesses the economist studies. For I think it may be fairly shown that even from an economic point of view it is shortsighted to make these sacrifices too frequently or too lightly.[1]

From what I have said, it will be seen that the economist has in the past too readily resisted assumptions

[1] *Vide* "Æsthetics as an Economic Factor," in my *Economic Factors in Modern Life.*

of "injustice" when the circumstances have seemed to him inevitable, which, indeed, in the particular conditions of his day they may have been to a more or less extent, as in the case of slavery, child labour, and sweating. The economist may feel that an existing state of affairs is a true economic equation, without any moral implications being valid, and yet at the same time he ought to be patient with accusations of "injustice" which would only be really valid in a changed or better state of affairs. For it is humanity's task to improve itself, and progress surely means nothing else. "We work not to acquire, but to become," and as Lincoln said of men, "I don't think much of a man who is no wiser to-day than he was yesterday," so we may say it of eras, which have like qualities of biological responsibility, of pharisaism, and of parasitism to other eras, past and future.

The economist has a great opportunity for contribution to the validity and possibility of the Christian ethic. When every allowance has been made for the spiritual value of poverty, and contentment therewith as a soil for Christian virtues, and when every warning has been accepted as to the perils of riches and contentment therewith, it still remains true that grinding toil is not uplifting to the human soul, if it allows no opportunities for real self-expression, for wonderment, and for thought and free action. But, as wealth advances, the most inimical to Christian virtue is the risk of a sense of injustice in maldistribution of wealth, of envy, and uncharitableness, and of an undue ambition to get rich quick, and to get something for nothing. Possibly the lesson of history is that it is better to be all worse off, provided we are all much alike, just as bad self-government is better for happiness than good government by strangers. I should be sorry to accept this as a final lesson for the future, because that kind of self-deception ought to yield to the solvent or corrective of better education. We cannot permanently impale mankind on its own past weaknesses. But let no one assert that it is easier to be good if you are poor; we ought to have outlived that pretty cant of Paley and his school. Indeed, I like much better the prayer, by Juan Louis Vives, for "them in Poverty," published in 1578 in a *Book of Christian Prayers*, and translated from the Latin:

> They that are snarled and entangled in the extreme penury of things needful for the body cannot set their minds upon Thee, O Lord, as they ought to do: but when they be disappointed of the things which they do mightily desire, their hearts are cast down and quail for excess of grief. Have pity upon them, therefore, O merciful Father, and relieve their misery through Thine incredible riches, that by Thy removing of their urgent necessities they may rise up to Thee in mind.
>
> Thou, O Lord, providest enough for all men: we, through our naughtiness, niggardship, and distrust, do make them private and peculiar. Correct Thou the thing which our iniquity hath put out of order: let Thy goodness supply that which our niggardliness hath plucked away. Give Thou the meat to the hungry, and drink to the thirsty. Comfort Thou the sorrowful. Cheer Thou the dismayed, strengthen Thou the weak, deliver Thou them that are prisoners. Give Thou hope and courage to them that are out of heart.

It has been indeed true that poverty and riches have no absolute meaning – they are only relative to a particular age or place. What was abundance and satisfying in the Middle Ages would be regarded as abject poverty to-day. Ideas of housing conditions which are the minimum fit for human beings change with every generation. There is no evidence that the capacity for happiness or virtue changes equally with them. It may well be that, if we look at the whole economic complex of a complicated civilisation, we are making it some day more difficult to be happy, and perhaps even good – in the more exalted senses of that word.

But clearly the task of the economist of to-day is more and more to work out modified Utopias, and to determine by controlled experiment and *ad hoc* examination what would really result from universalising or generalising some particular betterment of motive and of environment or opportunity, and their reactions. He can then give correct aims and possible goals, and the discontent he can properly engender will be a reasonable, a divine discontent.

The Christian teacher can co-operate to solve life's economic problems in many important ways. First, he can give a great zest to discover the better way. He may not, indeed, provide the better brains for economic analysis, but he can hold up the object, enthuse the goal, praise the endeavour. Secondly, he can provide and inspire the *temper* of the enquiry or method – sustain with the patience of the distant aim; encourage again from the rebuff and reverse; purify the motive from the popular success and mercenary ideal; give singlemindedness and self-sacrifice to the research worker and the most perfect humility before facts, and gird the whole effort about with humanity.

In the third place, he can insist on the recognition of the good elements in all the conduct of the peoples studied, and give breathing-space to all other motives besides those of self-interest. Again, he can insist on generalising from, and trusting to, the prevalence and permanence of the higher standards of conduct in economic affairs – by trusting men he may turn the quixotic into the customary. But, fifthly, his greatest contribution is in his own field – to change the human heart by that incomparable dynamic which is the evidence of history, so that those standards may indeed become general, so general as to affect the average conduct of the individuals in human society, that all the generalisations of economists about them may become out of date and unworthy of the new day. Thus he may give even the mathematical economist a new sum to do, and a new graph to draw.

It is the task of the Christian to watch economic affairs closely to determine – or "spot," if you like – the critical point and condition that will bring an evil or wrong result out of a practice or a trend that may lead either into good or into bad; he can have an attitude towards the drink problem, towards the stage and censorship, towards the gambling instinct – an attitude which is not so intransigent as to be useless in a practical world, but is a calculated and reasoned determinant towards economic, as distinct from moral, welfare.

Moreover, by championing the humdrum but real virtues of everyday life he can make a vast direct contribution to economic good. For the prevention of waste, the economy of overlooking and supervision required through faithlessness and defective workmanship, are direct economic factors as well as Christian virtues. In the relations between the several factors of production, all so supremely dependent upon each other, he can introduce dignity, and co-operation in place of scorn and enmity – perhaps the most productive economic factor that is yet only half explored, and certainly not exploited.

I have indicated that human incentive and response can be changed over whole periods of time, and therefore Christianity can make a great contribution to economic life and society. It is a principle, not a code, and therefore it must watch over economic change, like the growth of "big business," and infuse it with its own characteristic impulses and ideals. But it can only do this through the individual life, and it demands so much more than meat for man. As Jacques Maritain says so eloquently:

In the social order, the modern city sacrifices the person to the individual; it gives universal suffrage, equal rights, liberty of opinion, to the individual, and delivers the person, isolated, naked, with no special framework to support and protect it, to all the devouring powers which threaten the soul's life, to the pitiless actions and reactions of conflicting interests and appetites, to the infinite demands of matter, to manufacture and use. [1]

But there is a higher aim even than adapting man to the new order around him, and that is to make a new order within him. In the words of the same author:

It is heartbreaking to see so many intelligent creatures looking for liberty apart from truth and apart from love. Needs must they then seek it in destruction; and they will not find it. And all over the earth the mystics and saints bear witness to the love which gives liberty. The deliverance for which all men long is only gained at the end of the way of the spirit, when love – a measureless love, for "the measure of loving God is to love Him without measure" – has made the creature one spirit with God.

[1] Jacques Maritain, *Three Reformers.*

V

THE ECONOMIC BACKGROUND OF THE GOSPELS [1]

Two texts were chosen: Matt. xx. 6–7, the Parable of
the Vineyard, and Mark xii. 14, the question of the
tribute money.

I have three reasons for being here to-night:
First, I am a convinced believer in the importance
of this series of addresses. A right knowledge of the
origins of the New Testament is by far the most
important matter for the average church-goer to-day
if he is to get his beliefs into proper relation to
modern life, and if he is to get right guidance for
practical action and not make the same mistakes as
his forefathers.
Second, the economic aspect of these origins is so
important that it cannot properly be omitted from
such a series.
Third, while I do not suggest for a moment that I
can do it as well as Mr. Chappel would, at any rate it
ought to come easier to me to work in this field.
There is a great difference between the material for
this address and that for the three preceding. Those
of you who are acquainted with the field of knowledge
covered so far by Mr. Chappel will realise that there
is an enormous mass of facts, and will appreciate, as
I have done, the fine craftsmanship which he has
shown in their selection, and his great skill in getting
the right emphasis where otherwise there might have
been confusion. In this instance the facts are not so
well known. There is sometimes more conflict, and
inference is more often necessary.

[1] Address at the Wesleyan Church, Beckenham, being the fourth in a
series on the literature of the New Testament.

Three preliminary questions. Why do we want to know? How do we know? What do we know? First: Why is it necessary to know anything about the economic background? I hope none of you will be frightened by the word "economic." There is nothing mysterious or alarming about it. How you get your living, whether you like your job, whether your hours are long or short, whether your wage is much or little; what you can get for it, whether you are out of a job; all these things are your economic life, and to put no cant upon it, however religious you may be, they fill ninety-five per cent. of your time. Anything you say must be influenced by them, and anything that is said to you must have regard to them. So we can well ask about the teaching of Christ: How did it come to the listener, and what did it spring from?

Where do we get our information? It is not easy to build up from the Gospels themselves a coherent picture of the social conditions of the times, although Dr. Ryder Smith has made a very good account of the Bible doctrine of wealth and work. The Gospels rather add useful points, and suggest questions for answer, some of them almost unanswerable. Remember that the rest of the New Testament tends to deal with economic environment rather different from that in Palestine – letters written from and to places in the Græco-Roman world, where economic conditions were certainly different from those which surrounded the life of Jesus. The Gospels did not set out to be text-books of science or economics, and we ought not to expect exact descriptions or guidance from them. The general Epistle of James gives a good notion of the ideas prevalent about the relation of the new religion to problems of rich and poor. Actually the sources open to readers in general are not numerous – Josephus is important except that his imagination is rather active where such cold statistical facts as population are concerned. Other historians give some glimpses of the country. There was a very interesting letter written by one Aristeas to an Egyptian, which is the most important connected description we have, dated probably some years before our Lord. Great masses of material exist in the contemporary Hebrew writings, closed to most of us. Joseph Klausner's great work, *Jesus of Nazareth*, is a most thorough collection of such learning – it is a life of Christ entirely from a Jewish standpoint, but in the matter of description of social conditions it has few tendentious strains such as we find in the treatment of doctrine and teaching.

Anyone who is used to economic history can make some reasonable inferences from the isolated facts-I shall not weary you with authorities for all I say, but I shall try to indicate where I am relying on my own judgment. An American writer, Dr. Grant, has very ably summarised the chief material for us, and I am much in his debt.

First of all, a rapid bird's eye view of Palestine as it then was – neither quite like the Palestine of to-day, and certainly different from the Palestine of much earlier times, and here I must refrain from overmuch detail. Picture a land about the size of Wales, rather hilly and well forested, with fertile valleys. Once upon a time, to desert roamers it had seemed a land "flowing with milk and honey" – this would convey an exaggerated notion of its riches, for it was only just self-supporting, and needed unremitting attention to maintain its productivity. Ordinary crops of grain and the vine, fig, and olive were fairly abundant. But during the Assyrian deportation irrigation ceased, the terracing of hillside, which maintained a surface of soil, fell into disrepair, and the violent winter rains washed the slopes and the soils into the valleys (Proverbs xxviii. 3) – a prelude to the barrenness of to-day. Nevertheless, often Palestine seemed to outsiders like a garden, and one needs to realise the dense population that depended upon it to appreciate that the appearance of abundance is not everything. It was still predominantly or essentially agricultural, but rapidly becoming less so – the drift to the towns is commented upon as a growing evil. History repeats itself. Aristeas says, "The towns of considerable size, enjoying a natural prosperity, tend to be well populated, to the neglect, however, of the rural districts, since all men incline to a life of enjoyment, and it is only natural to pursue pleasure." He compares Alexandria, where the King had to make an order that no one from outside could stay more than twenty days. Handicrafts were numerous – over forty are mentioned – but they were subordinate in importance. The craft descended from father to son – "a carpenter and the son of a carpenter." It is noteworthy that Jesus drew nearly all His illustrations from agriculture and open nature, and hardly any from handicrafts, though He was a carpenter. The chief export was almost certainly fish, pickled or salted; the Lake of Galilee was especially important. Oil, and probably wool, were important too. Sheep were abundant, and the shepherd was a familiar figure. On the whole, judged by modern standards, the country was very self-contained, but there was little margin against bad harvests. In fair times fivefold, and in special places a hundredfold, were the farmers' yields. Herod had to import wheat from Egypt and Cyprus for the cities during famine years. In good years, fruits of the olive, vine, and fig gave a margin for exchanging for goods of other lands. But demand was never far away from supply, and often large numbers of people went hungry. Lentils, beans, and such vegetables were the chief food of the poor.

Mineral wealth mattered less then than it does to-day. Apart from copper, which was abundant, there was not much of such wealth. (Lead and tin were rare.) Timber was plentiful, and soft building materials were available. Palestine had all the essentials of a varied standard of life, on the rather low and slightly precarious standard of those days. It was, by its position, a highway or bridge between great nations, and there was a natural contest always going on between the trading facilities that this fact afforded and the exclusiveness of the Jews and their religious rules against exchange with Gentiles. The roads were kept open, however much the foreigners were hated. Highwaymen or brigands flourished on the trade routes. But trade flowed through self-contained Palestine, and affected that self-supporting stay-at-home people very little because of its religious exclusiveness. "The upright Israelite must not purchase any article that has had contact with idolatry" – no business dealings with Gentiles for three days before festivals, no money loans either way; no letting of lands and houses. Outsiders looked on the Jews as uninventive in the midst of their natural resources. Josephus said the Jews showed no tendency towards international trade. Certainly they had few Oriental luxuries. But the Jews abroad had even then a reputation for narrow dealing and great wealth.

The absence of native gold and silver meant there was no coinage of their own – it was foreign coin that circulated, and this could be doctored or debased at will by powers outside. Its purchasing power could be altered without any say by the inhabitants. To-day, this would be a fatal subservience. But then, the self-sufficiency of the main wealth, agriculture, and the prevalence of barter (in the parables, loans were repaid in kind – "100 measures of oil") saved the situation. Besides, the Roman Government did not actually permit coin debasement. Capital was not abundant – the Temple seems to have been the bank – probably the money-changers gave some credit as well, and took care of valuables. Money-changing of foreign coinage lent itself to some sharp practices and ill-gotten gains. The Parable of the Talents shows deposits with bankers and the receipt of interest. It was a sin to charge interest, but this only applied strictly to transactions between Jews. To put money with Gentiles could only be compensated by high rates of interest. The question of the religious legality of interest has only been cleared up in this country in modern times; for centuries the Bible was quoted against the practice. This dominated civil legality. In 1571, the Act of twenty years before, which had prohibited all interest as "a vyce moste odyous and destestable, as in dyvers places of the hollie Scriptures it is evydent to be seen," was repealed. Obviously the accumulation of business capital on any large scale was impossible without it.

Perhaps enough has now been said about the natural conditions. Economic life means much more than nature; political conditions may modify it seriously. The two great facts that made Palestine an unhappy and desperate country were over-population and over-taxation, and these are the basic economic facts behind the Gospels. In numbers the population was very dense. In character and balance it was most unsatisfactory. It does not perhaps convey much to say that the population probably numbered $2\frac{1}{2}$ to 3 millions, unless we relate it to a country of like area with primitive agricultural arts. They were a prolific race, and the population kept up to the very edge of the food-supply in good times, without the relief of emigration or foreign decimation at that time. They were bottled up, as it were, in their own narrow territory – the land promised by God to Abraham and his seed for ever – the Land of Promise where all should be fulfilled. Who, holding the faith, would want to leave it? Dr. Grant says, "Jewish territory is always over-populated. This is almost an axiom of political history during the Christian era. Ancient Palestine was crowded to its very limit. And if we add to this the numerous representatives of the Roman military establishment in Palestine, the soldiers and officers and their families, if we add the annual influx of pilgrims, coming by the thousands, and mostly poor, it is not difficult to conceive a situation in which the menace of over-population became an actual danger, with scarcely any remedy at hand."

While this question of over-taxation is of extraordinary importance in the background, I do not want to tire you unduly with the facts.

The hurt to their pride, both racial and religious, through foreign domination was, of course, important; when this domination expressed itself in taxation it became galling; where people get no visible *quid pro quo* for their taxes it becomes "unjust"; when the taxes are "farmed" in the wholly obnoxious practice of the East, and the "farmer" or tax-gatherer extracts a lot more from the people than he pays over, you have the problem of the psychology of over-taxation in its acutest form.

Just a word about this farmer. It has been the custom, and still is, in parts of the East, for a Government, after prescribing the taxes that are to be paid, to farm them out for a lump sum. The farmer takes the full responsibility for collecting them, and, if he gets more than the lump sum payment agreed, it is his profit; if he gets less, he has to "stump up" the difference. The gospel publicans were not the great princely farmers, but probably the sub-farmers for the districts. They had every reason to indulge in sharp practice and to be extortionate. It was such people who would be the highest bidders for the job. Think of the attitude of mind of the ordinary people to such a person in their midst, the channel of their substance to the hated foreign power! Then the publican mixed with strange people. There were taxes on everything. A tax on the street-walkers with whom the publican had to consort to collect his money – what a combination! To be a friend of "publicans and sinners"–have you got the sting of it?

But there is much more than psychology affected –
there is actual harm to economic ability. The Roman
officials, with the best will in the world, could not
affect more than a part of the situation; the Jewish
nation, by their own law, had got themselves into a
difficult position which took no account of civil or
military requirements. At this time there were two
distinct systems, civil and religious, paying no regard
to each other, and neither capable of being modified
because of the other, but crushing in their joint
effect. The local reigning house of Herod had to be
supported, and his taxation was very heavy, made
up not merely from the produce of the soil, but
also from tariffs and customs duties on merchandise
passing through. There were also taxes on sales, road
and bridge taxes, poll taxes for "enrolment," and the
like. Feeling was engendered not merely by the
weight of the taxes, but the way in which they were
raised and their destination. You will remember the
extraordinary complicated series of religious dues
that were imposed under the Old Testament system.
These were not to keep up civil activities or armies
and navies, but went to support the hierarchy of the
priests and the Temple staff. You start with the original imposts of Deuteronomy, and then later those
that the priests themselves established securely, and,
of course, it was made of religious importance that
the punctilious and full requirements of the law
should be satisfied.

The scribes took care to interpret every point in this
elaborate code in favour of the vested interests, and
in time it became an iron-bound system. Just to
enumerate the various imposts is illuminating as a
reminder. The sin-offering, the thank-offering, and
the shew-bread, the first-fruits of grain, fruit of all
kinds, "the best of the fruits," are said to amount to
a tax of two per cent. of the harvest, naturally a much
larger percentage of the profits. The tithe, you will
remember, applied even to mint, anise, and herbs.

Besides this, we hear of a second tithe imposed by the rabbis; the first-born of animals; special payments for first-born children, equal to two weeks' wages for a labourer; some of the best parts of the animals slaughtered for food, and part of the wool crop; payments for release from vows; a kind of personal poll tax comparable with Peter's Pence, and annual wood gathering for the Temple, with, of course, the "free-will" offerings at the door of the Temple. In addition to these, there was the local support of the poor, and local religious efforts and schools.

The total effect of this was terrific. Wellhausen says, "What originally were alternatives, were thrown together; what originally were left free and undetermined, became precisely measured and prescribed." The Romans took no notice of all this, and the Jew had to pay his tribute money on top as an addition to all his true and rightful obligations. The Church authorities were in no mood to modify their requirements because of the Roman demands. They held the view of the Mosaic law that "Till heaven and earth passed, not one jot or one tittle of the law should be relaxed." It was inconceivable to make any modification because of an outside burden. It has been reckoned, as an approximation and of course not exact figures, that the total taxation of the people must have been round about forty per cent., and it may even have been higher. I have no quarrel with this estimate; I think it is reasonable.

Now taxation of such a percentage on poor people is crushing in the extreme. We regard ourselves as heavily taxed in this country, but the burden on an income of £2 per week is only about one per cent. direct and twelve per cent. indirect, by far the greater part of which is on alcoholic drinks and tobacco, which corresponds with nothing in the Jewish position, and can be avoided. This total of thirteen per cent. is the worst we have to show as a parallel. Moreover, we get economic value for economic sacrifice in all our social legislation. The money comes back to us in other ways.

If you want further details of the enormous number of imposts, you can find them in such a book as *Jesus of Nazareth*, by Joseph Klausner.

So much for a view of conditions. I have no time to describe the social classes – the hirelings and un-employed, or casual labour, the slaves or bondmen; the smallholder agriculturists and fisher-folk; the priestly and legal community; the governing classes. You know of them all separately. You must make your own picture.

We shall ask, apart from Christ's view of social conditions, what were the current social and econ-omic ideas? What were the social aims? Many people seem conveniently positive about these. We can only glance at one or two of their favourite illus-trations.

The Parable of the Labourers in the Vineyard. The Unemployed (Matt. xix. 30–xx. 16). Every conceiv-able lesson has been drawn from this strange parable: the theory of work or maintenance – which leaves out of account how many could have been continuously supported out of the produce of the vineyard: the parable has no hint of social relief of unemployment; there is no evidence that the unemployed were paid a penny a day from the vineyard profits when there was no work to be done there. Then comes the prin-ciple of a flat return for all toil, regardless of time or skill – the old doctrine, "From each according to his capacity, to each according to his need"– or complete social solidarity – ignoring the fact that there was no discrimination here by need: Ruskin's interpretation – a fixed living wage – disregarding the absence of evidence as to what it bought. Was it a living wage? Another gives a spiritual interpretation, viz. that desert of eternal bliss is not a quantitative measure – "by grace are ye saved"; death-bed repentance earns the same heaven as a whole life of virtue.

You will note the human touch – the grumbling was
not that the last hour workers got as much as those
who had borne the heat and burden of the day had
been promised, but that these did not get much
more. But the parable was a reversal of human judgments – it was not a social judgment by Christ or a defence of a particular economic idea. "The Kingdom
is like unto." It illustrated the principle of God's
mercy, which does not proceed upon hours and skill
and productivity. It did not say this principle on
earth was right or wrong, or ever existed in practice;
it was a hypothetical illustration of a divine principle,
probably all the more emphatic because it was unlike
a suitable economic method, and therefore paradoxical. "The first shall be last and the last first."
Peter had just asked, "Lo, we have left all and
followed Thee. What then shall we have?" It is much
more likely a true interpretation that this was a gentle
way of getting the disciples' service on to a spiritual
plane, or a correction of their arrogance, than that
it was a programme or prognostication of the perfect
economic society, and its methods of distribution.
Whatever views you may hold on that economic
problem, the parable is hardly an adequate basis in
the absence of supporting evidence of Christ's view –
no such support seems to be afforded by the differential rewards of the Parable of the Talents.

The Parable of the Unfaithful Steward (Luke xvi.
1–13). No one can deny the difficulty of the teaching
of this parable. The steward is not praised because
of his integrity of spiritual action, but because of his
foresight and worldly wisdom. He wasn't praised by
Christ, but by the employer in the story. If even a
wicked and unjust steward can feather his nest in
this way to provide for the future, how much more
should the children of light use earthly mammon for
the highest ends. What is money for? It is to help us –
not hinder our spiritual good. There is no economic
lesson or social programme whatever in these words.

You might as well say the parable blesses absentee landlordism and the evils of landed parasitism.

In the Parable of Dives and Lazarus, the poor man and the rich man get their positions reversed in heaven. The Pharisees were lovers of money, and had been scoffing. It is not stated that Dives had been particularly wicked or Lazarus particularly virtuous to deserve this, though we may infer that Dives' fault was ignoring the need of Lazarus. There is no hint of reversal of fortune in this world; it is the "poverty-piety" equation familiar from Jewish literature – see also the Epistle of James. The famous reply to the Pharisees and Herodians, "Render unto Cæsar the things that are Cæsar's, and unto God the things that are God's," has had much put upon it; e.g. the root idea of two final authorities, Church and State, and, therefore, twofold taxation. The question was a crucial one. The answer "No" would have meant, "Here is an anti-Roman agitator; well within Pilate's net." "Yes" might mean weak traitorship to the Jews' dearest cause, which was the true Messianic hope of emancipation from the yoke. But he didn't quibble or evade; he said, in effect, That's temporal and earthly politics; think rather of the greater spiritual things. Acquiesce and free your mind for the greater tasks. Dr. Grant says, "If Christ had been a social revolutionary he could not possibly have answered in these words, or with the emphasis they conveyed."

To the Jewish writer Klausner it was the critical turning-point in the people's faith in Him. The masses thirsted for freedom from the Roman bonds. Jesus, so far, had been fearless, driving out money-changers, attacking scribes and Pharisees. Surely He couldn't boggle at this! Klausner curiously thinks the reply was intended to insult the foreign Emperor as the antithesis of God. When we notice that the people supported Him at the purifying of the Temple, but did nothing to save Him three days later, the change is hard to explain; unless we assume that His answer about the tribute money proved to the people that not from this Galilean Messiah could they hope for national freedom and political redemption. The Messianic hope was religious and vital, but it was a conflict of faith with terrible economic conditions. In John's account of the trial, Jesus makes clear his own idea of His purpose: "My Kingdom is not of this world: if My Kingdom were of this world, then would My servants fight that I should not be delivered to the Jews." The soul of truth, He disclaims all political or revolutionary aims in conditions in which they were surely, if ever in history, fully justified. The people had real temporal and economic wrongs – Jesus might well have boiled with indignation and given a programme of rebellion and release. What was, then, His idea of His own Kingdom?

His Kingdom. We have to account for the complete absence of any appeal to social betterment by revolution or even constitutional means. It is only possible from the religious point of view. The Pharisees also were not revolutionaries, and the oppressed people got weary of looking to them. Poverty, the effect of faithfulness to divine law, would be recompensed by riches – in heaven. Right acceptance of the world's situation of injustice is almost a certain passport to better times. The well-to-do for centuries have put this to diabolically good use.

Blessed are the meek, the persecuted for righteousness' sake, for theirs is the Kingdom of Heaven (Matt.v.9–12). This poverty-piety equivalence in the Epistle of James carries this conception a stage further – it is not merely the persecution and oppression by poverty for the faith, but a traditional glorification of poverty as a virtue in itself and as a theory of society.

The Jewish eschatology was, "The servants of God now suffer affliction, poverty, oppression, and possess their souls in patience: hereafter, wealth, freedom, satisfaction shall be theirs." This is not a proletarian dream. "The only programme for the oppressed is a further patient endurance of wrong, till the reign of God is perfectly established." This was the cardinal point of view of Jesus. He never minimised the spiritual dangers of great wealth, but He never condemned it when it was held with responsibility. The rich young ruler's prescription was personal to his own soul. It is not practicable for everyone to sell all he has and give to the poor, for someone has to buy, if things are to be sold. The proposition that the precious box might have been sold and the proceeds given to the poor was not accepted – a spiritual value was put higher. (It was a hard saying, that – "The poor ye have always with you"; not much of a social programme there!) Besides, some rich person must presumably buy the precious box. You cannot get a social scheme by pushing the difficulty one stage farther on. Against rich men as such in themselves, Christ had no word. Zaccheus, Martha, Lydia, Joseph of Arimathea, Philemon, possibly Paul, might otherwise have had no place in the Church. There is no evidence that they were expected to divide their possessions. It is true that in the main the rich rejected Him – so few got their wealth by legitimate means, or, if they did, used it properly.

Jesus, in current affairs, supported the *status quo*. The publican, so hateful a profession as the tax farmer, was told to extort "no more than that which is appointed you." The oppressors, the Roman soldiers, "Do violence to no man, neither exact anything wrongfully, and be content with your wages."

So Christ's teaching actually offered no escape from oppression here. He took the Jews' Messianic hope of a deliverer and spiritualised it. The idea of pain to-day as the purchase-price of blessedness hereafter has been a dynamic for centuries. "The old clear conviction of the utter insignificance of this life when compared with the life after death" has weakened, says Graham Wallas. The trade-unionist miner or factory hand is certain sooner or later "to ask for a measure of blessedness here and now." We have to look for the eternal value of His spiritual teaching, not in the social and economic programmes, or even ideas of particular ages, but in the developing force internal to all change. If He had laid down lines of social organisation, His plan would have been superseded again and again.

It may be a hard doctrine to you, but what is economically inevitable cannot be morally wrong. The highest practical morality is relative – relative to economic possibility. You cannot go to the Bible to prove what is the best form of embodied Christianity. Each age has to work out that sum for itself, and because it gets a different answer it has no right to be supercilious about past ages.

Take slavery. The case for slavery was satisfactorily proved until modern times from the Bible. It may be possible, as far as I know, to make a formal case still. I cannot say; I have not tried it. At any rate, there is something to be said for the view that the ancient world could not have done without it. Now take this picture: "How sweet the name of Jesus sounds." What a hymn! What depths of spiritual insight and knowledge! What intimacy! What immediacy! Something that can sound the depths of experience through the ages. Now see the writer of it – a captain of his ship, singing hymns in his cabin, holding prayer meetings, putting down swearing amongst the crew, and underneath him all the time a weltering, sweltering mass of African negroes herded under conditions that we should not tolerate for the lowest animals.

Now walk down near by here, pass our Keston Church, turn to the right on the 'bus route to Westerham, turn over a stile on the left up to the Holwood height, and see there the great tottering old tree, and, underneath, the seat, carved on it the record of the great decision by Wilberforce at that spot to devote himself to putting right the great slave wrong. Both Christian in spirit, but how different in outlook! You cannot prescribe in advance where the spirit of the teaching as distinct from the letter will lead you. The divinity of Christ lies in His power to give the eternal principle which can advance with every change in economic conditions and make new institutions. I do not know what the logical application of this principle will be in future ages. It will be, at its best, this spirit divided into the economic conditions of that time. Those conditions will be mainly what the world decides to do about its population, their numbers and distribution, and what science can do with the food-supply.

All this does not mean that we have any shame in social idealism – far from it; that it is not our duty to get the best and sanest political view; that we ought not to strive for every scientific advance in enriching the material world. All these will give the New Testament a fresh chance of expressing itself in new forms, but what we do learn above them all is the supremacy of the moral kingdom.

VI

In the beginning, God.
And ye shall know the truth, and the truth shall make you free.

Three preliminary points before I open my subject:
First, that this is my second, but also my last,
appearance in this capacity. I only take upon myself
this duty under some pressure from Mr. Chappel,
and because it is possible that the same words from
a layman that he might utter may, for some strange
reason, achieve a purpose more fully than his.

Second, in what I say concerning Scripture I shall
not go beyond what is to be found in the publications
of the Society for the Promotion of Christian Knowledge, and what is taught in our theological colleges
and, indeed, to the boys in our public schools. I am
aware that some of you may not be quite in line with
these three tests, but I only ask you to believe that
I am in no sense an innovator, loving different things
because they are new. In what I say about science I
shall give those renderings of its rapidly changing
ideas as faithfully to generally received knowledge
as I can. I am in a difficulty about language. What
may be novel and difficult to some of you will be
over-simple to others. I think a half-way course is
not very satisfactory. I shall endeavour to put most
of what I have to say in terms that can be understood
by all, but there are certain passages which I shall
not attempt to simplify, and must express in modern
terms for those of you to whom those terms convey

[1] Address at the Wesleyan Church, Beckenham, being the second in a
series of addresses on the Old Testament.

meaning. I know it is said that there is nothing that cannot be expressed in simple terms, but this is sheer affectation. It is true that all the great things of life and experience that are repeated through the centuries can really be put in Anglo-Saxon words, but, when the mind is exploring the processes of knowledge and thought, the vocabulary of a thousand years ago is wholly inadequate, and, indeed, we must invent our shades of meaning and of distinction as we go along.

In the third place, I want you to remember all through that my subject is not religion and science, but the much narrower one of the Old Testament and science. The former and wider topic contains many vast problems which are excluded from the latter; for example, a comparison of what our faith has to say on such problems as the divinity of Christ, the Virgin Birth, and the Resurrection, with scientific thought. Even more striking is the doctrine of immortality which is nowhere found or taught in the Old Testament; there are one or two glimpses of the idea in the Psalms and the Prophets, but on the whole it is true to say that the Hebrew religion had no doctrine of everlasting life. If it were not that my subject were thus confined, I could not possibly attempt it in the time.

Science is not some awful mystery. It is organised common sense, ordered knowledge, found by experiment, tested by experience, reconciled and consistent in its parts, and yielding the general principles which make further progress and statements of what will happen possible.

The three great concerns of science, since what we call "science" has come into being about the last three hundred years, have been: what do we know about the universe about us, what do we know about the earth itself, what do we know about life upon the earth and its development? Now we come to ask ourselves, "What does the Old Testament tell us on these subjects?" We shall find that, although the discussions as between the Old Testament and science have been going on continuously for the last three or four hundred years, there have been three great culminating points or crises corresponding to these three aspects, and each of these represented a more or less self-contained contest. But why should there have been a contest? In the first place it is necessary to study the conditions into which scientific knowledge of the universe first dawned.

Why do we need to go back 300 years?

First, because what we call science to-day began about then. Medicine was cradled in magic and mumbo-jumbo; astronomy and physics were in the arms of astrology; chemistry began with alchemy, love philtres and the elixir of life. Second, because there was built up that wonderful complex of realistic biblical imagery through Milton, Bunyan, etc., which, working through artists like Gustave Doré and a host of others, coloured the whole anthropomorphic thought of our own fathers and, indeed, of many of us in our early days – indeed, so much so that many of you would be hard put to it to say whether a particular notion you have was really in the Bible or not!

You must try to conceive the mental outlook, not merely on religious matters, but on natural events before the scientific era. Everything was regarded as settled by authority. Some ancient great man had pronounced, and no evidence of the senses was asked for or, if it were obvious, was regarded. Take such a simple thing as the fertilisation of plants. It must surely have been seen that, when the blossom on a tree was blighted or destroyed, no fruit results. So the sequence of flower and fruit must have been known by everyone from the earliest times. Yet the real causal relation between them was not understood or discovered until the seventeenth century. Except for Herodotus, who seems to have had a

glimpse of the truth 500 years B.C., the Greek phil-
osophers taught that fertilisation was unnecessary –
for example, that both the male and female date
palms bore fruit – and they held beliefs which could
have been shown to be quite wrong by observation
or a single experiment. Equally, with all other plant
knowledge, they were content with the haziest and
most traditional views when a little observation could
have made it precise. Towards the end of the seventeenth century the real facts about fertilisation began
to be discovered and put on record, and, in the first
half of the nineteenth century, the mechanism of
fertilisation was completely analysed and understood.

There were, of course, at all times, men of enquiring
minds who experimented and observed closely, but
they were few and far between, and often regarded
with grave suspicion, banished, or otherwise ill-
treated. The great Roger Bacon anticipated many
discoveries in optics, and yet he had practically no
influence upon the world for 200 years after, when his
namesake, by no means so great a scientific mind,
gave the scientific method a send off from which it
has never since stopped. Think of the great open
courtyard by the white-marble, leaning tower of Pisa
in the year 1591, with its marvellous group of
architectural beauty just as we see it to-day. A young
professor made his way to the top, then carefully
dropped from the parapet at the same moment two
solid balls, one a hundred times heavier than the
other, the crowd of learned seniors and great scholars
seeing with their own eyes that the two kept together
and reached the ground at the same moment, thus
smashing the traditional knowledge of many centuries. Had not authority said that one would fall
one hundred times as fast as the other? The learned
ones indignantly retired to their studies to prove
dialectically that the evidence of their own eyes was
all wrong, and this inquisitive young man, Galileo,
must really be stopped at all costs. Where would all

learning and scholarship be if this sort of thing went on? It was impertinent and subversive of all order.

This is not merely an illustration of the attitude of mind of those days, but it is also, perhaps, the beginning of modern scientific method. Now come down to our own times and our own country, and see one who is possibly the most original experimenter of all time, performing what is now an elementary experiment in electricity, before a large audience. He passes a magnet near a coil of wire, and a slight current of electricity is produced. It is uninspiring and unconvincing. "But what is the use of it?" said a lady. Then came Faraday's historic answer, "What, madam, is the use of a new-born baby?"

I am not sure that, having regard to the age in which we live, this attitude of mind towards new scientific truth is not often more to be deplored than that of the poor learned professors of Pisa in their day.

In earliest times the official representatives of religion and science were the priestly craft. They mixed the two. They were jealous of encroachment. In 500 B.C., Thales began to suspect and teach that there were principles or rules at work in nature – laws we should call them – and that they could be discovered by observation, and not merely at the whim of gods to be propitiated and "squared." The priests for centuries opposed such encroachment. It has been said with some truth that the great religious influence of St. Augustine was outweighed in its advantages by a single sentence that riveted this mode of thought upon the world for a thousand years, so widely was it used as final. "Nothing is to be accepted," he wrote, "save on the authority of the Holy Scripture, since greater is that authority than all the powers of understanding." At other times he insisted that Scripture not only gave no false information, but gave all that was wanted. No one was allowed to observe, much less experiment – only to elaborate, to the final degree of absurdity, poetical or descriptive phrases in Scripture. What is the science about the world so derived? The earth is flat, founded on an underlying sea (Ps. cxxxvi. 6, xxiv. 1–2; Gen. vii. 11). It is stationary (Ps. xciii. 1; cv. 5). The heavens are like an upturned bowl or canopy above it (Job xxxvii. 18; Gen. i. 6, 8; Isa. xl. 12; Ps. civ. 2). The circumference of this vault rests on pillars (Job xxvi. 11; Ps. civ. 3). Sun, moon, and stars move within this firmament specially to illumine man (Gen. i. 14, 18). There is a sea above the sky (Gen. i. 7; Ps. cxlviii. 4). Through the windows of heaven rain comes down (Ps. lxxviii. 23; Gen. vii. 11). Within the earth is Sheol, where dwell the shadowy dead (Isa. xiv. 9–11). This whole cosmos is suspended over vacancy (Job xxvi. 7).

For centuries there were isolated murmurs from rather independent spirits that the earth was round – they were scornfully crushed as opposed to authority, and absurd and atheistic. One divine sketched the whole plan of the universe: a great box divided into two parts, one over the other – in the lower, men dwelt; in the upper, God and the angels arranged stars and pushed the sun and moon backwards and forwards; a great mountain at the end hid the sun during the night. He said God would send to hell all who questioned it. Others dealt with the absurdity of men being upside down on the other side of the earth. St. Augustine said there couldn't be anyone there, for Scripture speaks of no such descendants of Adam, and, since St. Paul had said the word of the preachers had gone through all the earth, and we knew they had not been to the antipodes, there couldn't be any antipodes, and anyone who contradicted him gave the lie to David, Paul, and therefore to the Holy Ghost.

Early in the sixteenth century, simple Nicholas Copernicus, living on the borders of Poland, declared that the current ideas about the sun revolving about the earth, and all the elaborate mechanism invented to account for the movements of the planets, were wrong. He was very quiet about it, and with his few friends nursed his ideas for thirty years – he knew what the persecution of the Church would be. His great book was kept back by the printer and was brought to him only when he was dying. He feared even for his dead body, and directed that his tombstone should not mention his scientific achievement. It was even then some time before Bruno dared to speak of it within reach of the Pope – the consequences were short and sharp. Copernicus had made no mistake about that. Bruno was imprisoned for six years in the Inquisition dungeon and then burnt alive. That would surely be an end of such talk of a round world moving around the sun! People had objected to Copernicus that, if the planets moved around the sun, then Venus would have phases like the moon, according as the sun's light fell on her face opposite us or on one side as she moved to a position half-way between. Copernicus agreed, and said he could not answer the objection, but surely God would answer it. God did answer, through Galileo's little telescope. This discovery let loose a terrific abuse, and the shadows of the mountains and valleys on the moon, which showed that the moon shone by reflected sunlight, simply capped everything. Didn't Genesis call the moon "a great light"? At once the abusers carried the thought of the world not being the centre of the universe to an illogical extreme: "Then the other planets must be inhabited!" But how could those inhabitants be descended from Adam, and what about Noah's Ark?

Galileo all alone – on the other side the whole Church! He was tried: theology pondered for a month, and then declared, "The first proposition that the sun is the centre and does not revolve round the earth is foolish, absurd, false in theology, and heretical because expressly contrary to Scripture."

Galileo avoided the dungeons by agreeing to conform and keeping silence. On a new Pope's advent, he broke forth again. Once more he was tried, and signed that famous recantation: "I, Galileo, being in my seventieth year, being a prisoner and on my knees, and before your Eminences, having before your eyes the Holy Gospel which I touch with my hands, abjure, curse, and detest the error and the heresy of the movement of the earth." It is said that he murmured as he rose from his knees, "It moves all the same."

It was not merely the Catholic Church that took up this attitude towards new knowledge; the vigorous Luther and the gentle Melanchthon both denounced Copernicus in striking terms and with abundant logic. It was not until 1835 that books with heliocentric ideas were taken off the Roman Catholic Index of Forbidden Books.

In fairness to the Christian Church, it must be remembered that there was no properly attested science of observation and experiment – astronomy in its infancy was in the hands of astrologers, and astrology was physically fatalistic in a way that was repugnant to Christian teaching. Small wonder they distrusted observation and scientific method. I refer later to the subject of this determinism and the later Christian suspicion of the deterministic fatalistic tendencies of physical science. It is curious, of course, that the Church was at that very time elaborating a system of spiritual determinism of its own, just as dreadful and repugnant to us. Basing himself on some elements in Pauline writings, St. Augustine had constructed a fairly closed system of spiritual fatalism, and then Calvin tightened up every screw in it and blocked every loophole so that all mankind was divided into two rigid and determined sections, the elect and the damned, and these two classes were by no means the same as the good and the bad.

The second awakening as to the true nature of Old Testament literature came upon the question of the creation of the world, and its age. You will remember that well-meaning Archbishop Usher in the seventeenth century made a calculation of the chronology of Bible events, showing that the world began 4004 B.C., and this, with the seven days of the Creation, was the full life of the world and all its wonders. These dates got into the margin of the Authorised Version and were accepted by millions as the inspired Bible itself. This fact alone was responsible for infinite difficulties of faith and disillusionment and added to the bitterness of the conflict between believers in the Bible and the new and growing knowledge.

Lightfoot, Vice-Chancellor at Cambridge, and a learned Hebrew scholar, after a laborious search of the Bible, claimed that heaven and earth, centre and circumference, were created altogether, in the same instant, and clouds full of water, and man was created at 9 o'clock a.m. on October 23rd, 4004 B.C. Within two hundred years, Egyptian exploration revealed that a civilisation and culture of a high order existed on the Nile considerably before this date.

The coming of the fossils really began the trouble, for it provoked serious thought. Every kind of explanation was forthcoming. They were God's rejected models of his work – or outlines of future creation – sports of nature. Or they were specially put into the earth to provoke man's curiosity and test his faith. Even in recent times an eminent naturalist, in his anxiety to save the literal account in Genesis, has urged that Jehovah tilted and twisted the strata, scattered the fossils through them, scratched the glacial furrows upon them, spread over them the marks of erosion by water, and set Niagara pouring – all in an instant – thus mystifying the world "for some inscrutable purpose, but for His own glory." The existence of noxious and dangerous things in creation always gave rise to grave discussion, and was put down to man's disobedience. Sin accounted for all things hurtful to man. Even in John Wesley's time it was brought out with great force that before Adam's sin "none of these attempted to devour or in anywise hurt one another"; the spider was as harmless as the fly, and did not lie in wait for blood. This picture of an entirely vegetarian world lasted until geology revealed the remains of large numbers of carnivorous creatures, many having remains of animals in their stomachs, all extinct long ages before the appearance of man upon the earth. It was also orthodox religious belief that all snakes stood erect and walked, and even talked, before the Almighty's curse, until the remains of fossil serpents of long ages before man's appearance made men think otherwise. The differences in species among animals gave rise to much difficulty. All the animals were supposed to have been created in the beginning, preserved in the Ark, and continued without change. But, as zoologists found more and more species, the Ark was made bigger and bigger until it was held there had been a human error in measurement. When, across the oceans in Australia and America, entirely different kinds of animals were found, never seen in Europe and Asia, the puzzle was how they could have migrated from Ararat over such vast spaces of water, and many ingenious explanations were given.

With the approaching end of the world, Augustine thought all study of nature and animals futile, hence the wildest and absurdest views of animal life were current and lasted for centuries. No one checked up the facts. "Too much prying into the secrets of nature was generally held to be dangerous for body and soul."

Dr. A. D. White says: "Neglecting the wonders which the dissection of the commonest animals would have afforded them, these naturalists attempted to

throw light into nature by ingenious use of scriptural
texts, by research among the lives of the saints, and
by the plentiful application of metaphysics. Hence
such contributions to knowledge as that the basilisk
kills serpents by his breath and men by his glance,
that the lion when pursued effaces his tracks with the
end of his tail, that the pelican nourishes her young
with her own blood, that serpents lay aside their
venom before drinking, that the salamander quenches
fire, that the hyena can talk with shepherds, that
certain birds are born of the fruit of a certain tree
when it happens to fall into the water, with other
masses of science equally valuable." You can find
plenty of evidence of the hold that this had upon the
imagination in the sculpture of our abbeys and
various churches.

The discovery of America led to many strange
problems. By the middle of the eighteenth century
the great Linnæus had numbered 4,000 species of
animals, and men were everywhere impressed with
the difficulties involved in naming each of them by
Adam, and bringing them all into the Ark. Moreover,
the space required for the different kinds of food,
whether the animals were admitted by twos, as stated
in one part of the Bible story, or by sevens, as stated
in the other! How could animals so sluggish as the
sloths of South America have got away from Ararat
so completely and travelled so far? By the middle
of the nineteenth century, the wisest men in all the
Churches had given up the struggle. But they had
been profoundly helped by the new knowledge
about the Scriptures which came from the study
of the writings of the ancient peoples and a more
systematic examination of the Bible itself.

Until modern times it was not realised that nearly
all ancient peoples have preserved some sort of
traditional explanation of the beginnings of things,
often very poetical, or very primitive and very
fanciful. The book of Genesis is really a "collection

of short stories," and it has preserved two distinct accounts of Creation, which have many points in common with the accounts in Babylonian folklore, and a few points in common with other cosmogonies, as they are called. But, speaking generally, it can be said with confidence that the Hebrew accounts are by much the most dignified and beautiful, are actually nearer to nature, are free from degrading and un-worthy associations, and, above all, are dependent upon the idea of the One God – a most remarkable advance.

This early beginning of the Hebrew faith is indeed worthy – it is the cradle of our own faith in the One Supreme Being. In the primitive and faulty keeping of that little tribe with its genius for religion, the civilised world has become emancipated from the old beliefs in many gods and goddesses. I wish I had time to describe some of those other Creation stories. But it will be enough to focus attention on these two. It is, I believe, true that many educated people still do not realise that there are actually two interwoven stories in Genesis (chapters i. and ii.) so full of contradictions and contrasts that no real science of the beginnings could be based upon them if we had no other. In the same way the story of the Deluge, as a single story, is full of discrepancies until we realise that two stories are interwoven. Again I should like time to be drawn into the comparative Deluge stories of other lands – the accounts occupy 258 pages in Sir James Fraser's work on *The Folklore of the Old Testament*. I will only ask you to read the story of the Chaldean account discovered in 1872 at Nineveh on the tablets, and compare it with the two interwoven accounts (J and P, as they are termed) in Genesis. There are two distinct styles here. J distinguishes between the number of clean and un-clean animals. P makes all alike be taken in by pairs. P makes the flood last one year and eleven days, and J sixty-one days. J is crudely anthropomorphic.

P maintains a high transcendent God, with no account of Noah's sacrifice.

In a similar way, the Joseph story is full of contradictions until we realise that two documents are interwoven.

Shall I now illustrate the differences in the Creation accounts?

The contrasts between the two Creation accounts:

(1) The first account in order (but later in time) emphasises the creative word. The second says nothing of this, but God "makes" or "forms" especially clearly – the words are quite distinct in the original.

(2) The first dwells on the six-day process; the second has no trace of this division, or a creation week of seven days. Indeed, it refers to the "day" when the Lord made the heavens and the earth – and the author of this was evidently unacquainted with the first account or he might have said "days."

(3) The first account gives three first days to the elements, and, second, to the separate movements of light, and creatures of land and sea and air. In the second, man is made from the dust of the earth, and then a garden is planted and trees grow up.

(4) In the first, the waters bring forth fishes, marine animals, and birds (Gen. i. 20), but in the second, both land animals and birds are declared to have been created, not out of water, but out of the ground (Gen ii. 19).

(5) In one, man is the end and aim of creation; in the other, he is the beginning, coming before the animals.

(6) In the first, man and woman seem to be made simultaneously; in the second, God creates woman as a consequence of man's loneliness and the unsuitability of the animals as companions. In the first there is no trace of the creation of woman out of man, as in the second.

(7) The most striking difference is in the conception of God. Elohim, in the first, is majestic, dignified, and aloof. Yahweh, in the second, is "more human, acts and speaks like a man, walks in the Garden, is puzzled at man's behaviour, and discovers his secret by cross-examination" (James).

Our translators thought they had a single continuous coherent record, and so they unconsciously minimised differences which are more readily visible in the original Hebrew. To take one instance – Gen. ii. 18. God said, "It is not good for man to be alone. I will make a helpmeet for him." Then follows an account of the creation of the beasts, etc., and Adam's naming of them, and the conclusion that they were not a helpmeet for him, and the consequential making of woman. The Vulgate is ambiguous on this, but Luther almost deliberately adjusts this to the order of the first chapter by wrongly translating it "for when the Lord God had made every beast of the field, etc." The German text has suffered from this exceptional difficulty. Dr. Moffat's translation makes the original clear, that God first made the animals as an experiment in helpers which was not satisfactory.

You will see, therefore, that, if we are going into details in the assertion of the biblical supremacy over science as a literal account of how the world came into being, a difficult choice has to be made, and the very fact and act of choice is destructive of the infallible basis or theory of literal inspiration. You can understand why one feels a little impatient in these days when we hear it reiterated, "Why do you want to destroy people's simple faith in the plain simple words of Scripture? You destroy their faith in the Bible." The fact is, without the aids of modern research, and a proper conception of the Bible story, it is full of difficulties which need not exist.

I find I made the following notes some thirty-four years ago in the margin of my Bible which will serve to show the then state of Christian view of the reconciliation, so far as it was available to a boy in the books of an ordinary home and accessible libraries.

Biblical proofs that "day" does not signify twenty-four hours, but an indefinite period:

(1) Gen. ii. 4. "In the day the Lord God made, etc." The word is "yom."

(2) Deut. x. 1. "Hear, O Israel, thou art to pass over Jordan this day." They did not till his death.

(3) Ps. cxlv. 8. "As in the day of temptation." Here it was forty years.

(4) Sun was not appointed till fourth period to rule over the "day." How did the division exist?

(5) If we understand "day" as sunrise to sunset, how it varies in different parts of the world – at the poles a whole year.

(6) Gen. ii. 17; John viii. 56; Rom. xiii. 12. "In the day thou eatest thou shall surely die." "Your father Abraham rejoiced to see My day." "The night is far spent, the day is at hand." No specific period.

(7) The heavenly bodies were created, according to Job xxxviii. 6–7, before their light came to the earth.

(8) Ps. xcvi. 4; 2 Pet. xi. 8. "A thousand years in Thy sight but as yesterday." "One day is with the Lord as a thousand years, and a thousand years as one day."

(9) The seventh day is not even yet concluded. God still resteth. John v. 7 and Heb. iv. 4, 11.

(10) Fuerst's lexicon observes that "yom" translated " 'day' only exists in derivative senses and is used for a period."

It is the custom now to regard all this as beside the mark, and to state frankly that a day of twenty-four hours was really meant and intended in these accounts. I agree that it does not matter very much when once we have recognised the true character of the early part of Genesis. But, while doubtless both translators and readers mean a literal day, I am not so sure that

the original writers or recorders were necessarily
so exact in their thoughts, and there is no reason why
a general, figurative idea of durations of time should
not have satisfied their minds.

Forty years ago, too, men were still struggling to
fix the order of the creative events in the first account
with the order in science. But, again, this is now almost irrelevant, although, as I have said, the Hebrew
tradition is vastly superior in its approach to
naturalism.

I must touch lightly upon the third great crisis or
conflict, the repercussions of which are felt in our
own day, that relating to the evolution of life and the
antiquity of man with his lowly origins. From the
unpretentious mansion in the quiet country near by
Beckenham – indeed, some of Darwin's letters bore
the address, "Downe, near Beckenham"– came words
seventy years ago which were to shake the whole
world. The affront and menace to religious faith
seemed terrible. But I am glad that, with so many
other aids from other directions to a change in
attitude, all the thinking elements in religious life
came to accommodate themselves to the new truth
much more quickly than in centuries gone by. I am
glad that Darwin rests in Westminster Abbey, close
to Sir Isaac Newton. After all the vituperation that
had been heaped upon him, it was a worthy recognition of his Christlike temper and character. I am glad
that that house is now a national possession in the
British Association, and I dare to prophesy that, in
a hundred years time, Downe will have as many
visitors as Stratford-on-Avon.

The full implications of evolutionary ideas are not
yet clearly worked out. But enough is definite and
accepted to give a new view of man's origin and
destiny, in my judgment more noble and impelling
to sacrifice and service than the old. Here, however,
I leave my discussion of it, for it takes us away from
the subject, the Old Testament.

Let us now look at several of the difficulties which have arisen in simple and faithful minds.

Fst. The thought that to destroy the idea of instantaneous creation out of nothing, and to provide as a substitute a gradual unfolding, is to belittle the Creator and His power.

There is nothing intrinsically belittling to our view of the Deity in thinking Him the ordainer of laws. One has very rightly said it is easier to think of the power which can call a rose into being than one which can ordain a process by which roses shall for ever make themselves.

Is the Bible account after all so inconsistent with natural processes, and causes at work, as well as its direct declaration or fiat?

Consider these passages: "Thou art my Creator" (Job xxxii. 22; xxxv. 10; xxxvi. 3); "The people that shall be born [created] shall praise the Lord" (Ps. cii. 19); "Thou sendest forth Thy breath, they are created" (Ps. civ. 30); "Remember now thy Creator in the days of thy youth"; "The Lord hath created a new thing in the earth" (Jer. xxxii. 22); "For Israel hath forgotten his Maker" (Hos. viii. 14). There are many other passages where the function of creation or making is assigned to God, in which natural causes are obviously at work, and not the instantaneous fiat. It seems to me not inconsistent to imagine that the writers of Genesis felt dimly that fiat and process were not incompatible. Or shall I say that it is hard to affirm that they had a clear idea of fiat as distinguished clearly from a natural process? It is so easy to read into early records a distinction which is so clear to us, but which to them was unformed and unnecessary.

In Ps. xlviii. 5–6 there is the passage about the sun and moon and stars and heavens praising the name of the Lord, for He commanded and they were created. Moffat's version goes on, "He set them boundaries that they should not pass." Or, another says, "made a decree." This comes astonishingly near to a conception of natural law for an ancient writer, who had not learned to generalise process or progress.

Second. "You are always destroying our simple beliefs and giving us nothing in return – religion goes to pieces." Of all the extraordinary and ungrateful and irreligious and fatuous contentions, this seems to me the most extreme.

God has blessed men's efforts for new knowledge to a remarkable extent. The Bible is now a clearer and more helpful and intelligible document than ever it was. I have not much patience with the people who let the old slip grudgingly from their fingers while they are too lazy or blind to grasp the new truths and the new Bible ready to their hands.

Third. "It is too bad of God to have plagued His people for centuries with deceptions and to have abused their simple faith in the word He gave them. He could just as easily have revealed the truth in the first place by inspiration. Why didn't He?"

Well, science has continually expanded and shown that what was a few generations ago apparently the whole truth is only a part of the truth, to be qualified and added to, relative and conditional. So, if any explanation of the genesis of the world satisfactory to the mind of a scientist in the sixteenth century had been put to the early Hebrews with no knowledge of mathematics, geometry, or mechanics, only just emancipated from the plurality of capricious deities, it would have been wellnigh unintelligible to them. If an account satisfactory to the literal minds of the average educated people of the mid-nineteenth century had been put there it would have been wellnigh incredible and like a strange language to Bruno and Copernicus. It is hardly too much to say that an account of the constitution of the universe in terms satisfactory to 1929 would have been almost moonshine to the readers of 1850 or even 1890. Because, to be intelligible, a statement of the facts must have the background of all relevant knowledge and experiment.

Fourth. The assertions made by science in relation to the Bible which some of you may find distressing, and which you continue to reject, are all of one piece with the body of scientific knowledge which so profoundly modifies your daily life. I am not quite sure, if you treat it with such contempt or doubt in the one sphere, you have much clear right to use electric trains and light, to have a wireless set, to rely on X-rays at the hospital, or to do half the things that are new to this generation. I was brought up on the conservation of energy and the conservation of matter – one is merged into the other now – and the combination isn't true any longer. The corpuscular theory of light was then altogether displaced by the undulatory theory. Now, to explain matters, apparently we have to invoke both, and often to hold incompatible ideas together. The doctrine of the atom gave solidity a meaning, and now the atom fades into infinitely small solar systems and there is nothing solid at all, only infinite varieties of energy and motion. The Euclidean geometry made everything so final and clear with the majesty of the inevitable, the rigidity of the unalterable. Who can forget the intellectual flash, the mental click of the forty-seventh proposition – all inevitable from a few self-evident first principles – a proof like nothing else in life. Now with relativity everything bends and curves and stretches under the strains of motion and position, and nothing "stays put."

The world as looked at through the growing monopoly of physical and chemical science and the materialistic dogmatism of the 'eighties (not indeed amongst the real leaders of thought and science) was one of the most depressing exhibitions in the history of human thought, almost matching in intolerance the religious persecutions of the sixteenth century.

Now we see that quality is an essential in any

explanation of life and the world and is almost entirely missed by physical science – even in the scientific realm the science of physics and chemistry have to be supplemented by biology, physiology, psychology, anthropology.

A recent writer says: "A time will come when physiology will invade and destroy mathematical physics, as the latter has destroyed geometry. The basic metaphysical working hypothesis of science and practical life will then, I think, be something like Bergsonian activism."

In the *Children's Newspaper* of this week, I read: "Everything points with overwhelming force [Dr. Jeans says] to a definite event or series of events of creation at some time or times not infinitely remote. The universe cannot have originated by chance out of its present ingredients, nor can it have been always the same as now."

That is a profound saying, and it leads us to believe that, whether Dr. Jeans thinks matter is melting away or not, he must believe in the possibility of some process beyond all our imaginings for carrying on this wonderful created thing.

This is a striking passage from his book: "The primary matter of the universe appears to consist of elements whose existence we are only just beginning to suspect, and to exist in the state of almost completely broken-up atoms, a state of matter which, again, was not contemplated before 1917. Indeed, our whole knowledge of the really fundamental physical conditions of the universe in which we live is a growth of the last quarter of a century."

If we know so little of matter, may it not be that it has immense surprises in store for those who will know much? In any case, as Dr. Jeans says himself, "we cannot be very confident of any ideas we form about a universe which we discovered only the other day. Sooner or later the pieces of the puzzle must begin to fit together, but we may reasonably doubt whether the whole picture can ever be grasped by the human mind."

Science and discovery have shown, beyond recall, that the primitive ideas of Genesis are not a close representation of what happened, in a scientific sense. They were indeed adequate to the religious needs of the people of that time.

But what science puts in their place is not final: it is continually being amended, refined, made more and more exact or more complete.

When I was a boy, physical determinism was the ultimate and inconceivable, but inevitable, bugbear of all thinking minds on the problem of life and destiny. Even natural selection as the basis of evolution and betterment and progress was a mechanical explanation. To-day the horizon has opened in an astonishing way, and materialism is the least satisfactory theory of the world. Even on its own ground the veil between matter and spirit has become so tenuous and imaginative that at one point they become almost convertible terms.

When you reach the root of the matter, nearly all the problems between science and religion are problems of determinism and, shall we say, freedom of the will. Is everything that ever is, to be rolled up in the womb of the past and present, and life and time merely an unfolding, or does nature or human consciousness transcend the ideas of cause and effect and give us new phenomena which have no adequate cause?

If our minds are constructed to think in terms of physics, mechanics, and chemistry, and this natural science, or even the mechanical theory of natural selection, then we cannot put our finger on any point that admits of a state of affairs without antecedents from which it must have resulted, and a closed system of determinism is the inevitable result in some form or other. This determinism is undoubtedly true over a very large part of the field of change and development, but emergent evolution gives greater scope or escape from it than any doctrine that we have had hitherto, whether we take it in the form which Bergson gives it in *The Vital Spirit*, changing the course with the course, or in *Emergent Evolution* by Lloyd Morgan, or in that difference in the inner qualities of every cell according to its actual setting and the corporate whole in which it finds itself. Any one of these is a sufficient escape from the horrible cage of forty years ago. I think that, in an early stage of life and consciousness, determinism is true to a very high per cent., and that there is freedom of the will only to a negligible point. Freedom of the will is a growing phenomenon with the development of human consciousness – that is, with spiritual progress. We are still the creatures of habit tied in by the possibilities of our ancestry and our environment, so that we cannot be and do anything that we like, but within the narrow range of possibility left to us, our freedom is greater than ever, and, rightly used, with every century it is widening the possibility more than ever within which it acts. So that conscious control of ourselves by knowledge and psychological or spiritual agency is, in itself, the greatest factor in reducing the human element in our lives. I believe this is the real meaning of "And ye shall know the truth, and truth shall make you free." So the doctrine of the freedom of the will is to me relative to the age in which we are talking, and the limited God of the Hebrews – after all, no man can have a God bigger than his own idea of a God for all effective purposes – was a Deity quite insufficient for our modern ideas. I passed a courting couple the other night and could not help overhearing the girl – I imagine she would be nineteen or twenty – till I got out of earshot. They were not talking of love, and it was not difficult. "Oh, the Bible," she said, "I am fed up with the Bible. What is the good of a God who hardens a man's heart, and then bats him on the head because his heart is hardened?" Everyone of us must have sympathised with this point of view when we have been trying to make the most of those early developments of the idea of God. But let us not be supercilious about the Hebrews. They had laid hold upon the great monotheistic idea. They had a genius for religion. Their tiny race was the cradle of the mighty truth. They were miles, or should I say centuries, ahead of all their contemporaries. If they appropriated this God to themselves and made a tribal god of Him in a way that is repellent to us, and invoked His aid in their bloodthirsty adventures, whether right or wrong, at any rate they did no more than children do with "me and mine!" The problems of the Old Testament and science properly viewed are now almost negligible. They are interesting, but not critical. The contest has shifted its ground, and I think that all to the good.

The chief cause of the breach between science and Christianity is "the overstepping of bounds." Theologians overstep the limit when they think they are in a position to restrict scientific investigation on the score of biblical assertions, as, for instance, in prescribing the method scientists must pursue and the results at which they must arrive. "The theory of verbal inspiration, while given up, still casts its bewildering shadows far over the modern mind" (Schmidt).

Scientists overstep the limits when they put the results of their researches at the disposal of an anti-Christian view of the world or think the axiom of causality excludes teleology.

Do you realise the astonishing age in which you live? They were great phases in the development of living consciousness when the "mind" began to think in three dimensions, to exercise conscious control over its own processes, and then to communicate with its fellows in such a way as to make a common action possible. We are now entering on a parallel period, possibly many centuries, even greater in the development of thought and life.

First: after long processes of thinking in three spatial dimensions, plus a growing ability to think in terms of time, we are entering a stage when, more and more, advanced minds are working, in snatches and with great difficulty, in a fourth dimension. Most of us are only able to think in terms of relativity and the quantum principle laboriously and for a few minutes. Some day it may be second nature and all life will be transformed.

Second: conscious control and direction is developing from the individual to the race. It fumbles in eugenics and social biology. But the conscious direction to particular ends of a new-found control of population is the most momentous possibility of our time.

Third: communication between our own forms and stages of life is a commonplace brought daily to a more astonishing perfection. But men have begun, by scientific method, and persistently, to try to bridge the gulf between our own and other consciousness, as we call it, in another world. They are beaten back by frauds, by errors, by the shadows of their own minds. We who are critical are not sure whether the small deposit of apparent truth which remains means much or nothing, whether it is scientifically significant or not. But the effort itself is significant, and its ultimate success over millions of years would be no more wonderful than the past achievements of God's development of this universe of dead matter, life, mind, and the infinite soul of man.

VII

"A POINT OF VIEW"[1]

I think I ought to begin with my point of view on
"points of view." Truth is so many-sided that even
the most gifted and most industrious cannot hope to
have first-hand knowledge of more than a few of its
aspects. In our endeavour to relate the significance
of our personal contacts with the others which we
receive at second-hand, we take much trouble to
weigh evidence and judge credibility and reliability
in others whose testimony we have to consider.
Then, in becoming responsible for a description of
the "truth" about any subject or object, we often
deliberately subordinate the small section of our
intense personal knowledge – which we suspect we
may overrate in importance or unconsciously regard
as crucial when it may be incidental – and deliberately favour and emphasise what we acquire and
adopt. We keep a tight hand on our "point of view,"
lest we be accused of unscientific treatment or a
bigoted standpoint. But, since we inevitably exclude
or belittle any knowledge or views that are actually
repugnant to our general scheme of truth or any that
contradict our own field of personal observation and
reasoning, the result does still represent our "point
of view," catholicised as far as we have the grace or
scientific strength to do it. It must inevitably be so,
since for each observer his own personality must
be the centre of experience! A friend was asked the
other day what place he thought the most interesting. "Any place that *I* happen to be in," was the
reply – not egotistic, but representing the subjective
character of all opinion. But when I am asked to

[1] Broadcast as the fifth in a series of "Points of View," 1930.

express my "point of view," I feel that I am free from the usual scientific obligation to blend the observations of everyone else with my own. Like the observer in the old story, if I happen to be leaning against the leg of an elephant, and I know nothing about the rest of the animal, I can describe it as "like a tree." I feel something like a youngster left alone with an assortment of good things, and with no obligation whatever to study the family's wants or feelings. I become more of the artist and less of the scientist.

When I examine my "point of view" thus isolated, I find myself envying some of my predecessors in this series, because I cannot honestly express myself as positively about many things as they have felt able to do. There are numbers on which I feel I am still collecting evidence – I haven't heard the case through – before, even to myself, I give a provisional verdict. On others I have made up my mind, but I am ready to reopen the case on the slightest provocation. Here I can only state a present opinion, without much indication whether to me it seems final or only a "carry over." Nor can I indicate the road travelled, and how much evidence has been weighed, and whether the balance of evidence to me is emphatic.

Most "points of view" have dealt at some length with "democracy." Merely as a principle of government, I think democracy can be easily overrated – we have reached it too soon. First, the average individual is not well enough educated, in the sense of knowing what is really good for himself, to enable him to weigh an apparent direct good against the unseen indirect harm that it may do him through its effect on society as a whole. He will cheerfully vote for some boon for himself which will react on the whole health of the community on which he depends, and this applies to rich and poor alike; nor has he a good balance between present and future boons. Second, the art of getting the best thought effectively to the top, and to the position of practical

effectiveness, has not yet been discovered. In intellectual matters, in democracy, brute force still
prevails. But, like others, I hope against hope that
toddling democracy will teach itself to walk steadily
before it breaks its neck because it cannot. Certainly
"government of the people, by the people, for the
people," as a principle, is to me about as long as a
piece of string, unless I know something about their
standard of moral and intellectual judgment. Nevertheless, when it can be clearly said that it understands
the issues involved, I trust democracy, and I believe
heartily in its principles. For I have no great confidence in the complete purity of motives of any
known autocracy, or in the intellectual skill, in
managing a complex world, of any alternative yet
evolved.

My point of view for the main issues of daily life
is frankly economic. That does not mean that it is
materialistic, still less pagan. I know well enough
that the economic is only a small part of the whole
rounded and complete life of the individual, and
that what is due for imagination, affection, sentiment, and religion, outweighs in ultimate value any
"nicely calculated less or more" of a few groceries,
or the difference between a seven-and-a-half and an
eight-hour day. But, at the moment, in this country
especially – for many of the nations on a lower
standard of life are happy enough in their way –
the economic issue dominates. We have fussed over
it to such an extent that it is like a nail in the shoe –
until it is removed or flattened we can neither read
poetry nor admire sunsets, nor listen to sermons,
nor even be reasonably sweet-tempered. The other
elements of the good life are difficult to attain, so
long as we have an unsettled economic problem.
It is quite possible for the full and rounded and
happy life to be unattainable even with the best
standard of living in the world, if we have a "grouch"
– a ground for comparative discontent – which

obsesses us. So the economic point of view to me is
the most important, because it is "in the way."
The preacher will say there is another course open
– to make people care more for non-economic
values – and the problem will then cease to worry
them. I do not believe it, so long as it is a question
of really misunderstanding the facts *about* economic
goods, rather than merely being too fond of them.
But there is an additional reason why the economic
viewpoint is supreme just now. It is that we are in
real peril, and a serious breakdown of our economic
society – which will endanger all our other values –
is far from being impossible.

The "bee in my bonnet" – my point of view – is
that the most urgent problem of the day is the
stability of the unit of monetary value and measurement – that is, of prices. It transcends in importance
the problem of unemployment, of industrial unrest
and co-operation, of crushing taxation, of industrial
advance and rationalisation, of international relations,
because it underlies them all. A just and skilful settlement of problems in any one of these fields can be
ruined if this central problem is not solved. We had a
standard of value that changed by forty per cent. over
a period of some twenty-five years, and then changed
back again to a similar extent over a like period, in the
Victorian era. That was just tolerable, for changes
then mattered far less than they now do, but in itself
it accounted for much difference in economic for-
tunes. But we are now feeling the effects of a change
of twenty per cent. in money values in five years –
the most striking change of modern times as a
phenomenon not confined to one country – with no
kind of guarantee or evidence that it may not continue
on a like scale for years to come unless we get control
of it.

Such a fall in gold prices – prices measured in a
gold standard – is peculiarly dangerous to this
country, for several reasons. First, we are the most

dependent on foreign trade, because we have arranged our industrial structure over many years past so as to supply exports to a wide range of foreign customers at competitive prices. A heavy fall in world prices necessitates readjustments in costs, which we are not economically or politically in a position to secure with the necessary promptness. If we are securing a high standard of life for our wage-earners in competition with lower standards abroad, it can only be kept up by higher individual output and efficiency. Every fall in the price-level makes the task more difficult, unless the output and efficiency per individual is simultaneously increased. Second, our wage settlements are on a large scale, and tend to remain fixed until large or striking events precipitate change. Meanwhile, unemployment is the corollary of an unadjusted position of a competitive or unsheltered industry, both as against a competitor abroad or a sheltered industry at home. You cannot permanently have a British worker getting goods costing £3 per week as his reward when a Continental worker gets goods costing £2 a week, unless the output and efficiency of the British worker is fifty per cent. greater. You cannot permanently get capital to flow into the British industry to secure four per cent., where it can secure eight per cent. elsewhere, because of that very attempt to balance unequal conditions. You cannot permanently have the unsheltered engineer, receiving 50s. per week, riding from his works in a tramcar, at the front of which his less skilled colleague, as driver, works less hard for £4. Third, the National Debt charge and other commitments fixed in terms of money form an excessively high proportion of our national income. The proportion becomes higher as the national income expressed in money falls, unless the total quantity of production is at the same time substantially increasing. We have added well over 1,000 million pounds sterling of real weight to the National

Debt during the last few years by this cause alone.
Fourth, the most important possible single cause
which can bring down the whole Reparation structure, with its dangerous political reactions upon
good faith and inter-Allied debts, is further appreciation in the value of gold. The average "Young
Plan" annuity of 102½ million pounds is not very
different in real weight of goods and services from
the normal "Dawes Plan" annuity of 125 million
pounds as envisaged by the experts in 1924.

It is clear to me that, unless some machinery can be
rapidly evolved for making the measure of value
sufficiently stable, so that contractual settlements
painfully arrived at on a just basis (between nation
and nation, between borrower and lender, between
debenture holder and ordinary shareholder, between
the provider of work – by hand or brain – and the
provider of capital) will all "stay put" for a reasonable
period, a stage of great difficulty is ahead of us. This
stability is a matter of international action, in a field
where identity of view as to the nature of the problem
is lacking, and still more the nature of the remedy,
so that the disposition of the least progressive may
well dominate the situation. I hope more from the
successful establishment of the International Bank,
and from the co-operation that it will induce in the
finance of nations, than from any other source. It is
of more importance to the future of civilisation than
a settlement of Reparations or than an immediate
reduction of armaments. But it is a matter in which
democracy, as such, is helpless, and has no advantage
over any other form of government, except to make
it more dangerous not to achieve a solution.

I had many years' experience as a Civil Servant
with the preparation of schemes and the elucidation
of principles for different Governments and Ministers
of all complexions. I have also had many years as
a student of statistics and economics, and I have
found that I could keep my studies nearer to the

truly scientific the further I kept from party programmes and political presentations (with their
absence of those half-tones which are the realities
of economic life). These have unfitted me, I fear, for
the joys of political warfare, though I appreciate
the value and necessity of political and party divi-
sions and the impossibility of getting along without
them. From my point of view, there is still much to
be popularly realised about many basic facts of
economic life before we can put the economic problem successfully on one side and apply our minds
and souls more unreservedly to other issues of life.
A whole group of these relate to the true nature of
wealth and exchange, and we need clearer ideas
about the connection between individual output and
the standard of living; about the connection between
what we put into the pot and what we can get out
of it; about the fallacy of the "lump of labour"
theory (and about the short time conditions in which
it is true); about the connection between the level
of real wages and unemployment; about the reactions
of scarcity and the failure in the long run of "making
work," and of trade restrictions; about the effect
upon the individual real wage of the undue proportion of the ordinary family budget spent in
alcohol; about the sources and supply of new capital, and its necessity; about the conflict between
the economic comfort of immobility in individual
trades, and the value of mobility to the community;
about the negligible effects of dividing still further
the gains of the few among the many; about the
effects of large-scale production abroad; about the
position of research; about the effects of direct
taxation upon prices; about the connection between
visible and particular imports, whose objectionable
features are seen, and unknown and general exports,
whose importance is unrealised; about the reaction
of social humanitarianism upon our economic future;
about currency and credit; about the economic waste

and overlapping of our distribution system and about
the futility of financial jugglings in amalgamations
and flotations, unaccompanied by physical changes.
Until there is clearer thinking on these matters, or
until obscure thinking about them no longer serves
to prevent intelligent action – that is, until things
have no longer to be made popular or acceptable
before they can be made effective – I do not think
democracy can get into its stride. Not until then will
the field of government cease to be cluttered with
economic difficulties so that we can turn our attention more successfully to other and higher issues.
The citizen of the future must have a better appetite
for slightly bitter facts, and be less prone to deny
the existence of any fact affecting himself that is
not sweetened to his taste; he must have better judgment in deriving a proper course of action from those
facts, and he must devise a better machine for giving
effect to that judgment in a practical programme.
Then I believe democracy will be a great success.

I have no faith in Socialism as a panacea, although
I believe that nothing for common service begins to
be efficient until it has a touch of the official or
bureaucratic about it. I do not particularly object to
the common supply, by national or municipal means,
of service that is wanted on uniform lines in circumscribed areas. But I think it folly to argue from
success in certain of such fields to success over the
whole. Often the very success of Socialism in limited
areas is parasitic upon individualism as a whole. The
fact that we want to ride in trams, or to post letters
consistently on an average that can be relied upon,
forms a basis for a type of control, especially if backed
by the general credit, which is wholly impossible of
universal application. The fact that each of us has
the glorious liberty to spend £1 in ways which may
call into action the resources of any part of the
country or of the world is, in the last analysis,
the reason why even the most intelligent form of

Socialism must be impracticable. If we will consent to buy only what a Government has prescribed, and at a prescribed price, and not to leave it unbought, then Socialism, generalised, can begin to have a chance.

There are two other major issues which, from my point of view, dominate practical but non-economic life. The first is that we have completely failed so far to harmonise our growing instinct for social humanitarianism and equalities with ultimate social strength and survival. Ethics and biology are in conflict, as we know well, but we refuse to recognise it in practice. I agree with much that Sir James Jeans said upon this question. The constant effort to relieve and support the weak, or to obtain the advantages of corporate action in which individual responsibility is often hidden, and the way we strive "officiously to keep alive," are both fraught with the probability of a real nemesis in a few generations. Amongst the less fortunate in the community are those who have fine qualities but who have been victimised by fate, to help whom is a real social investment, with a fine social dividend; but there are also many who are underdogs through improvidence, irresponsibility, and general inherited weakness. Our all-round policy of making things smoother for the less fortunate does not discriminate, and it will bring inevitable nemesis for the race. In its economic aspects the problem is closely related to the eugenic. Making it easier for the less vigorous stock to survive and multiply is bad enough; but putting the burden, as we really do, upon the more vigorous stock, so that they are unable to do as well for themselves as they might, doubles the evil effects on the balance of the population in future. This is no plea for leaving undisturbed by graduated taxation extremes in the distribution of wealth, especially of inherited wealth. But it does point clearly to the dangers of heavy social expenditure at the expense of the reasonable rewards accruing to first-class enterprise, leadership in brainwork, risk-taking, and thrift. Every transfer of wealth in this area "counts two on a division." There is something eugenically wrong here and now, without waiting for ultimate consequences, when a first-class honours graduate lecturing on chemistry, or doing research work, is getting little more than the man who cleans the laboratory windows or minds the building. When those of the former class pay heavily towards the education and social service of the latter, the gravity is emphasised. The economic machine is often unfair, but, where two workers are fairly getting the marginal result due to their respective contributions to the economic whole, no considerable transfer can be made from one to the other on compassionate grounds without some evil consequences ultimately arising. The brutal truth is that hard weeding, pruning, and thinning are essential for all vigorous growth and improvement. I saw recently an account of a special national "preserve" for chamois in Switzerland (from which carnivorous animals were excluded) maintained by the Government; the herd gradually deteriorated until a few wolves were introduced, and a definite improvement to the best standards was then quickly manifest.[1] And yet the humanitarian instinct and practice is the finest flower of civilisation, and tenderness for the weak and unfortunate a real differential of the Christian belief. In my view, the way out of the dilemma in practical affairs will be found along eugenic lines. By all means let us do all we can for those whose lot is genuinely unfortunate, and temporarily so – subject to a more practical desire to let natural economic results follow economic slackness in the individual – but let us discourage in every possible way the multiplication of the stock from this section of the population, and refrain from

[1] Professor MacBride, "The Herd Instinct in Animals," *Eugenics Review*, July 1929.

over-weighting the best stock. In other words, we must be as tender as possible to the ills that are, but as ruthless as possible, realising the utter mistakenness of a humanitarian policy, in all matters relating to the generations that are to be. The practical working out of this compromise is a first-class problem for the next few decades. But two factors press it on, one helping a successful solution and the other uncertain. The new-found possibility of a conscious direction of the birth-rate, and possibly soon the sex-rate, is an economic engine of vast power and even danger; the establishment of universal peace will make the purely economic inter-racial competition more ruthlessly eliminating. No doubt warfare that depended upon physical prowess and courage was once of some biological value in weeding out the weakly, but modern warfare, eliminating the best manhood of both sides by the impartial cruelty of machinery, is distinctly dysgenic, and there is not necessarily any question of the survival of the fittest about it. The nation that eagerly puts a premium upon individuality and enterprise, and does not deaden all to a common level, is the nation with survival value in the new economic substitute for the biological effects of war.

The other great problem is the machinery of government. The present task in its complexity and variety is too vast and detailed for the apparatus. Nearly every Minister has too much to do on his own responsibility. The time of Parliament is very ineffectively spent; vast issues have to be decided in a short allotted time. There is no certainty that the best thinking will come to the top in practice. It has to be capable of easy and attractive presentation. It stands very little chance unless it is aided by the very different and subsidiary art of exposition. There is a story of a member of Parliament who delivered a most thoughtful and original speech that fell completely flat and had no influence whatever. By way of experiment, the identical speech was made on the following day by a practised orator, and its effect was profound and immediate.[1] In a real thinking community such a dependence of matter upon manner would be impossible. Part of the truth about the machinery of government is that we have not discovered the secret of the "economical transmission of power" in mental force comparable with what we have done in physical force for steam and electricity. The art of thinking, in the individual, is in its infancy, and not very much of our educational system yet deals with its direct improvement as a definite process with its own technique. But when we come to the methods of organised thinking the waste of power is enormous, and the result very much a matter of hit or miss. The best quality material put into a machine may be ruined by defective working and bad design. But a perfectly working machine of election and committees and references cannot produce anything greater in quality than the real material of thought that is fed into it. There is no royal road to a solution of this problem, which is common both to politics and industry, but much more skilled attention must be given to it. The whole of our past practice has been too traditional and empirical, and it requires intensive study. Equally, too, the way in which invention and research are financed and get into practical operation in industry is still too opportunist and haphazard for a scientific age. Popular voting and desire cannot control the facts and findings of chemistry, but it still plays a great part in what is "acceptable" in economics. The future progress of economic practice must rest on a more scientific use and widespread understanding of statistical methods, which cannot be bullied or coaxed into preconceived notions and wishes.

[1] Kinglake and Peel, *vide* White's *Inner Life of the House of Commons*, or *Memories and Reflections*, Earl of Oxford, i. 55.

I am profoundly moved by the littleness of the economic and political issues in the larger view of life and destiny. My archæological and antiquarian instincts give me a sense of history which sees happiness and purpose and moral progress persist in the most diverse conditions. Economic content is all relative and comparative in the most limited way. A ten per cent. difference between the fortune of a man and his neighbour is potent to disturb the spirit, where the knowledge that one is four times as well off as one's prototype a hundred years ago, or twice as well off as one's neighbour in Southern Europe, fails to touch the imagination. Our powers of adaptation are remarkable. The luxury of one generation becomes a basic necessity of existence in the next. I see no satisfying conclusion to economic and scientific progress without a moral and religious background.

I can never quite understand why the public think that a popular novelist or even a playwright must necessarily be an expert in religious guidance, or any ultimate philosophy. To me his point of view is one item only in a great synthesis. I have a profound regard for the findings of physical science and astronomical speculation, and a constantly growing feeling of their inadequacy as an explanation (or justification) of life and the universe. More and more the great framework of "pointer readings" and measurable entities which science has elaborated requires a metaphysical philosophy to give it meaning. It tells us more and more about existence in one or two dimensions. But the things that make life real are qualitative, and elude all physical record and measurement – love, goodness, beauty, and even vitality. Physical science seems to tell me about as much concerning the prospects of immortality, or its nature, as a blind man can about a flower. The facts of consciousness and instinct and the data of psychology must be included in any scheme of thinking

that is to be satisfactory as a long-run solution.
William James, at the time he was the greatest expert
of his day in religious experience, admitted that his
own was meagre. But that of others existed as a fact
to be accounted for – it could not be pooh-poohed
away, and behind it James inferred a reality.[1] On the
broader aspects of religious thinking I am a modern-
ist with no great differences from Dean Inge, Bishop
Barnes, Canon Streeter, and Professor Eddington.
I have an instinctive belief that what works or makes
a difference has in it real truth. You call this pragmatism. So when we come to the impetus and conduct
of daily life I am, after long mental meanderings,
more unashamedly "pragmatic" than ever, though I
know well why pragmatism is discredited as a pure
philosophy. I am a convinced believer in the permanent value of organised religious institutions, in the
preservation of the religious instinct in society, and
in the practical "canalisation" of moral force. We
shall let them decline at our peril. It is a matter of
relative indifference to me that the literal meaning
of words, creeds, and hymns lags somewhat behind
modern scientific conceptions, so long as they carry
a moral force, which moved our fathers, over to the
average man of to-day, and without which he is a
sorry creature. I have no passion for a new edition of
any great hymn-book following every new book on
astronomy or the atom. Fancy trying to get public
worship and moral exaltation and spiritual immediacy
by way of collects in the vein of Herbert Spencer or
Haeckel ! The pulpit has a more difficult task to-day
than ever, but a more essential one. In all the larger
problems of mind and conduct I find that the story
of the life and death of the Galilean peasant, Jesus
Christ, when I have done all with it, both constructive
and destructive, that modern knowledge suggests to
me, still remains the most startling challenge to
thought and purpose. Unless we have faced the issues

[1] *Letters*, vol. ii., pp. 210–15.

He raises, and found some place in our scheme in which they are consistent, we have no satisfactory "point of view." In my philosophic and scientific mentality I know all the absurdities and snares of anthropomorphism. The scientific mind cannot understand why the Absolute, the First Cause, must be a Deity like a superior human being to the average man. But the average man can only think comfortably in anthropomorphic terms, and, after all, I am spiritually a democrat, and the spiritual world exists for the average man and the clever ones are only his servants. There is little to be gained by the complete unity of the Churches. They need to be rationalised into a few essential forms. The removal of vestigial remains of past ideas which have no longer any significance, and consolidation into several main types of worship and appeal, will make for vitality. And continued vitality with a living appeal and high moral sanctions, and a dynamic which can touch the average man who is neither a scientist nor an intellectualist, is of the highest importance in the survival value of the community. In my teens I was caught in pure thinking by the sheer arrogant determinism of the physics of that day, but in the pure practice of life I rebelled at its stark absurdity, as much as any master of the art of practical living has rebelled against philosophic idealism. The way out has come through physics itself, even if we have to get into the recesses of the atom or the far reaches of the universe to break the chain of determinism. In philosophy I am content with emergent evolution and all the other modern refuges from scientific predestination. The modern doctrine of the complete sacrifice of the interests of the individual for the good of the future race, although in some respects a worthy ideal, is not sufficiently practical as a guide to conduct. We know little enough what will be "good" in the future of the race. A reasonable balance is necessary between the feelings of the present and the supposed interests of the future. On the whole, in self-sacrifice the needs of others in this *present* age come first. Similarly, the notion that the moral incentives arising from a belief in personal survival are less worthy than those which are evoked by collective immortality or race survival seems to me quite unwarrantable. The fact that personal immortality has no deep roots in the present findings of physical science seems to me almost irrelevant.

The two most significant things that make this age a great one to live in are the conception of relativity and the approach to spiritualism. A few people can think painfully now for a few minutes at a time in four dimensions, but when it becomes a common background to men's minds in the far recesses of the future the whole universe will be different. A few people to-day are battering at the doors of the unseen world. I do not know how much significance is to be attached to the tiny residuum of their efforts which will satisfy modern tests of knowledge. I have no personal faculty for the pursuit. But I do feel that it is the *will* to do it, and the method and the effort, that are significant. In the slow process of evolution their ultimate success in developing two new senses for the mastery of all knowledge would be no more remarkable than the marvellous universe of life as we grasp it to-day that has come to us from such unimaginable beginnings, and yet the ultimate significance of that future may be just as unfathomable.

VIII

THE CITIZEN OF THE FUTURE [1]

When men peer into the future, as H. G. Wells may do from time to time, we usually get anticipations of the world men will live in, the advance of invention and its effect upon men's lives, the Utopian institutions and conditions that we shall evolve – a picture of fancy and delight which gives the thrill of romance and touches the borders of credulity. These pictures are based on an underlying conception of progress in society, and very rarely do we get any suggestion that civilisation may go downhill. The Robots and Butler's Erewhon gave a hint of the problems of mechanisation, but most of our prophets are incurable optimists. They do not often have much to say about the man who will inhabit that world, his character and disposition. But we have to lead towards him, and shape our ends. What will he be like, this Citizen of the Future?

How far ahead is my future? Not so far ahead, I think, for the picture I draw to be unreal or fanciful, giving us to-day no impetus and no incentive to begin to make it; but on the other hand, it should not be so close that we can see only ourselves slightly larger and better, but still ourselves, with all our weaknesses. Shall we aim at four or five generations hence? What will be the characteristics of the citizen of that age?

The leading characteristic will be, I think, a far greater sense of civic responsibility. For he will have a much keener appreciation of the solidarity of society and of the whole civilised world, which will bring a sense of shame if he feels that he is the weak link in the chain, that to-day is quite the exception

[1] At Epsom, Ebbishan Hall, on Citizen Sunday, December 1929.

and not the rule. For the sense of solidarity or of collective quality may be conceived in various ways. A good society may mean at least three things. We may liken it to a bag of shot, which we may call *good*, meaning that there is a very small percentage of bad or misshapen shot in it, and the removal or betterment of these will improve the reliability of the whole. But they are independent units, and their interdependence is *statistical* only. Or we may compare society to a machine in which the whole functions badly because of one defective part – a badly made piston-rod or a badly centred wheel. But remove this, and substitute a perfect part, then all the other perfect parts perform their action perfectly in a perfect whole. The parts are independent, but they have an interdependence which is *essential*. But, better still, we may liken society to an organism of which the parts are cells, and, if one group is diseased or injured, the others are not only impaired in action, but may become diseased and die too. This is the physiological or functional analogy for society which will give that acute personal sense of responsibility to the future citizen. The sense of solidarity will include not merely intense interdependence in economic life, but in their whole moral, mental, and philosophic development, national and international, and this sense will be a new common denominator for a civic responsibility. To treat one's individual fitness, not as a question of personal pride or shame, but as an element of regimental religion; to see that one is completely fitted, not to earn the most, or enjoy the most, but to fill the allotted place the best; to feel uneasy and ashamed if the civic machine of which one forms a part is not working smoothly – these are elements which will belong to that new order of citizenship, and they will be active, not because the citizen will wish to be thought well of as first in the race, or hate to be thought ill of as last in the race, but because the health and ill health of the whole and the efficiency of the whole will be an impersonal ideal towards which the personal contribution is vital.

It will not mean that independence and personality will be less respected; far from it. A recognition of essential and valuable difference will be more gladly given than it is to-day. Dr. Glover said, in *The Influence of Christ in the Ancient World*, " Independence is a great thing, but a depraved sense of equality is not the way that leads to it, as Greece found to her cost." The notions of the nineteenth century which Graham Wallas has called the intellectualist fallacy will be quite superseded, although they will then be much nearer the truth. We have been all prone to the view that by some mysterious alchemy the ballot-box and democratic representation would distil leadership and wisdom out of masses of ignorant and prejudiced individuals under the mob influence and sway of partisanship. We are slowly becoming emancipated from it. The citizen of the future will have passed beyond the cruder democratic ideals, and the history of our times will have shown him that, failing certain important individual characteristics in the people, they can be led as fatally astray by democracy as by any autocrat. His superiority in public affairs will be due to the fact that the formation of opinion will have a technique, and be in itself scientific, instead of being haphazard or induced. In the manufacture of any product, the machine must be right, and well adapted to the desired end; it must be well designed and also well made; it must be regularly fed with material; the material must be the right kind; there must be something to make the machine "go"; and, when the product is delivered, it must be used and usable. All these are but analogous to the processes which must precede right action as the result of scientific processes of thinking. The art of thinking in the individual is quite empirical at present – no one

knows precisely the kind of mental discipline that is
necessary for original and progressive and inclusive
thinking – just a few have the knack, without quite
knowing how.

Let us first take the material. The citizen of the
future will have a genuine aptitude for facts, and
a distinctive attitude towards them. He will have
a horror of false facts and misjudgments. He will
not give a mental verdict first, from habit, or
liking, or impression, or influence, and then select
the facts to make his case, or save his face, or perhaps
honestly only see the facts he has learned to look for.
He will know that if he tried to form a well-balanced
judgment from first-hand knowledge of all the relevant facts on all the subjects that came before him,
even in the ample leisure left from his daily work,
he would go mad in a week. So division of labour in
selection and preparation of facts, and in the earlier
processes of thinking upon them, will be most
consciously and deliberately undertaken, and discharged as a responsible trust, just as responsible as
the handling of other people's money by a bank.
So he will be far less partisan towards facts, and his
choice will not be determined by the tint of the
glasses he may wear. He will have such self-control
that he will allow for his own personal equation.
Then he will have become emancipated from what is
to-day a terrible drawback, and will not be blunder-
bussed into believing things by the trick of repetition, the imposition on the subconscious, and all the
paraphernalia of the publicist of to-day. He will not
accept that "B's tyres are best" merely because he
sees the statement a hundred times a day; and
advertisement will consist in making known the
existence of particular goods, and in certified and
carefully worded statements of their average, not
selected, performance. The creation of public opinion
by megaphone processes and slogans will be first bad
form, and then inimical to its own case.

The citizen will be careful to judge matters from a non-personal standpoint; he will know where the other man's shoe pinches, and be *conscious*, in a sense to-day we hardly understand, and only reach in rare moments of objectivity. He will be less obfuscated by an array of facts, and not get hot and bothered if he has to keep half a dozen in the air at once; his technical mastery of their manipulation and arrangement, and his observation, will be highly developed. This will partly arise from practice, but also because he will have orderly principles of arrangement, and a sense of proportion and importance in selection. "William James once said in a vein of good-natured irony: 'To Bryce all facts are born free and equal.'"[1]

In history, as in science, there is no democracy among facts; all, it is true, have the same right to be understood, but some facts are of vastly more significance than others. The scholar, for whom all facts are of significance, and all of equal significance, never understands anything, though Nature is kind to him and conceals from him that there is anything to understand. Conversely, I have heard genius described as the instinct for the fact with meaning, for the real factor; and it is this that every true historian and every real man of science will seek.[2]

The seen facts will no longer have the tremendous advantage over the unseen facts, either in their favour or against them. To-day we either hate strangers amongst facts, and heave half bricks at them, or else we go to the other extreme, and every fact has honour save in its own country. You remember the darkie who had been called before the bench on a rather serious charge, and the judge explained to him that he ought to be defended. The accused asked whom he might have, and the judge saw several advocates in the court and said, "Well, there's Mr. Smith over there, or Mr. Brown just here, or there's Mr. Robinson upstairs." The prisoner

[1] Lord Oxford, *Memoirs and Reflections.*
[2] T. R. Glover, *Influence of Christ in the Ancient World.*

took a good look at Smith and Brown, and then ex-
claimed, "Guess, judge, I'll have Mr. Robinson."
This is the attitude of many novelty-hunting and
intellectually snobbish people towards facts – they
have no use for the tried and proved facts under
their noses. Many facts cannot be directly apprehended by the senses, or by observation, yet they are
most important of all – they are statistical facts,
averages, percentages, modes, medians, coefficients
of dispersion and correlation, and they are pregnant
with meaning to those who have learned to handle
them, and the very devil to those who haven't. The
citizen of the future will furnish his mind with them.
He will make a far greater use of the public libraries,
using them as a part of the civic machinery, to come
to a ripe judgment. He will have his own tool-box
of books, of course, but he will know the value of
communally owned reference – the truest communism. With the greater efficiency of industrial life,
and perhaps the wise spending of his money, he will
have emancipated that four or five shillings a week
given to waste now, and a library will be a com-
passable asset of every home. So the citizen will hate
to let bad facts into his thinking mill, because nothing
good can come out, and he will have organised new
ways of getting his facts. The permanent "fact-
finding" commissions of America are a germ of this
development. All this I conclude as the logical out-
come of some generations of better education, of the
breakdown of isolation through the broadcast, the
cinema, television, and universal rapid air travel;
through the failure of merely popular representative
government, and of organised Press opinion through
drapery catalogues masquerading as purveyors of
factual truth. There will certainly be more than one
newspaper where an intelligent idea of what has
taken place at a meeting, and the serious ideas
expressed, can be found, in place of one or two
humorous bits, or engaging "stories" which were

the least important features to the serious followers of the movement.

Next we must look at the machine of judgment or thinking. The most carefully selected and beautiful facts will be ruined if they are fed into a bad machine. The first essential is to distinguish fact from thought about fact. Hobbes said, in a most memorable phrase, "No discourse whatsoever can end in absolute knowledge of fact," but of course to-day the world of idea is becoming the world of facts to us; still, however, the distinction remains valid and important over a large part of the formation of opinion about "what ought to be done next," and practical living may still be distinguished from speculation about the ultimate constitution of matter and force. In that future day there will be two great advances; first there will be training for thinking as a practical art, as for work or a profession, and each will be taught to find his own knack or vein along which the best results can be found, and thinking will no longer be regarded as something that every gentleman can do by instinct. The distance that has to be covered to reach this point can be visualised only by reading Graham Wallas's *Art of Thought*. But the range of thought and its apparatus will be wide, right into the fields which are specialist to-day. We have made a beginning, for the small boy of to-day babbles with ease and without pedantry of ohms, watts, volts, cycles, thermostats, moving coils, the heaviside layer, vitamins, air pockets, high pressures, magnetos, and frames of reference. Clutton Brock said, now many years ago, in *The Ultimate Belief*, "We think of the man of science or the artist, if not of the saint, as a being with peculiar gifts, not as one who exercises, more precisely and incessantly perhaps, activities which we all ought to exercise."

Secondly, thinking will be organised, so that, instead of vast efforts failing to come into the focal point of general recognition, and dying, almost wasted, so that many thoughts have to be born many times, till one survives to manhood and self-assertion, every infant thought will get its chance of survival. But there will be birth-control in thinking, and no pseudo-thinking will get rushed into print and clog the time and energies of men. A canalisation of thinking, an elaborate but natural referencing, will make the thought product richer and full of energy. But competition will be keen, the standard high, and selective criticism high-toned but severe. Men will no longer mistake "busyness" for business, and an active mind will, as in Lord Oxford's story of a certain divine, have the activity "not of hinges, but of wheels." Thinking will have direction and purpose. There will not be incessant motion without progress. I believe that it will have considerable freedom from personal bias, and be more impersonally logical. I heard it said of the renowned logical acumen of French politics that it will demonstrate that "C must infallibly follow A and B; *we like C, therefore A and B are true.*" Most of us can spot a false syllogism and an undistributed middle term in a three-line statement, but, if it is tricked out into a large volume, it will take most of us in. The thinking citizen, I have said, will refuse to exercise his thinking except on good facts, knowing the damage to his machine to use bad material, and his proportion will be good. He will use instinctively the different types of proof or evidence appropriate for the subject-matter – the mathematical or identity type, the physical or measuring type, the statistical or modal type, the religious or subjective type, the historical or converging type, the legal type, and the circumstantial type – most of which are thoroughly jumbled up to-day.

Thinking will be recognised to be what it actually is – hard work and highly personal. "God gives the nuts, but the squirrels have to crack them," is an old German saying. Thinking will be recognised to be what it actually is – the most acute pleasure. An American writer on a strictly utilitarian plane said recently:

Intensive thought is required in order to conceive its splendid possibilities, and human nature will always be human nature. Thinking has never been a popular pastime. It is conceivable, however, that in some future time youth will be taught that the most intense pleasure that can be experienced by a human being is the sudden conception of a new thought, and that even the grasping of an idea already known which, like a random butterfly, has eluded the pursuer, provides a rare satisfaction.[1]

The citizen of the future will achieve a real poise between holding to past ideas and practices and emancipation from them for new needs, and he will carry this, not merely into science, art, and music, but even into religious faith, where he will not be un-Christian even if he has travelled far from verbal creeds of to-day. Canon Streeter says very wisely:

In his attitude to the religious authorities of the day Christ was a revolutionary. The notion that it is the duty of a religious man to accept uncriticised anything that the past has held venerable and sacred, finds no support in Him. Christ was conspicuously a critic of tradition. He was constantly condemning accepted conceptions of God, accepted canons of morality, and, above all, that ecclesiastical tradition by which the word of God, then as so often since, was made of none effect.[2]

The debt to the past is one we can only satisfactorily discharge by putting posterity equally into ours. Whatever we may owe to particular ancestors and their efforts, our generation and environment "enjoys life as a whole at a higher level and of a richer quality because of the acquisitions of all the preceding generations."[3] As Professor Pigou says, "Environments have children as well as individuals," and the

[1] F. W. Shibley, *The New Way to Net Profits.*
[2] Streeter, *Reality.*
[3] C. E. M. Joad, *The Meaning of Life.*

future citizen will have an environment which will be
the lineal descendant of the environment we at this
moment are creating. The evolutionary and biological
significance of this will some day be recognised, and
the necessity for scrutinising most severely every call
of pity, charity, humanitarianism, and social relief,
which makes life easier in one generation but burdens
future generations by the processes of thwarting the
hardy and ruthless efficiency of the survival of the
fittest. The balance of the "true good" between one's
own generation and one's responsibility to the generations yet to be will be more consciously made by
the citizen of the future. Beyond the safeguards of
negative eugenics, which will then be in full swing,
I am doubtful whether the secrets of positive
eugenics and human and social Mendelism will even
by that age have become a practical programme.

I am not so clear in my mind as to where my future
citizen will stand in relation to the aims of life and
the "realm of ends." He will have a definite programme for social development and government, but
I do not know whether the new physical science
will not have left him more helpless than ever as to
the final meaning of the universe. I do not think that
sufficient time will have elapsed for new senses to be
markedly developed with which to approach and
master reality, and particularly whether spiritualism
will have any scope for the ordinary individual. But
I am sure that *direction* will be the quest of that day.
One can procure a car, one can learn to drive – both
these I have postulated – but this is useless without
the motive power and somewhere definite to go.
Life will be less negative, I believe. The social virtues
of avoiding will be less the test of "good form" than
positive achievement, and individuality in direction
will not be frowned upon as eccentricity – even in a
public school.

In that day, the problem of a stable measurement of
value will have been practically solved, memory

being still acutely alive to the ghastly escape from complete shipwreck that civilisation will have had because of its intellectual and democratic cowardice in facing it. Mental power in thought will be more general, and Aristotle less of an Everest than he still is to-day. Men will, as they have at last begun to do to-day, recognise, and not persecute, genius in their midst. "Civilisation as a whole gradually moves up to the level from which the voice of the genius crying in the wilderness was first heard, and the children posthumously ennoble the man whom the fathers starved or crucified."

The citizen will, at any rate, have got beyond the hobbledehoy stage of regarding enjoyment and progress as a function of speed in moving about, and an incessant wandering of the eyes, and titillation of new scenes. The pool of silence will be sounded by the West as well as by the East, by Christian as well as by Brahmin. The new quietism will be as potent for rousing moral fervour, not merely for a few chosen spirits, but also for the man in the street, as tambourines and collective singing to-day. Men will be able to listen to a sermon over twenty minutes long without somnolence, boredom, a relapse into golf reminiscence or visionary balance-sheets.

The future citizen will have a right sense of work, thinking not only of its dignity, but of the joy in it. "The best worship is stout working," said Carlyle. He will be better adapted for it by vocational choice. Again, the pool of silence will serve, not only spirit, but brain and muscle. He will have outlived the fad of worshipping as a man "devoted to duty" the one who drives on till 6.30, and will think much more of him if, by exercise of brain and ingenuity, he can find a way of getting away fairly at half-past five, realising that long, continuous hours often result from muddle and lack of drive, and often create them. He will have a little more respect for the man with his heels on his desk and creation in his brain than for the man with his head over the desk and lead in his spirit. Both Lord Balfour and my friend Owen Young have been most devastating as thinkers when their bodies have been at an angle of twenty-five degrees from the horizontal.

Practical brotherhood will be a more general achievement, for men will *care* more, and realise, even from a personal point of view, the reactions upon themselves of disability in others. But pity will extend not merely to distress and trouble in others; it will be just as solicitous for inefficiency and overweening pride, and the underlying causes of distress. Solidarity means more than common suffering and common prosperity. For if we are aiming at self-realisation we are failing abjectly. To forget ourselves and our vanities, and lose ourselves in the cause and the chain of life, is to achieve a real end. Brotherhood has to be extended to the unseen and unknown in our own age, and, ideally, to the brothers of generations ahead, and our actions are not brotherly if they are inimical to either, however sweet they may look to the poor blighter next door. Unselfishness is a bigger problem than charity. "Spiritual education," says Clutton Brock, "is an education in moral, intellectual, and æsthetic disinterestedness."

To the future citizen, quality will count as much as quantity, and we shall revert to the two mites. All the great things in life are qualitative. Streeter says:

> The essence of personality and of its inward life does not consist in quantity, but in quality. A man's passion for his lady love takes up no more room in space than his affection for his great-aunt; the difference is one of intensity and quality, not of size.[1]

I am not competent or rash enough to prophesy what discoveries science will have made, or how man

[1] Streeter, *Reality*.

may live. But in gauging man's development I have tried not to "think of a number, and double it." I have steeped myself in contemporary eighteenth-century thought, and tried to make a jump forward not wholly out of keeping with the lessons of the past, and what I have dared to prophesy has been, in my judgment, the development of tiny seeds now planted or the logical adaptation to the conditions that are in sight. Perhaps I have unconsciously drawn upon the recognised Utopias, or the standard criticisms of to-day. At any rate, I agree with H. G. Wells, in *The Open Conspiracy*, that "Our antagonists are confusion of mind, want of courage, want of curiosity, and want of imagination, indolence, and spendthrift egotism. . . . These are the jailers of human freedom and achievement."

To sum up. The citizen of the future will find out more, think and judge better, have clearer aims, and weigh the spiritual aims of life against the material, with greater success; he will work more wisely – perhaps I should say sagaciously – and he will do more of it for love – true love of himself, love of humanity, love of the future in a developed race-consciousness, and the glory of God.

IX

If all forms of transport were subject to one authority, which was responsible for the application of new capital in the most appropriate way in the general interest, including the interest of the providers of capital, then, whatever the drawbacks and other disadvantages of such a system – and they would be many – we should expect to find a whole apparatus of discrimination and determination, to enable proper decisions to be reached, which is completely absent under our present system. Such a body would be failing in its duty if it extended one form of transport – other things being equal in the matter of service – instead of another which would have involved less expenditure or given better results for the same outlay. The system that we actually have to-day claims to have the public virtues of severe competition within each particular form of transport and severe competition *between* the different forms – a competition which extends, not only to the financial results, but to the scientific progress in each. Where the competition is not or cannot be perfectly free, then a considerable measure of regulation originally intended to be in the public interest exists. Where competition is free, but is bringing its own nemesis in public inconvenience, a small measure of regulation is being introduced. We are now beginning to get the glimmerings also of co-operation. There is no guarantee under such a system that any one section of transport, in ignorance of the true costs and

[1] Inaugural Address as President of the Institute of Transport, on Monday, October 14th, 1929.

scientific position of the other, may not embark large sums of money upon projects which may be quickly rendered obsolescent by an imminent advance elsewhere; or, alternatively, may not *fail* to embark large sums of money for fear that obsolescence will come about through some suspected advantage or scientific improvement that is likely to arise, but yet actually does not arise, in a rival form of transport. Are these communal blunders avoidable?

Assuming all the virtues that the nineteenth century attributed to *laissez faire* and unrestricted competition and its hatred of regulation, we still have to face the fact that in the one case, looking at our economic interests as a whole, there may be a great waste of capital due to its piecemeal application. Even within one industry each independent enterprise fancies its chances of success over that of its neighbours. There are too many going in for extensions on a boom, and a lot of capital is invested which, with more co-ordinated interest and better foreknowledge of the aggregate supply, would never have taken the particular form that it now assumes. Capital so rendered obsolete, and duplicated, or so wasted might very well have been applied to other human needs in quite a different order of preference. There is not now so much new capital coming into existence that we can afford to misuse or misapply any large proportion of it. It is true that less capital might be forthcoming if there were no great attractions of high speculative profits to be snatched by superior promptitude or ability or luck. But, on the other hand, the sight of many industrial failures and the risks of total loss tend to restrict savings in other ways. On balance, *probably* security or an experience of reliable results, rather than a lottery, will procure the larger fund, and *certainly* the net fund finding a proper destination serving the true interests of the community will be greater.

Taking the point now that for fear of the unknown

in the other forms of transport, we fail to advance as rapidly along any particular line as we might, some opposing considerations arise. It is clear that a single autocratic mind or control might wish to conserve its particular assets *beyond* the point of potential obsolescence until their working life was exhausted before bringing in new forms and alternative methods, and so would hesitate to destroy its own capital before it proved physically necessary. Thus by ultra-conservatism it might deprive the public of advantages which under another system they would begin to enjoy earlier. On the other hand, where competition in the past has been fierce and many people have burnt their fingers, a different kind of reluctance may creep over each line of advance. The fear of extending an existing capital equipment, because of its potential annihilation by some rumoured or suspected scientific change or advance in another field, may be a very real one, especially in days of large units and many alternatives. Unnecessary time may be taken over testing out comparative advantages, not in systematic and immediate laboratory fashion, but in the hard realism of objective capital expenditure and loss. We have to-day gone a long way beyond the stage of imagining that the ruinous cheapness of commodities, or services supplied below their real ultimate and long-distance costs, is any lasting advantage to the public. It may lead to violent reaction in combinations and monopolies which will hold up prices; or to tariffs, with many political and economic ills; or to the general economic reluctance on the part of new venturers to enter a field which is strewn with the wrecks of past disasters. A single economic mind and control, to which I have referred, in its ideal form, would weigh up the advantages to the public, as a whole, of the better services obtained by a premature scrapping and annihilation of capital as against the alternative and unseen services which the public would get in other directions by the application of new capital to other objects supplying new services, which is capital now required or used for superseding old capital supplying existing services. But the seen is always so much more easily grasped than the unseen, though it is not necessarily so potent, and, if it is Utopian to think of a single-minded ideal control free from bureaucratic disadvantages expending the whole capital for transport in the most advantageous way in transport, it is still more Utopian to think of that economic mind going beyond what would be the most favourable balance-sheet and profit and loss account *for itself*, into making sacrifices inside its own activities for the sake of the larger good beyond itself, especially where such larger good is intangible. I fear, therefore, that the question of the greatest public advantage from the accumulation of expenditure of capital as a whole is too distant a dream for us now. We must learn simpler lessons first. At the moment, we might take as our Utopia the greatest public advantage for the capital expended in the particular sphere of transport, and leave the comparison of this with other uses of capital until we are in a fair way to achieve this nearer goal. At the moment, the various forms of transport, while over part of the field complementary and assisting each other, are also over another large part of the field alternative and competitive. It would be idle to suggest that, in the agencies supplying the latter field, there is yet any general movement for single-minded consideration of the problems. We have not yet reached the stage when the shipping interests will say to the rail, "By expending x pounds I think we could make eight per cent. on a particular service, but, on the other hand, you would probably make ten, so, in the interest of the greater return on hard-won public savings, we will stand aside and you go ahead"; or, alternatively, "It will cost us a million to supply this service, but we think you could do it for

£900,000, so it is your job." Nor do the 'buses and the railways meet and say, "The long-run costs, including public expenditure, of doing this particular piece of work this way will be so much, but by doing it the other way it will be so much less – let that point decide the issue." Far from this, we are still in the glorious stage of trial and error, only dimly conscious of each other's true costs; not always fully inclined to equate them in a scientific spirit and certainly with no precise knowledge of the comparative value of potential scientific advance, which is the keynote to an economical investment of capital in the best form. Even governmental application of capital to transport itself is quite empirical, especially if it has responsibility for one form and not for another. How much more is the application of capital by a hundred different agencies?

For the first time the Institute has abstracted from a number of other hitherto quite separate services, a common function, and agreed to look at that common function more by what it represents as a single idea of economic service, than by the varied ways in which it is discharged. All the sciences and public services and businesses use statistical methods, specialised for each, and those methods can be abstracted and generalised into a set of principles in a science for common application to all kinds of material, and this science then becomes the handmaid of the other sciences. So when the civil, mechanical, and electrical engineers, surveyors, economists, manufacturers, merchants, accountants, and financiers "hive off" from their respective spheres of thought all that has to do with transport, and bring it under one study and roof and mode of consultation, or consideration, they do not relinquish their respective professions, but they cultivate a new and common hinterland. Professor Whitehead has said that new abstractions are the most powerful engines of advance in thought. Accountancy was such an

abstraction "in the concrete." How powerful has
been its advance since it has been separated from its
several different practical manifestations! I would
say, too, that the process of making new territories,
by focusing attention on what have hitherto been
boundary regions between different territories, is
equally important. If we have been looking intently
at two different points of interest, where the edges of
our vision, almost out of focus, have just met, it is
likely that we know very little precisely about that
blurred middle area. Let us now make that boundary
the special object of our gaze, with the former objects
on the edges of vision, and we must necessarily by
the new focus obtain a new sharpness of knowledge.
So economic geology, economic geography, medical
jurisprudence, chemical biology, all represent new
and productive fields of concentration of thought.
The Institute of Transport represents, first, the
abstraction of the idea of a particular service, however
performed, and, second, a new territory for study
which is at the same time a part of the territory of
existing professions and businesses. We may reasonably expect that in due course it will induce appropriate reactions in thought which will be a consideration of identities more than differences. Of course,
if the Institute is a collection of different and often
competing interests, each of which studies only its
own particular field, it will fail in its object. It will
give nothing more than the past has done. But in
course of time it will be almost impossible for inter-
acting influences not to be felt. Propinquity is the first
law of understanding. The "Here's a stranger, let's
heave half a brick at him" spirit must gradually
fade as the stranger becomes familiar. It may well be
that the older members of the railway, shipping, and
road interests will never talk the general language
of *transport* easily – they will always have the accent
of the old home, and the point of view of their own
calling. But the young men, who will become masters

of their several crafts of transport in the general context of a single over-riding science of transport, will some day form a body of men whose thoughts move interchangeably in its several forms, to whom co-ordination, correlation, collocation, and colligation will be second nature. Instead of thinking of co-operation as a risky sacrifice of interests, or a mere insurance against loss, they will think instinctively of the most appropriate and economic form of transport for a particular task, and any deviation from it, or duplication of it, will be unscientific and repugnant. But nothing is gained by attempting the second day's journey before the first is run, or even planned. What is the immediate possibility and, therefore, the immediate duty?

I consider our earliest attention ought to be given to see that the *pressure* of scientific research is applied equally at all points of the problems of transport. If in one form scientific research is constant and insistent and automatic, while in another it is occasional and apologetic and forced, then we can never be sure that we have really learned the right lessons, and chosen, for a given purpose, the most appropriate instrument. Each branch of transport ought to know what are the chief problems that are before the others, and how they are being tackled. Each ought to have available the results of the other's efforts, in a common language. Not only are these results and efforts to a considerable extent now locked up *within* each form of transport, but even between the several separate scientific fields in each kind of transport, the mechanical and the electrical, chemical and physical, there is often not too clear and clean a contact. Even between the several departments of a single railway there may be little community of thought and effort. Moreover, the common waste of scientific research, the burial of negative results in individual cemeteries with no tombstones, is as marked a practice here as elsewhere in industry. For advance to-day is really not so much fishing about for a lucky discovery, as the patient elimination from a field of total possibilities, and a record of other people's negatives is a valuable contribution to anyone entering any such field of research. Who, in fact, takes the lead in pressing for improvement and experiment? Does the drive come from inside or outside? Do experts in the transport industries ache for specific discovery, and, if so, do they go outside for the solution, and with what response? Or do they evolve it themselves, or join forces? Or does pressure for change come mostly from outside, and, if so, what reception and facility does it get?

On the whole, in the field of pure theory and scientific application, drive is not lacking. There is sufficient interest in the various forms of propulsion, Diesel, turbine, high pressure, and other variants, to secure scientific progress. The evolution of the internal-combustion engine has had its impetus because of the immense commercial gains for the pioneers of each advance. But it is a common denominator of economic application that is lacking, and here the science of comparative costing is in its infancy. For, if a more powerful locomotive, after paying regard to capital cost, after allowing for bridge strengthening, for different coal and water consumption, and for maintenance, and for differences in track maintenance and rapidity of stock-usage, gives a certain new unit of economic effort to move merchandise overland, what limits of cost and performance must some new high-pressure equipment on a coasting vessel, now under scientific enquiry, actually reach to be equal to that unit? And is that task scientifically within reach? At present it is trial and error and supposition, but comparison may obviously be made much more certain than it ever has been. The chief difficulty is that it is rarely a straight comparison of the cost of single identical service, and the economic problem of "joint supply" is involved in one case, while the other partner in the supply for the other transport agency is different. The cost of the given merchandise transport overland may be well aided by some further service which fluctuates, and which the vessel cannot touch, while, conversely, the vessel may wander afar and pick a living elsewhere in its off season, where a specialised railway-stock cannot. An even pressure of scientific research over the whole field is essential. Comparison of the results is essential. These can only be compared in a common language of economic costs and efficiencies. When this has been done we can possibly say that hard-won savings have been applied to the best point of public advantage. A true costing of road and rail costs for a similar service, down to their ultimate essentials, including public costs, has hardly yet been made. Yet a wise community would try to make it before embarking large sums of social capital. Everyone understands the necessity for research in production, and securing lower costs. But transport costs enter into production costs in all the materials and processes. They certainly also enter into price for distribution to the user. Anything gained in this field is equal in value to the gains in the direct production. But, with mass production at single centres in lieu of small production in a number of places, economies in the unit production may be offset by the longer haulage of materials and the distribution and transport costs must tend to be larger relatively to pure manufacturing costs. Uneconomic conditions in the transport costs tend therefore to be more important if less obvious.

If we consider the initiating force which brings about a change, it may be difficult to say what predominates. First, take a *general exterior change pressing for particular new applications*. Some invention or discovery of a general principle has to find numerous particular applications before it can be produced economically. It presses its potentialities upon each possible industry, and each may be sceptical of its applicability to its own case. The inventors or developers try to adapt and prove its suitability without perhaps very adequate means of finding the exact variations necessary, by experiment. I remember, when the "lightning fastener" was invented, much ingenuity was spent in devising ways in which all kinds of industries could use it and then proving the use to them. Some of those industries were quite slow in realising its possibilities; in others its competitive possibilities were economically limited by first costs, until it had attained a sufficient output elsewhere to lower them. So another industry specialises in ball or roller bearings. It knows alone what variants are possible from its existing specifications. But the industry invited to use it alone knows what are the several qualifications it must have to succeed (by cost and otherwise). Neither side is likely to succeed by itself. It needs a very real partnership in the research and the experiment, between the one with a generalised *supply* knowledge and the other with a particularised *demand* knowledge, to hit upon the right application.

In the case of anti-friction bearings for rolling stock, experience abroad had demonstrated that there were various advantages, and there was much research and a good many designs, but, while the results were good for slow speeds, there had been no great success of an economic character for fast passenger-work. At later dates, however, the railways of Sweden and France went a good deal further and claimed a 14.5 per cent. saving in tractive force. In Czecho-Slovakia it is claimed that the weights of the trains for a given power were increased 17 per cent. by roller bearings, with large decrease in maintenance costs. I am not sufficiently expert to know how far these mechanical improvements have prospects of complete ultimate success, but here we may notice an example of the highly inter-related character of scientific improvement on economic direction of capital. A definite advance in this direction may be converse to the problem of locomotive design and may obviate any increase in weight and tractive power, with the possibly consequent problem of further capital expenditure on bridges – two very important problems in costs which may well turn the scale against rival forms. But my point here is rather that, intrinsically, the pressure for considering such a matter as ball or roller bearings has come, and, in the nature of things, probably will continue to come, from the technician seeking new applications for his principles. We might imagine the impetus coming in the following order. The commercial side say to the operating, "There must be, in order to meet rival forms of traction, substantial reductions in rates, and these can only be obtained by reduction in operating costs"; then the operating experts "pass the buck" to the engineers: "If we can have longer and heavier trains we can meet these demands." But this becomes a question of greater engine-power as against the possible wastage of double heading, etc., and the mechanical engineer passes on the problem to the civil engineer by saying, "We have reached the limit of what we can do within the existing load gauge and allowable weight on axles," and this then becomes a problem for the civil engineer to make his track and bridges suitable for this new demand and discover what the cost will be. On finding this prohibitive, the problem might then be transferred back to the stock to see whether the required conditions can be made within a reasonable cost on the lines of removal of friction. But I doubt if much happens in this way. I see no reason why pressure should not come along mechanical lines by costing, searching out for alternatives, much more than it has done in the past. With highly divided and technically distinct sciences, there has been a tendency, of course, for each to think of the solution of a financial problem only within the limits of itself. There is a much greater tendency to-day to unify scientific problems. The introduction to the Report of the Bridge Stress Committee refers to the interaction between questions of bridges and of locomotives, and this illustrates my meaning: "No maker of locomotives is greatly concerned with the structure of bridges, nor has any builder of bridges possessed adequate opportunities of experiment with locomotives in motion. The complex relation between the two has, therefore, never been completely understood; nor can it be until the need for a co-operative effort becomes fully realised." The work of this committee is a standing example of co-operation on a purely physical, mechanical, and mathematical problem. I think we have to go even further and to deal with the economic costing of each alternative. I will revert to this problem a little later.

Another example of improvements coming by way of an independent industry seeking for applications for its product and pressing them upon transport is the carborundum sanding portable machine. It may be that in time the desire to speed up and to economise on the facing of axle-box guides and general surface-finishing would have brought about an enquiry initiated from the railway end, but there is nothing to prove this.

There has no doubt been, over a considerable field, a large amount of improvement obtained in this way, e.g. the reorganisation of work in wagon shops on progressive lines brought about much quicker times for passing the stock through, and an important limiting factor was found to be the process of painting and drying. This bid fair to throw away a good part of the time economy that the other improvements would have given. Here at once was an incentive for research into various painting materials in order to see how far speeding up could be effected. The company was sufficiently strong in its scientific equipment to carry out these experiments itself, in order to test at the same time any other essential qualities for the particular use of paint, and after considerable experiment, the necessary processes were discovered and applied.

Such an instance as the testing of the bonding of wheels to be efficient in the case of track circuits, and to avoid "false clear" incidents, raised special problems of testing for their low resistance values. Here the problem was placed mainly in the hands of an outside firm, which received the details of the required performance and then co-operated with the railway's technical staff. It may be said that this is a very common form of procedure obtaining where the quest comes from the transport industry itself. In the electrical field particularly, it may be said that no great advance on broad electrical principles owes its discovery to railway work and workers or research workers, but that the problems in technique had been handed over to research associations as general problems, with representation from the railway technical departments, while problems in mechanical application have often tended to be dealt with by direct contact with manufacturing establishments.

It would, I think, be correct to say that, while, in locomotive construction, improvement has been mainly from within, impelled, of course, by continually advancing operating requirements, and while the same is true to a large extent in telegraph and signalling, yet, in matters of electric traction and power utilisation, most of the drive in discovery has come from general electrical research outside. This doubtless is due very largely to the fact that, whilst railway companies have their own locomotive and carriage shops and have always, to a large extent – the larger companies at any rate – built their own locomotives and carriages, their requirements have not been of sufficient volume, so far, to warrant the manufacture of heavy electrical plant or machinery.

They have rather proceeded on the lines of utilising the developments, as these become commercially feasible, resulting from research on the part of the manufacturing firms. The interests of these firms are directly bound up in such developments, but are of increasing importance to the railways, who, realising this, contribute largely to various research associations.

In locomotive practice the standard main-line engine has developed gradually from the old single driver to a six-coupled type, due to the heavier loads to be hauled, and the avoidance of double heading; and, for the heavy goods and coal traffic, eight-coupled engines are generally in use – and engines of the Garratt type, where the weight is distributed over more axles, are now being introduced for this class of traffic. Banking engines having ten-coupled wheels are in use for steep gradients. The use of modern heavy locomotives has necessitated the reconstruction of many bridge structures. The increase, in boiler pressures, and the use of superheaters, has conduced to the efficiency of the locomotive in recent years. One of the most important improvements in locomotive design, viz. the more correct balancing of the driving wheels, and the consequent elimination of abnormal stresses on bridges and the general hammering of the permanent way, is now being effected as a result of the enquiry into the impact on bridges by the Bridge Stress Committee, who found in their investigations that the impact or "hammer blow" of the locomotive had a very great effect on the stress on bridges.

In civil-engineering practice much of the progress and development on British railways during the last twenty years has been due to the co-ordination of the chief engineers of the various railway companies. This materialised in the formation of the Railway Engineers' Association (a private association), instituted in the year 1902.

It may be claimed on behalf of the railways that the labours of this association, and of the Association of Railway Locomotive Engineers, materially assisted the British Engineering Standards Association, incorporated in 1918 and previously formed in 1901 by the Engineering Standards Committee of the Institution of Civil Engineers, Institution of Mechanical Engineers, Institution of Naval Architects, the Iron and Steel Institute, and the Institution of Electrical Engineers.

But in certain aspects of civil engineering the initiation has been from outside.

Steel manufacturers are experimenting in the production of stainless and silicon and other alloy steels. Silicon steel has high tensile properties, and its use in bridges reduces the dead weight of the structure, and is thus useful for long-span bridges. A high tensile steel of British manufacture is being used in the great bridge now being built over Sydney Harbour, but this steel has not yet been standardised for general use in British railway practice. It has, however, been used for several large bridges in America and Germany. Steel manufacturers are also experimenting in a steel having about .2 per cent. to .3 per cent. of copper in its composition. It is claimed that this steel is less liable to corrosion than ordinary steel, and its use in bridge work, and even for rails – say, in wet tunnels – is being advocated. It is slightly more expensive than ordinary mild steel, but, excepting the added copper, is virtually of the same structure and quality. It is used in America for bridge work where the native ores contain copper in suitable quantity. These developments in steel have been largely due to the enterprise of steel manufacturers, and cannot be claimed to have been wholly initiated by the railway interests in this country.

Not by any means can all scientific advance, however, be made either by representations from outside bodies on application of new principles, or by the

discovery of new needs which are put to outside
technical bodies or manufacturing establishments;
there remains much that can only be done upon the
spot, by the highly trained research-worker having
his laboratory in the establishment itself. Commercial
production has benefited very greatly, for example, in
foundry work through using the heavy-oil engine and
high-pressure steam plant, but these results cannot
immediately be obtained by the chemist or physicist
just being put down in the middle of the works and
asked to look round; it needs long applied study,
and much faith in the expenditure of experimental
capital. Again, the plotting and planning of such
work, and its subsequent control by people with
commercial instinct is in itself a fascinating study in
the interaction between scientific possibility and
human psychology. There is an equal danger in the
desire for immediate commercial results by the
general manager, and the liability to scientific stunt-
ing in the long distance by the uncommercial scientist. A recent critic says, on the subject of the wear
and tear of steel rails, in which there seems to be a
considerable division of opinion as to whether any
real progress has been made for many years: "Most
of the railways conduct experiments of various
kinds, but there is little or no collective use of the
result, and it is doubtful whether in the end they lead
anywhere. A standard specification is a dead hand to
initiative." And this writer in *The Railway Engineer*
makes a great plea for railway research. There is no
doubt that collective experiment and collective testing have made considerable headway, but collective
research far less. Research probably receives far
greater attention in America and Germany in industry generally—Germany because her only way out
in industry is through mass production and rationalisation, and America because she is rich enough and
has such spontaneous imagination to indulge her
wealth. The President of the Institution of

Mechanical Engineers in 1927 dealt specially with this point.

Our several means of scientific advance are as follows: 1. The individual scientist. 2. The firms' research departments (e.g. the Bell testing establishment has 4,000 investigators and assistants). 3. The National Physical Laboratory. 4. The universities. 5. Such bodies as the Non-Ferrous Metal and Cast Iron Research Associations.

It is doubtful whether the last named receive enough support, and especially whether we have sufficient "bridges" and means of rapid communication between their work and actual industrial operations.

The great defect of individual research departments' work is, of course, that the history of failures or negative results, which is so valuable, is completely lost. There is an enormous waste in duplication of effort, and in general there is not a large enough view, nor is the problem sufficiently seen in its "pure science" aspects.

In general it may be said that progress has not been due to work involved by the daily duties of the people in the workshops and factories, and, moreover, the administrative head has generally only spare moments to apply his mind to such problems. It is quite true that many useful suggestions come from those who are in personal contact with difficulties and failures, for their correction; but, if a good process is working smoothly, it takes the abstraction of a relative outsider to suggest that a radical change is possible and is worth looking for. The process of comparative costing is one of the modern means of jogging us out of our ruts and asking new questions.

Research on scientific lines is required in every branch – it is not confined to physics and chemistry, but extends to all functions.

In my view, there should be in every department and business – whatever we may expect by suggestion and illustration and question from those responsible for running things, as they are, to the best advantage – some minds set aside for considering change and improvement, and for experiment. The type of mind is often different; its abilities grow by what it feeds upon; it evolves a technique and knack and process of discovery and elimination; it gets a "feel" for a line of success; it learns to see the wood despite the trees! More can be accomplished by ten such minds on a problem in its most favourable setting, getting three yards into the problem, than a thousand men, with their many daily occupations, snatching a few moments of amateur application and each getting three inches into it. The readiest co-operation between the two types is wanted, but the drive, the concentration, and the technique of a select corps, as the cutting edge of discovery, is essential. The effect upon the daily worker ought not to be that of making him feel he has no part in advance of thought. Rather, in practice, it breaks down the self-complacency of the "practical man," who often either belittles the possibility of better ways or else has an undue craze for everything new because it is new, with the risky lack of discrimination which accompanies that mood. The practical man has been well described as one who practises the theories of fifty years ago. He often considers himself strongest where he is really weak. As my darkie friend says, "De trubble wid de man what knows it all is dat he talk so much he ain't got no time to get no information." Professor Whitehead says, "If you have had your attention directed to the novelties in thought in your own lifetime, you will have observed that almost all really new ideas have a certain aspect of foolishness when they are first produced."

The grouping of pistons, cylinders, feeds, gauges, and a hundred other parts into new forms and combinations, to make a new machine, we call invention and scientific research. The grouping of different types of men and physical agencies into new combinations we just call "organisation." We tend to restrict the idea of scientific research to the physical sciences. But, rightly, any generalised knowledge, with principles for application at all points, becomes scientific. When does the ordinary adaptation of his resources to the local demands, by a trader or manufacturer or transport agent, become something that can be dignified by the name of scientific research? My answer is, When it ceases to be trial and error, empirical, and proceeds by recorded experiment, under control, to general principles, capable of general application as a new way of doing old things, or a way of doing new things. In order not to create false impressions, the research corps may be termed "development" sections, but they must proceed by the scientific methods of recorded experiment, and establishment of methods or principles which have identical effects.

The type of research that goes to proper rate-fixing may very well be termed scientific. Fundamentally, railway rates are based on the class of commodity and the distance it is to be carried, but, in actual practice, many other factors have to be taken into consideration in arriving at the numerous rates which the British trading public seek daily. This necessitates a widespread research possibly undreamed of by the average layman.

As a first step, the facts are viewed in their local aspect, and, when it is found that the revision of a rate or the adoption of a new one is practicable locally, then the considerations are extended to the wider field of similar traffics passing in other directions or in other parts of the country. Taking an illustration of a large contract for which tenders are sought – those interested in securing the contract necessarily require to know the lowest price they will have to pay for getting the goods delivered from their works, and they naturally apply to their own local railway official as to what the rate will be. In all probability a number of similar enquiries will be made in respect of the sale contract emanating from many places served by different railway companies. It is essential that these should all be concentrated for consideration at one central place, so that the price quoted for the transport from each place will not only be reasonable, but equitable as between the various applicants. To ensure this, all facts in regard to the tonnage involved, the distance to be conveyed, loading per wagon, facilities for collection and delivering and handling, whether competition exists with other means of transport, have to be available, and these are subjected to close investigation by those responsible for fixing the charges to be made.

A phase in which careful research is necessary before old rates are altered or new rates adopted is in respect of port areas, or areas devoted to the production of such staple commodities as iron and steel, cotton, etc. Trade has been built up from the ports over long periods of years, and the cost of rail transportation between area and area has become more or less stabilised, having regard to the needs of the trades with such places.

Now let us consider in what way the railway officer applies the principle of research to his terminal depots. How can it help him here?

Again the whole question resolves itself into one of cost – the cost of passing merchandise from road vehicle to wagon, or vice versa, as rapidly, cheaply, and efficiently as possible.

Let us bear in mind that whilst many existing depots have been made more efficient with the installation of up-to-date equipment, the possibilities of expansion are limited by the very nature of their own existence; they were created to serve particular towns, neighbourhoods, etc. The traders using them were all in close proximity, and the inevitable crowding in of the depots has made their expansion all the more difficult. To do anything in that way to-day, in many cases would involve buying up valuable properties and compensating displaced tenants, creating the additional burden of providing an adequate return for the capital expenditure and necessary maintenance. When, therefore, the traffic using a station grows beyond the existing capacity, the railway manager is forced to consider ways and means of quickening the processes inherent in the work to be performed, so that an increased volume may be dealt with. How can such problems be overcome? – by the employment of more labour? Yes, to an extent it can be done, but only to the extent to which the manual strength can operate freely. As soon as freedom of movement is interrupted, so does trouble arise, and, the more freedom is restricted, so does the speed of operation become slower and slower.

Knowing this, how does the railway manager cope with the business increasing beyond the capacity of his accommodation? He considers whether his cartage vehicles can be placed more closely to the wagons to which the goods have to be transferred, to lessen the distance the goods have to be trucked across the platform; he considers whether the composition of his gangs trucking the goods can be modified, whether he has too many men barrowing, and not enough loading the goods in the wagons and vans; and, by these and other means, he endeavours to quicken his speed of handling and avoid enlargement of his equipment.

Notwithstanding what may be done on these lines, however, there comes a time when additional accommodation must be provided – the capital expenditure must be faced – and then research plays an even greater part.

In formulating the plans, consideration is given to other points, including:

(*a*) Laying out the shed so that the smallest possible distance will be covered in trucking from cart to wagon, or vice versa.

(*b*) Placing the rail lines in the shed so that the largest possible number of wagons may be berthed alongside the platforms for loading or unloading at one time, minimising the time occupied in resetting the shed with further wagons as, during such periods, of course, handling operations cannot be performed.

(*c*) Planning the entrances, exits, and roadways, so that the movement of road vehicles may be unhampered and at all times flow in conformity with the movement of traffic to or from the rail wagons.

(*d*) Surfacing the platforms with materials giving the maximum wear and presenting the minimum resistance to the passage of the barrows, the latter factor being one of some importance in obtaining the maximum service from the manual labour employed.

So we find again that research must come first in planning a rail depot, in the same way as it must in planning a highly complicated chemical-producing plant.

What has been said in regard to the construction of depots applies equally to mechanical appliances to be used therein. For instance, in the years that have gone, fixed cranes, or cranes such as gantry cranes working only within circumscribed areas, have been quite sufficient to meet all needs. The use of such appliances, however, involves the placing of the load to be lifted in close proximity to, and within range of, the crane – a process frequently causing delay and inconvenience to other operations. To get over this, experiments have been made with mobile cranes which can be manipulated at any point and at any time with little or no interruption of other work. Development on these lines will undoubtedly help in facilitating terminal operations, and research will play its part in deciding what types are most suitable for the particular work to be undertaken.

A word might be said here in regard to the latest method adopted by the railway companies for improving transportation over their systems – I refer to the general use of the container. By utilising such receptacles, goods can pass from sender to consignee untouched by the railway companies' staffs, and, with the complete elimination of handling, damage or loss is almost equally eliminated. Containers have proved their worth, and provision for adding to the existing stocks is now an established feature in the railway companies' programmes of development; in fact, experiments are being conducted with the object of devising other types for traffics not hitherto dealt with by this method.

Some of the most important matters now under physical research, which may be of far-reaching importance on the development of branches of transport in which they are *not* used, are:

In the case of steamers, the question of motive power and fuel, now in a state of flux, with the range of applicability of high-pressure systems; in the case of docks, the handling appliances; in the case of roads, motor design and the net costliness of road maintenance; in railways, the range of electrification, locomotive types and high-pressure boilers, wagon capacity, braking, and lubrication. But, for the non-physical subjects in all types of service, we need to know much more about the unit cost of operations and the limit of profitable expenditure on particular services, the economic life of "repairable" assets, the incidence of sickness and fatigue in labour. For all these subjects we need a more exact record of facts, and a uniform arrangement of them. We need a better equipment for testing them experimentally, and uniform, open, logical methods of deduction from these tests.

If the layman tries to learn the true comparative value of two locomotive types, he gets it from one, with exact figures, that A has an initial cost greater than B, but probably a longer active life; that B costs more for running repairs and maintenance. Another tells him that A is less in coal and water consumption, but B has more "up its sleeve" in power. Or that A has a wider general utility, and can run everywhere, while B has the economy of greater speed and less liability to breakdown. Sometimes one thing is in fashion and sometimes another, but it is almost impossible to reduce this comparison to a net economic balance from such impressions. It was expected that the institution of a system of costing of individual locomotives, in which all incidents are recorded, would enable each type to throw up a definite general trend of performance which in a few years would be valuable information in deciding on capital expenditure. But the advantage of precise knowledge came much earlier – indeed almost at once – and the large incidental economies resulting from the mere analysis of the initial facts justified the regular costs incurred.

The existence of this Institute will lessen the drawbacks of water-tight compartments in departmental practice, where there is no relation made between the different results of each. It ought to do something to prevent the lack of continuity and comparability in research. But, of course, above all, it ought to help create a type of mind which will fill the present need, men of general knowledge of principle, restless enquiring outlook, rigid scientific proof, with the knack of experimentation and deduction. How may it bring this to pass ? Here are some possibilities: First, by bringing the different interests under one roof and into a common Journal. Second, by the curriculum and syllabus for training of new entrants. Third, by encouraging the exhibition of the results of scientific research to each other. Fourth, by publishing papers dealing with comparative aspects, costs, etc., in its Journal. Fifth, by standardising the language and procedure of economic costing. Sixth, by joint committees for common work on comparative questions which shall not be experts defending points of view, but experts co-operating for the search of truth. Seventh, by a single-minded unity in presenting its work to the world. Competition will still exist between the forms of transport. But its preliminary heats will be fought out on the drawing-board, in the laboratory, and on the costing-sheets. The Institute will not do all this to-day, or to-morrow, but surely the results will come. If we cannot see the goal, at least we know the direction, and can set a course that meets the day's demands with the day's weakness and strength, but leads to the promised land.

X

The present position of management and direction in industry generally is a half-way house between the ideas of the middle nineteenth century, which are still working with some success, but rapidly diminishing success, in some industries, and the very different conceptions and needs of industry conducted on a quite different scale, both at home and abroad. The development is proceeding rapidly. It is partly a matter of psychology and education, and partly of economic evolution. The management of business is no longer regarded as something socially and intellectually inferior to professions, or requiring a less disciplined and rigorous educational equipment, and it presses into its service a much wider range of mental attainment. We find, therefore, that businesses can be successfully run to-day of a size and style for which the human material of management would not have existed fifty years ago, and thus development of new types has been facilitated. But, on the whole, the economic evolution has outpaced even this human change, and an authority has gone so far as to declare that the structure is evolving more rapidly than the minds of most of those who are responsible for its direction.

The increasing size of individual businesses has undoubtedly been mainly economic in its origin, inasmuch as, other things being equal, size has given definite advantages in production and marketing.

The change in the form of management of the

---

[1] Broadcast, in November 1930, as two of a series of talks on "Industry Looks Ahead."

typical business has been partly the result of the change of size, but, when once discovered and practised, has also often enabled the increase in size to be achieved.

A successful private business has rarely run into the third and fourth generation without some loss of drive and initiative. "From clogs to clogs in three generations" is a Lancashire saying that has analogies in countries so far apart as Germany and Japan. The distribution of new blood, or the bringing in of the trusted managers, has been facilitated by the joint-stock form of ownership, where the residual claims of the relatives of the previous generation have been represented by a part of the share capital. The business is now much less in danger of disruption and decline through the death of a part-owner than it used to be. This form of management, with a board of directors, and published and audited accounts, with shares having some degree of negotiability, has enabled new finance for extensions to be raised from outside sources and the general money-market. The rise of a special type of person, without capital, but able to manage businesses of different types, has helped greatly. Amalgamations with other businesses have been thus facilitated, and the emergence of the professional company promoter on the look-out for likely private businesses to be "floated" has hastened the process. Even the heavy death duties, which can much more easily be dealt with in the case of a negotiable shareholding than of the less divisible and less negotiable ownership of a private business, have done their part in promoting the movement. The percentage of profits made by private businesses, out of the total, changed from seventy to a little over thirty in a period of forty years.

Over the two decades prior to the war the number of separate colliery businesses went down by over twelve per cent., and the average profits rose by over seventy-five per cent. Cotton businesses diminished by nearly twenty-five per cent., and the average profits increased nearly one hundred per cent. Woollen businesses were down in number by twenty-five per cent., and up in average profits by some eighty per cent. Shipbuilding firms were down by eleven per cent., but the profits were up by over one hundred and fifty per cent. Brewery businesses diminished in number by twenty per cent., and profits increased over fifty per cent. Banks were fewer by over fifty per cent., but profits increased over one hundred per cent.

In the cotton industry, out of 221 concerns in 1884, 127 were private firms with a typical size of 20,000 spindles, the main type for companies having 80,000 spindles. In 1924, out of 203, only five were private, with 20,000 spindles as a maximum, and the main type for companies had 110,000 spindles. We all know how much further this process has now gone with the advent of rationalisation and the Lancashire Cotton Corporation.

It has been the staple industries in which the tendency to large-size production and to amalgamation has been most obvious, for private initiative and enterprise have always been, and still are (even under the form of small limited companies), the best adapted for developing new ideas and changes, until they have thoroughly established themselves. It is to-day not easy to raise money, even for a large company, to run an untried and pioneer process.

In the Victorian era, the typical private business was originally built up by a man of vigorous personality, who drove hard bargains, seized every opening and opportunity, and had little concern with total production and comparative costs. On a continually expanding foreign and home market, as a pioneer, over-production was not an ever-present danger, and he met with more success than his actual qualities of brain and foresight might have justified. But the most important feature was that he lived "lean and hard" and did not indulge himself in spending as his profit increased, for he turned it nearly all back into the business as new capital, the funds being hardly depleted at all by income tax, and not at all by super-tax, while death duties made no periodical inroads upon it. Virtually, of course, he never "enjoyed" it at all, and, apart from prestige and local power, economically, at the time, it was socialised as completely as if it had been extracted by the State and reinvested; though later, no doubt, in the hands of less industrious and more ambitious descendants, its character as saleable private property was more evident. But, meantime, it had achieved its purpose, for it had made business thrift the most cardinal of all the virtues. The aggregate of this saving was a very large proportion of the total investment of the country. The backbone of industrial expansion was in the staple industries of the North, where men cared less about the display of consumption than the display of production. Even in my own experience as a revenue officer at the end of the nineteenth century, I found that the style and size of a man's residence had a close proportion to his income in the south of England, but hardly any reliable relation in the north, where it was not an uncommon thing to find a well-to-do manufacturer still living in the little house that he had occupied as a beginner thirty years before.

The manufacturer and, indeed, the merchant had little knowledge of the total potential output of the industry of which he formed a part, still less of the probable available stocks at any moment. The aggregate of the actions of men all moved by the same impulse in differing degrees, each expecting to be in front of the other, tended often to come to something well in advance of true requirements. The available statistical material was not only scanty, but it was also much too late to be a guide to conduct.

The qualities required for success in a small-sized, very competitive business were highly individualistic – courage, quick decision, and initiative, with dogged perseverance, no little personal knowledge of all the different processes and functions discharged by those employed. But the employer did not need to possess, in any marked degree, conciliation, power to collaborate, the spirit of team work, and patience to work towards a co-ordinated decision. He was often successful in proportion as he knew his own mind, ignored others, and was even domineering and rugged. Now the man corresponding to him to-day in industry will occupy a salaried position as a departmental head, or a divisional chief of the separate works of a combine. In the first, he will spend a large part of his time fitting in his ideas with other departments to a common end, consulting, adjusting, urging, giving way, sharing responsibility – a considerable cog in a large wheel, instead of a small complete cogwheel in himself. He will thus require a whole range of new qualities which the individualist does not need. As Dr. Bowie has well said, in a very original and useful book just published on *Education for Business Management*:

In the past, the power to drive was important; the rugged, forceful, gritty type of man suited the venturesome days of the Industrial Revolution. To-day the man who is equipped to co-operate with his fellows, the man who can attach other men to himself in respectful affection, is called to leadership. . . . When the affairs of a business become diversified and complex, direct, personal control is no longer effective or feasible. The result is that young men must enter the portals of industry by a different door. There are not the same chances as in the past for men to use moderate amounts of capital to establish themselves in independent concerns. The opportunities offered young men have changed. The ability to take up a responsible position in a large concern is now taking the place of the opportunity for starting a new business on a small scale. The abilities required in these two spheres are different. The latter needs, above all, individual courage and initiative; the former, while needing these qualities, also requires a sense of co-ordination and co-operation. The brilliant soloist may make a poor member of an orchestra.

The individual proprietor has only to think and do and take the step – he need have no gift of exposition or making precise his ideas and estimates. But the departmental head, when he resists or supports proposals affecting him, or initiates proposals affecting others, cannot remain silent. He must give reasons for the faith that is in him, and, therefore, if he is inarticulate either in committee or by his pen, his usefulness is greatly limited. Now he needs the gift of clear expression; and the art of making a concise but comprehensive report, or of ready response in committee (almost unnecessary in the Victorian business) is almost essential in a modern concern. For, failing it, the other departments affected, and the co-ordinating management, are all hampered.

The divisional or local manager, again, requires qualities not necessary to the Victorian chief. He receives from a number of departmental heads the instructions and lines of policy and is relieved of responsibility for that kind of decision. Indeed, often the full reason for what he is directed to do cannot be clear to him, for he cannot see the whole map. But he has to give practical effect, in a hundred variations, to the general rules, and he may have to use discretion to vary them within limits. He gets the rubs and kicks of actual application to the worker, the customer, the public, which the departmental heads do not see or know in detail. If the variations are great, it is for him to take the initiative in drawing attention to the need for modification of general principle. He supplies the raw material on which decisions have to be made, and he is the sensitive conductor to realities. He has both less and more responsibility than the sole owner and manager. For he may be able to stand aside from all large discussions of policy, in buying, price fixing, and changes of supply. But he cannot just "please himself" how he runs his factory or his division – he must conform to his instructions on general principles, and "make them work" even if he doesn't like them. He has many bosses or advisers, and needs to be both teachable and dominating, both passive and active.

The leader and the directors who manage a large concern with many sections and functions have three main tasks; first, to determine and keep to the single aim of the business in its purpose and development (which no one employed individual in the business may necessarily discern all the time) and to see that the inter-relationships are all framed and directed to that end, and that all are pulling in the same direction. In the second place, they have to delimit function exactly, so as to prevent overlapping or gaps, or failure to give incentive or fix responsibility. This delimitation includes the problems of specialising in functions, as against complete area autonomy. In one case the manager of each works or each district may have complete responsibility, including control of labour conditions, of costing and accounting, of technical equipment; but, in another, he may have been divested of any one or all of these functions, which have been handed to specialists who control them direct. In the third place, the right types of men have to be chosen for each function, with the right types of blends of contacts and systems – for example, reports and committees. Some find that the modern business is constantly revising its contacts, and making new experiments in delegating, or making what has been a general function and everybody's business into a special or expert function.

Professor Marshall, in his enumeration of the chief requisites of the head of a modern business, put them in this order: (*a*) judgment, prudence, enterprise, and fortitude in carrying risks; (*b*) acquaintance with appropriate technique, and power to initiative advance; (*c*) power of organising in a system, but always as a servant and never as a master; (*d*) sympathy and resolution with subordinates; and (*e*) power to discern the best potentialities of each and to assign the highest work to them. These qualities are all wanted by heads of moderate business and by the departmental heads of large businesses. The main task of the chief and the directors is to assess them, and to determine at what point specialists are wanted and how to weld them into the team. The team has not merely co-ordination as its object, but the mutual stimulus and progressive force which results from the continual intercourse of high officials.

There are three stages for almost any amalgamation or great merger. At first the factories or units carry on much as before, until the new central management get to know each other, and then a process of high centralisation sets in, first finance, bank balances, and new capital expenditure, passing on through technical equipment, costing, purchasing, advertising, labour, and welfare, until nearly everything passes through the central mill. In this stage the central management gets to know actually what is happening and to establish uniform and standard practices, and to lay down common principles. After this stage the third process of devolution and delegation may follow, but the powers given back are usually restored in a different form, because the delegation is supervised by experts, e.g. a research department, or a technical engineering establishment, an establishment officer for labour conditions, a welfare supervisor, a publicity manager, with whom the local management must keep in a constant state of co-operation.

All this delimitation of function, intervention of experts, and existence of departmental management means that a new type of consultative co-operation is demanded, and touch is kept by committees to a much greater extent than hitherto.

The head of the business will no longer boast that he can do the jobs of everyone in the business as well as they can. He may have nothing more than certain important managerial qualities highly developed, but he is generally all the better for having had a complete grounding in some definite field, such as accountancy, or law, or engineering, in his first ten or even twenty years of business life. The appreciation of detail and the knowledge of the feelings of the man at the machine, or on the office stool, and the attitude to delegated authority, are all invaluable ingredients in experience.

Many self-made heads of business to-day, who left school early, are still impatient at the idea that business management has anything to gain from public school and university training. There is the "look at me – *I* have managed without it" spirit. But they forget that, whereas a hundred boys chosen at the leaving age of fifteen or sixteen, thirty-five years ago, have thrown up five, say, who can occupy the highest posts to-day, a similar choice of one hundred to-day would not so certainly do so in the years to come. The simple reason is that they would not be the same hundred. To-day the educational ladder and facilities are such that the best of the hundred in question will have passed on to public and grammar schools, and some of them to the universities, so that to get a strictly comparable *hundred* it is necessary to dip one's bucket, so to speak, into the three different ages. This refers only to the attempt to get the same native ability, and does not touch the larger question of the ultimate value of the further training and education.

*   *   *   *

It may be said that the newer tools now available in industry provide for finer measurements, judgment of the future by the experience of the past, and specialisation of function. The importance of the relation between direct expenses of production, which vary almost exactly with the volume of output, and the standing or overhead expenses which vary only slightly, has long been realised, and rough types of costing have long been in vogue for this purpose, and for determining profit on specific contracts. But exact measurement of everything in business that is capable of being measured, either by time, such as so many items an hour, or by volume, such as so much usage of material per unit of saleable product, or fineness, such as so many rejects per hundred of cartridges, or, above all, money cost per unit of effort, such as the cost of handling packages at a goods depot, is relatively modern, and does not extend much beyond the United States, the British Empire, and Germany as a common practice.

Lord Kelvin once said that we know very little about a subject until we have learnt to measure it. Costing is essentially measuring. There are no doubt many who still think it is an expensive fad, an academic exercise, and they have some justification where the plant and the output are so small as not to be able to stand the expense of a system elaborate enough to give useful results. Such a system would be very little more expensive for large plants and outputs and is, therefore, easily supportable by them. Critics are also justified, at least in suspicions, where costing systems are carried to an unnecessary degree of refinement, or pretend to absolute exactness where such cannot exist. But, in general, a costing system in a competitive business of fine margins must be quite detailed to give results that are valuable in management, and it is better to have none at all than a very cheap one, which only puts into figures what everyone knows already by the light of nature. Thus to know that a pound of artificial silk of average type has cost so much in labour, so much in materials, and so much for overhead costs, in a year, is nowadays of little value. It is necessary to know accurately the cost of each thickness of denier, and this involves a detailed system right through the works at every stage. It is also necessary to know the cost for much shorter periods of time, if costing is to be used to control and check manufacture, to direct policy, eliminate waste. Above all, the system should reveal process costs, that is, costs of each distinct manufacturing process through which the material passes. For costing enables a comparison to be made between the efficiency and expense of two different plants producing similar things by the same or by different methods – a comparison of two places at the same point of time. It also enables us to compare the efficiency and expense of the same plant this month with the corresponding month a year ago or two years ago – a comparison of two times at the same place. And the search for the reason for differences disclosed may reveal many things open to correction, long before they would be visible to the naked eye of management. For this purpose, then, a single cost for each product is not the ideal form, because a cost of £100 each revealed in two places might lead one to suppose that they had nothing to teach each other, and that all was for the best. But if there are four processes, A, B, C, and D, it may well be that the £100 total cost is quite differently made up in the two places, A and D being higher in the first than the second, and C and D lower. Thus A, B, C, and D may be 40, 20, 15, 25 in the first and 30, 25, 25, 20 in the second. Now, in the first factory the lessons of the second may perhaps be learnt by technical examination and applied in processes A and D, and, similarly, the second factory can learn new ways from the first for doing processes B and C. The result will be that the cost in each case can be reduced from 100 to 85. Process costing often requires careful physical storing, weighing and measuring devices at each plant, and this costs money; but the expense is often very amply repaid in efficiency. For costing not only reveals money costs: it shows consumption of fuel, current or oil per unit of use, percentage of waste, etc., and the various items of physical efficiency, as well as costs of handling at different places. It may be thought that the utility of such measurements is confined to the efficiency of day-to-day management, and does not touch high policy. But accurate costing is essential in determining the wisdom of large capital expenditure, particularly in substitution for less advanced methods of manufacture, involving lower-grade manual labour. I have known the final costs of a large highly elaborated factory in a populous, highly rated district, with heavy labour charges, run for a long time in equilibrium with the costs of the output of small units, in rural surroundings with water power, and cheap unskilled labour, with primitive machinery and favourably situated for raw material.

In the second place, fine and strictly comparable costing may be necessary before it can be determined which of the factories is the one to be closed down when output is excessive. I have known a board of directors, in the absence of such details, dispute, by the aid of sentiment, association, and mere impression, on such a question with equal wisdom and knowledge, and only the test of comparative costs has later on brought out the elements which are irreducible by improved methods, etc., and shown which factory has the greater potentiality for improvement.

In the third place, the higher management needs the help of costing results if it is considering a policy of radical expansion of output. Having estimated the demand schedule, or how much more the public demand will absorb at different levels of lower price, it has then to be determined what will be the net unit cost of increased supplies.

I have known cases where the search for the reason

for small differences in process costings has suggested subjects for scientific and laboratory research, with very profitable results, and a re-arrangement of lay-out frequently follows. Many businesses, particularly working in metals, holding stocks of raw materials which fluctuate considerably in price, have not distinguished between the costs of manufacturing and their costs in bearing such fluctuations, so that speculation results, affected by price, have been hopelessly muddled up with changes in efficiency, owing to the absence of cost accounts.

There are still many old-established businesses which have no such measurement. I met, not long ago, a manufacturer, of the fourth generation in a well-known establishment of moderate size, who boasted that he never had a return or a figure of any kind on his desk – he said he knew by instinct whether a machine or a workman was good, and whether he was producing within his price, and costing would only be a waste of money. Certainly few large businesses could carry on for long without accurate record.

Apart from the technique of costing, which is now highly developed and well established, the human element is important. Costs ought to be computed by workers who are independent of the management of particular units, but the management should regard it, not as an instrument of higher admonition, but as an aid to their own efficiency. I have known cases where, before the head office has received and examined the assembled figures and had time to ask the appropriate questions, the factory managers and technicians have already "got after" the tell-tale differences and remedied them. Moreover, the friendly rivalries between different establishments may be stimulated by the free use of this material, but as a rule it is only factory efficiency costs, as distinct from completed and "all in" costs, which are thus more or less common property. The value of costs is much enhanced if they follow hot after the period to which they relate. Greater elaboration is often little worth while if it involves undue delay.

Analysis is a very general term which applies throughout business records. For example, few businesses are now content to appropriate large sums for advertising without examining as closely as possible the results due to each kind of advertisement, especially in areas and towns. Comparative statistical records are, therefore, an important engine of policy. In the United States very large sums are spent in support of general statistical agencies. Business forecasting is a widespread exercise. But I suspect that the average business executive gets more of this kind of food than he can mentally digest, for the adequate use of such general material does not come by routine, but only by a special mental training which few managements possess.

One American development in big business is, however, of very great importance. Mass production involves the very utmost co-ordination between all the different processes, and a constant re-timing according to their variation in efficiency. As motor-cars come off a belt at something like one a minute, and all the parts are fed to the main stream by the departmental bays, a delay in any one, or insufficiency of materials, must hold up the whole process at terrific expense. If the orders fell off and the cars were not taken promptly away, the countryside would be choked in a few days. In the past ten years corporations like General Motors have developed their budget system to a very fine pitch of accuracy. Each of the many units of the far-flung selling organisation reports what is anticipated in its area as sales of each kind in the light of past experience and of local development and procedure, for each month of the year, and the aggregate forms the selling side of the budget. This forms the monthly target of every department, which makes the nicest possible adjustment to it, so that the year's budget lies ahead, in great detail, down to the anticipated monthly net profit from the department and from the whole business. This budget is not merely an interesting statistical exercise, with monthly excitement and departmental emulation in accurate prophecy; it is a guide to policy and a means of departmental check and control. Every material change or discrepancy gives a point for analysis and enquiry. The budget system is being extended to business of many different types.

In the working force of every business there are two possible aggregations: first, that of individuals each efficiently getting the best return he can for the work he does, or putting in not more work than is necessary to earn his money; second, the same set of workers animated with a keen corporate spirit, a real *esprit de corps*, able to feel that they can take a personal interest in the success of their co-operation, and can make suggestions for success, or for the avoidance of disputes. Hence a prominent feature in the minds of modern management is the choice and fostering of the best of the various means for creating this goodwill, and making effective the immense latent force of intelligent assistance through suggestion schemes, works, councils, profit sharing or shareholding schemes.

Then, again, the wide subject of industrial welfare, not merely run by just any intelligent person by the light of nature, but by specially trained officers who have a scientific knowledge of general results at home and abroad, and whose business it is to follow every development, must occupy a prominent place. This means not merely the study of working amenities, ventilation, etc., but spreads out into housing schemes, savings banks, magazines, and assistance to all kinds of activities promoted by the workers themselves, which help towards the good and full life which is the best background of industrial efficiency, and, indeed, the real goal of all economic life. The number of journals and societies now devoted to the development of these different movements is a sufficient indication that they take an important place in industry.

Compared with thirty years ago, the number of features in business for which either whole-time specialists or advisory specialists (or both) are engaged is very considerable. On the side of pure and applied science we have every stage, from affiliation with a joint research-business or association, to the chemists in the laboratories of the corporation, and technical officers who are the active agents in applying the results in the business. Then there are cost accountants and statisticians; establishment officers, who study the workers' conditions; transport, publicity, and insurance experts; legal advisers and departments; medical officers, etc.

If anyone imagines that advertising is a matter in which everyone knows what ought to be done by the light of nature, I recommend him to read Sir Charles Higham's little classic upon the subject in the Home University Library. In the same series, Dr. Myers's book on *Industrial Psychology* will show him what a wide new range of specialism is being covered by the Institute's experts – the psychology and physiology of rest pauses, boredom, and length of hours; the influence of lay-out and position in work; time studies; colour schemes; intensity of lighting; accident prevention, and the correlation between accidents and age, leisure, rest, and various other factors; vocational guidance and intelligence tests; the physical causes of damage and defective output. Dr. Myers says:

The aim is to discover the best possible human conditions in occupational work – whether they relate to the best choice of a vocation; the selection of the most suitable workers; the most effective means of avoiding fatigue and boredom; the study and provision of the most valuable incentives to work; the causes of, and remedies for, irritation, discontent, and unrest; the best methods of work and training; the reduction of needless effort and strain due to bad movements and postures; inadequate illumination, ventilation, and temperature; ill-considered arrangements of material; or defective routing, lay-out, or organisation.

One may sum up by saying that a few years ago the industrialist spent most of his time in the improvement and care of his machinery and capital assets. Now he is learning that even from a business or economic point of view, to say nothing of higher aspects, it is far more important to study the human material, in its psychological aspects, and to save from deterioration or abuse or unnecessary fatigue every human factor.

I do not say that we have only just turned from early Victorian carelessness and antipathy, such as was evidenced by the abuse of child labour, and the outburst by employers concerning the fencing of machinery. For a long period has intervened, characterised by great goodwill and good intention. But only of late years has it been recognised that every one of these features may be the subject of meticulous scientific scrutiny and experimentation.

Power, whether from oil or coal or electricity, is costly and precious. Its economic transmission and application with a minimum loss is a constant preoccupation of the engineer and inventor. Substitute thought for power, and it is equally true and important that it should be brought to the focal point of decision, and to its practical application in organised effort, without circumlocution, collision, and interference. This great network of specialists and departmental heads has to be bound together and directed in such a way that effort is not wasted in delay and duplication and multiplicity. What is the more effective medium of communication and interchange of thought? At one extreme we have a system of written minutes such as is appropriate in a Government department engaged in pulverising an Act of Parliament with scrupulous uniformity in its detailed application. At the other extreme we have the casual conversations and unrecorded decisions of small businesses capable of acting with swiftness and decision. The modern great business must have an appropriate blend of written record to fix responsibility and aid reflection, with committee work of a more or less formal kind, and individual decision and action. It will differ a little with different businesses, and their personnel, and should be constantly under vigilance to prevent the delays that follow so easily upon bureaucratic forms, or the inefficiency that may result from decisions and responsibilities too casually discussed or recorded.

It must always be remembered that hardly any business decision follows arithmetically and inevitably from the evidence. The technical and commercial case can always be worked up to a certain point, but there is nearly always a gap left to be jumped by the individual judgment. Hence the business "nose" is by no means obsolete, and its accurate sense is all the more important when business is on a large scale and a business judgment covers so large a field. No big business can be run to-day without a reasonable element of the bureaucratic; it is very unwise to try to conduct it without proper regard to the feelings and knowledge and *esprit de corps* of the workers; it must be democratic. But these two cannot do without a strong touch of the autocratic in leadership.

Modern industry must fail in its purpose if it does not give satisfaction to three sections of the community. These sections are by no means always distinct; a single individual often belongs to all three. First, the consumer and purchaser – he must not be the victim of big business by being victimised by price through rings and monopolies, or through the holding back of improvements by interested parties.

On the other hand, it is never in the real interests of the consumer that he should be debauched by floods of cheap goods produced under ruinous competition, with inevitable reactions in the lack of new enterprise to come to his service. He is much best served by a continuous flow at reasonable prices, affording good wages and good profits, but giving him the advantage of new methods and new discoveries. Second, the worker, by hand and brain – no industry is stable that does not give him a fair deal in wages and conditions, and fairness must not be judged on a moral basis, but on a strictly economic one, namely, the value that he adds personally to the product. In the third place, the shareholder and titular leader and promoter of the industry. Shareholders are now so diversified, so frequently changed, and so mixed, that one shareholder may often have holdings in various concerns in the same line of business. They, therefore, cannot be relied upon by any one business as being a purchasing force or even a good propaganda force. Their function tends to be confined to the supply of capital, and not to extend to the actual management of business or responsibility for its conditions. Someone is wanted as a centre or focus for all three. It is not to be wondered at, therefore, that there emerges from all recent literature on the subject one common note – that of trusteeship in the board of directors and the management. However purely a matter of business on a prosaic and everyday plan the writing may be, both in England and America, this note of trusteeship is inevitably reached, and the whole idea of trusteeship of these three great interests is gradually forming the background of all directorship and management of big business of the best type; so that almost unconsciously it is felt that the sacrifice in the interests of any one must react upon the success of the whole. No doubt there are many exceptions and reasons for combination by each in its own interests, but there can be no question that modern directorship and managership takes this trusteeship seriously, with a single eye to the efficient discharge of its triple responsibility.

XI

THE DILEMMA OF ECONOMIC CHOICE[1]
(*The Problem of "Transfers."*)

I. Introduction

In my remarks to-day on the subject of "Transfers" it is not my intention to go over the ground of analysis covered in the reports made to the Economic Restoration Committee. So much practical thinking will have to be done in the future, as the problems relating to this great international question slowly develop in actual life, that at the moment I shall better devote my time to a discussion, in the first place, of the *spirit* which should animate such thinking, the *attitude of mind* that will be most likely to lead to fruitful and useful results, and the *temper and method* of our study and search for truth. In the second place, I desire to set out some of those fixed and cardinal principles which, when we are immersed in the turmoil and detail of actual business, we shall probably be inclined to lose sight of, or even to doubt, but from which we shall stray or diverge at our peril. No worker in any field of thought can claim to be independent of all limitations. There are fixed features of topography, of physics, of mechanics, or of chemistry within which every constructive worker, however original or daring, must keep, if he is not to build a fairy-tale or a delusive hope. In the field of thought with which we deal there are limits of national psychology, of politics, of geography and history, and most important of all, because least obvious and yet most inexorable, are the economic

[1]Delivered before the International Chamber of Commerce in Brussels, June 1925, on the occasion of the presentation of special reports on the "Effect of Reparation Payments on Industry."

laws which must be like covered bones within the body of all organic thought that is to function truly. It is with the limits imposed by economic principles that I am mainly concerned.

In dealing with both these aspects, I shall draw freely on what seem to me the unfortunate misconceptions or mistakes of the recent past, and speak without hesitation of those fallacies in the present outlook of our different communities which cannot be too often combated, too openly discussed, or too vigorously denounced if we are to have better days for the nations of the world. I shall risk the criticism that, in my illustrations, I sometimes seem to travel wide of the subject, for the ramifications of the problem of transfers in trade and politics are so great that few widely held opinions are without some influence upon them.

II. The Transfer Problem Defined

Before I plunge into these two subjects, a preliminary word upon the nature of the problem itself may be desirable.

The most distinctive contribution of the Dawes Committee to the problem of reparations was not a programme of the sums which, over a period of years, Germany could properly be expected to produce, starting with a period of economic recuperation and working up to a period of normal economic prosperity; the main contribution was not even the setting out of ways in which that annual contribution should be raised, by a system of railway and industrial bonds, and the safeguard of the controlled revenues. The most important feature of that report was the recognition and emphasis of a *principle* which had hitherto been obscure or little understood by politicians and statesmen. The principle was, of course, that the production of economic values available for the use of creditors is quite a different thing from the obtaining of, and presentation to, those creditors, of general purchasing power or wealth in their own currencies. Germany may well be required and able to produce a large amount in material economic values, but, with insignificant exceptions, she can only transmute those values into foreign currencies through the ordinary processes of industry and trade. Some residents in foreign countries must be ready to give their own currency for those material productions, when Germany can present the foreign currencies so obtained to the Allied Governments. But, in ordinary foreign trade, goods exported are mainly paid for by goods imported, whereas, in this case, Germany will require to obtain foreign *currencies* for goods worth $2\frac{1}{2}$ milliards gold marks per year, instead of foreign goods in return. That is to say, she must be able to send abroad, in *excess* of goods which she imports, goods or services to this value. This is the famous *export surplus problem*.

If it were left to Germany to hand over in foreign currencies the proceeds of whatever she had found it convenient or easy to send abroad, the Allies' claim to reparations would have been undetermined and left to Germany's will from time to time. Equally, if it were left to the Allies to say from time to time how much in their own currencies they thought Germany could produce, and to prescribe such a sum independent of the exports, it might well be that the derangement of the exchanges would be inevitable. The Dawes Plan, therefore, prescribes a definite production of a quantity of German goods for export, actually taken by taxation out of all individual German ownership, though remaining, apparently, as a part of ordinary German trade assets until exported, and it prescribes an independent and expert body to control the purchase of foreign currencies for the Allies *at the same speed, or to the same extent*, as the surplus production is absorbed by Germany's customers.

As a matter of fact, since the export trade brings profit to *individual* Germans, and it is to the interest of such individuals to bring about the largest exports, the chances of success are much greater than if the Transfer Committee had to take possession of the goods in Germany and find customers abroad themselves. But so important are the reactions of exports, or the obtaining of foreign currencies, upon Germany's financial stability, that the process, under the Dawes Plan, is no longer to be left to chance, but is to be supervised by an International Expert Committee, who have both the interest of the Allies and of Germany's internal stability at heart. Their greatest task will begin in 1928.

The Allies mark account in Germany I liken to a reservoir. It is fed by an inlet pipe of known dimensions and flow, which is the budget and industrial contribution to the Dawes annuity under the plan. The outlet is the export surplus, expansible and of unknown capacity, under expert control and pressure. Its ultimate outflow depends partly on pressure from within and partly on suction from without. If the outlet proves to be smaller than the inlet the water in the reservoir will rise. If it rises to a certain level the ball-cock begins to shut off the inlet so that the outlet suffices to keep the water at that level.

III. *Our Attitude of Mind towards the Problem*

Be facts what they may, it is, after all, our *personal attitude* towards them that determines human destiny so far as that destiny is within our control.

The first essential is complete personal candour or honesty. – Wholesome collective thought must first have its roots in individual conviction, and personal conviction must be founded on honest and thoroughgoing thinking. There are far too many people thinking loosely and carelessly on this subject, far too few thinking cautiously and yet fearlessly. In England we have a proverbial saying about "the wish being father to the thought." Economic truths and principles have a nasty knack of not being as pleasant or rosy as our desires or our hopes. We experience every kind of temptation to wrap them up in pleasant language, or to ignore them or to hide them.

The economic truth runs counter to common and ready modes of thought – the practice antagonistic to it may be easy and, perhaps, for the moment pleasant. Such are all attempts to balance budgets by financial expedients, temporary loans, etc., rather than by resort to unpopular taxation. Such are all attempts to raise the standard of living without a general increase in output per working hour.

Again, we fondly hope the truth may not be *really* true – there may be some escape. "Economists" differ in degree in pessimism and optimism. It is natural to adopt the view most favourable to our desires. It was this tendency that led many of us to adopt without examination a number of the earlier ideas and projects regarding reparations promulgated by eminent lawyers and statesmen without economic training or statistical instinct.

The second essential is greater discrimination in our choice of guides. – There is no one of us but must depend, to some extent, or even to a considerable extent, upon the judgment and analysis of others. In ordinary affairs of life we should choose our chemist, our engineer, our geologist with great care and discrimination, and dismiss without difficulty the opinions and facts of ill-qualified persons. In medicine, certainly, how particular we are; we should not expect expert advice on the heart from an eye specialist. Yet any journalist or editor, by writing on economics, can influence public thought – even influence *us* who are on our guard. The rôle of economist can be readily assumed by men who have no aptitude and no training, who have had no discipline and no toil. Moreover, an expert in one economic field is assumed to be equally expert in others – but an eminent banker is not necessarily a skilled guide in all economic fields. When the subject matter is novel, even an expert in the older aspects of it may be disabled by his very experience. Take the recent vagaries of foreign exchange. I have known men whose whole lives have made them experts in the day-to-day "market feeling," but who have had very little grasp of the underlying principles or forces which determine exchanges to-day. One such, who has had a great reputation on the exchange market for twenty years, said to me recently, feeling there was some factor missing in his mental equipment: "Perhaps there is something in this purchasing power parity theory of the professors after all." Similarly, many successful business men have very slender grasp of the principles which underlie the movements of prices and gold values and trade fluctuations. We must be prepared to admit to our own minds the often unwelcome, or even the half-conclusive, results of theoretical analysis in place of easy readings of superficial facts.

The third essential is complete public candour. – Having learned how to ascertain a fact, and then how to face it, what do we propose to do with it ?

During the war, economic facts often had to be covered up – they might have given encouragement to the enemy, or destroyed the morale of the nation. Moreover, if we waited a while, something might happen which would put a better face on them and make premature disclosure a needless alarm. Much of this spirit has continued since the war, and, up to the present, economic statements are frequently subordinated to considerations of political convenience or national prejudice. If a truth has fed our desire or our vanity it has been openly displayed. If it has condemned the easy road that we wished to travel it has been carefully put into the background or wrapped up in such general terms that its popular appreciation has been blunted. I am going to enunciate the following unpleasant principle, viz. that the time has arrived when we should ask: *Is this economic statement true, or as nearly true as we can foresee? If so, is it also unpalatable?* Is it running counter to our desires and prejudices? If it is, let us no longer follow the natural and easy course of silence or suppression. The more unpalatable it is and the more unwelcome it is, the more let us emphasise it, or even exaggerate it, so that it should be brought home to all that we are living in a fool's paradise by nursing our wishes as though they were facts! We have had "make believe" long enough. We have long enough followed the principle that, if a statement does not appeal to us as being very pleasant, we should behave as though it were untrue. Perhaps I may put it on a more limited ground. If anyone is to continue to mislead, let it not be the economist. Let him speak out fearlessly and emphatically the faith that is in him, and let any glossing over or covering up that has to be done be the work of professional politicians and diplomatists who are responsible for introducing all the political and diplomatic elements. But don't let them call politics and diplomacy economics! I can hear it objected that sometimes the truth is too strong to bear all at once. It is true that a medical man might at times regard it as a criminal thing to tell a patient how ill he is, and that an atmosphere of optimism is half the way towards a cure or, if there is some slight chance of recovery, may make all the difference between success and failure. I will only say that with a shrewd patient this requires to be done very artistically or not at all, for the patient with a little imagination knows he is being deceived, and in his heart draws an even darker picture of the truth than he need. This may be an intelligible and even permissible line of action in the case of certain kinds of illness. It is not much good, however, where a surgical operation is needed, to go on giving pills, or prescribing a cheerful life. *Moreover, where the patient is following a course of life that is inimical to his recovery from disease, it would be folly to let him go on pursuing it.*

It is rather to this latter case that I would liken the sickness of nations, and I think that the economist in the position of the complacent doctor is acting from cowardice rather than from prudence if he does not say bluntly what his view of the position really is. We have all heard of prophets and preachers who have gained a temporary popularity through preaching fair and comfortable things, but in our hearts we think more of the man who has a deep sense of principle and sticks to it throughout all his practical utterances, putting the responsibility for departure therefrom upon those whose lives are affected.

We think over much of the domestic political reactions of unpopularity, etc., on the part of those who awake to facts for the first time. It seems the truth must be revealed only gradually and, we say, by inexorable facts.

Again, we think of reactions abroad against cherished political hopes.

But I submit that we have gravely overdone the supposed interests of domestic and foreign politics in obscuring economic facts. In the future of the transfer problem in industry let us face facts and principles and publish them.

The fourth essential is the daily recognition that all economic life for nations involves a choice between benefits.

National economic life does not consist, any more than individual life does, in having the best of everything. It involves self-denial of one set of advantages to secure others. No honest man who devotes himself to learning and study grumbles because he has not the skill, prowess, physique, the honours in certain circles, of the man who devotes his time and effort to outdoor sport. He has made his choice and abides by it. He rejoices in the advantages which his choice gives, without being unduly envious of the different advantages secured by a man who has chosen a different and incompatible course. Those who wish to devote thought to those mental and moral values in life which are outside the getting of material wealth cannot be surprised if a man who *specialises* in wealth getting, to the exclusion of other attainments, becomes richer than they. Similar broad choices have to be made by men in the expenditure of their incomes. Using the economist's language, they are always choosing between the relative satisfactions given by additional expenditure at the margin along different lines, to secure, according to their temperament, the highest aggregate marginal satisfaction. It must necessarily be the same with nations, though it is little recognised that different courses of action are often mutually incompatible, and that it is impossible to secure at the same time the full advantages of following both. It is unrecognised, because a nation rarely speaks with one voice – different sections are vocal at different times. Sometimes it is the governmental interest, or the taxpayer, or a section of industry talking as though its own interest were the total interest. We choose different courses, have different ideas, and yet seem to think ourselves entitled to the same results. For example, England enjoys the full liberty of the use of alcohol as a national habit, with the sense of individual freedom and personal enjoyment or indulgence which this use involves. The United States have deliberately chosen to deny themselves these advantages. We are informed on all hands that, conservatively stated, the economic results in the States are an improvement in production there of at least twelve or thirteen per cent. all round – put by many at a higher figure – that widespread house-ownership and distribution of capital savings are a consequence with considerable economic advantages. American employers, though chafing against the restriction of their *personal* liberty, would not go back upon this national choice. To them the game is worth the candle. I do not assert the same results would necessarily follow in England, but we have made our choice, with all its own advantages, and it is absurd to complain if the economic return to labour and capital is to a substantial extent less than the American, or if, in the economic contest in those foreign markets which compare us relentlessly, our strength and achievements fall short. We can have one or the other, but not both. Again, in England we have a network of trade rules and labour regulations which, we may assume, have been adopted because of certain advantages they are expected to bring. They are the British choice. If another country secures competitive advantages because of greater elasticity of practice, we cannot complain or expect it "both ways." A shipowner told me the other day of a vessel loading coal which at 12 o'clock the Saturday before Whit-Monday was fifty tons – or, say, half an hour – short of its minimum charter complement. The foreman was offered £10 to complete it and let the vessel get away, but declined. The job was finished on the following Tuesday, and the vessel got away on Tuesday evening's tide at a loss of a large sum. The time taken to turn a vessel round is an important element in transport costs and competitive prices. I am told that this would not happen in Germany. It appears that British ports are at an increasing disadvantage as against the freedom of German labour conditions, on the one hand, and the greater superiority of physical equipment of, and appliances in, the American ports, on the other. Our choice *may* possibly be arguably best on a *total* view, but we cannot expect to enjoy the best *economic* results produced by others by means we choose not to employ.

Again, the position of England to-day, with her excellent budgetary situation, and her very trying and difficult economic condition, is an object lesson in the kind of alternatives that lie before statesmen in the policy they shall adopt. Here we have a chronic unemployment situation – a million and a quarter men out of work, and largely supported from public funds. Here is a mass of men contributing nothing towards the productive fund of the country and being supported out of it. The situation would be intrinsically the same, though it would sound quite different, if those men were clad in khaki uniforms, subjected to daily drill, supported and paid out of the country's production, not by the dole, but by military payment. In other words, a large standing army, whatever its other perils may be, is not essentially different in its economic aspects from a large unemployment problem, and yet how different it sounds! Again, a very large number of these unemployed might have been given special State work to perform, and paid, through ordinary industrial channels, the full rate of wage. This, though impossible if the money had to be found through the State budget on the ordinary basis of taxation, would have been quite possible had we been prepared to steal the money required to pay them – silently and unobtrusively from the people who have saved money in the past, by reducing the purchasing power of their wealth. In other words, any country can maintain for a time a spurious appearance of prosperity and economic activity if it will resort to inflation and thus obtain the funds from one section of its inhabitants and postpone the day when that section will realise what has actually taken place.

I can say, without offending my French friends, that in an economic sense they have chosen to avoid the unpleasantness of drastic direct taxation of an open kind by a one-sided and hidden capital levy which has been used to pay for their greatly superior economic activities during the past few years. Instead of taking half of a man's francs away by direct process and spending them on national account, they have left him with his nominal francs, but made them half the value. The choice may or may not have been wise, or even inevitable, but it does not behove the French to envy the British budgetary position, or the British to envy the French employment position, without remembering in each case the price that has been paid.

Again, the United States industrial and import policy has been such that it has preferred to allow a free import of gold instead of competing commodities when debtors paid their obligations. It has chosen, wisely or not, between the claims and interests of its manufacturers and the necessity, expense, and economic risks of holding vast quantities of idle gold, which can only be real wealth to minister to human satisfaction when it is used to purchase goods (which then implies imports) or that supply of future imports which is implied by interests on foreign investment.

In most of these instances the choice is made by public and political opportunism between the troubles seen and immediate and the troubles unseen and postponed.

I emphasise that national economic life is made up of a choice between courses that are relatively incompatible, in which the full advantage of each cannot be enjoyed together, because a recognition of this is going to be in future a central feature in the proper attitude of mind towards the transfer problem.

IV. *What Actions or Ideas Will Make the Task of the Transfer Committee More Difficult?*

Now, I propose to set out, nakedly, those things which make transfers more difficult than they would be if such things were not present. I will not stop to consider whether such things do not possess countervailing advantages which will justify the choice of them after allowing for their disadvantages. This choice must vary for each country in its force and importance.

Moreover, we must not forget that what makes transfers easy at first might make them most difficult in the end. For example, it is conceivable that transfers could be made very easy if Englishmen and Frenchmen bought readily all German goods and ignored completely their domestic supply. But, if this brought widespread ruin and unemployment in a few years by the disuse of their own fixed capital and labour, they might later on be unable to buy anything from Germany at all.

1. *Government pressure to secure funds faster than trade policy allows.* – If the Allies were to prescribe that the surplus must take the form of wheat, they might make the surplus impossible. But they leave it theoretically free to Germany to export whatever she can make most readily, and what other people will buy from her. She may produce any quantity of goods for export, but they will not become an export surplus unless foreign countries want them and will buy them. The *first* important principle that emerges is that the purchase of foreign currencies with marks paid to the Allies cannot proceed faster than the physical surplus of exports is made effective. If an attempt is made to get it to proceed faster, depreciation of the exchanges is inevitable. The export of goods and services is the inexorable limit to the purchase of currencies and the payment of reparations in *cash*.

This is the first cardinal economic truth, and it has been a very unwelcome one. We have tried hard to dodge it, to think there must be *some* way in which Germany could produce dollars, francs, and sterling, if she would, which need not entail such a consequence.

2. *General tariff policy and a narrowing market for Germany.* – If German goods have a free market over

the widest possible area, the whole world demand is available to sustain price, competition, therefore, is not so ruinous to established industries, and a given quantity of German production ranks for a maximum yield in money reparations. The more given areas are fenced off and the German supply concentrated on a narrower population, the smaller is the aggregate demand and the *lower* must be the price which will dispose of the German production. This means that the export industries of the protected areas will have no chance, and it also means that German production to make a given amount of money reparations must be much greater.

3. *Selective tariff policy: exclusion of trade imports because they are similar to home manufactures.* – If the Allies were quite unlike Germany in their own productive power, fixed capital, and skill, they could receive Germany's reparation goods without displacing any of their own products. *Other* nations who make the same class of goods as Germany might feel the effects on their export trade. But, in so far as the Allies have industries similar to those which constitute the export industries of Germany, they must feel the effect of the reparation payments in increased and sustained competition.

The second economic fact is that, whereas ordinary imports, however competitive and inconvenient, do, in fact, compel an equivalent stimulus to some export trade, real though unseen, it is otherwise in the case of reparation payments, for the German imports must come, with all their inconvenience, to compete with our home industry, and there is no countervailing advantage, seen or unseen, to our export industry. We have to look in another direction for the advantages.

Such advantages must be found in our national budgets, where a given amount of expenditure can be paid for, after reparation payments have been credited, with a less burden of taxation. The general taxpayer has an increased purchasing power through the lesser tax-burden. What will he do with that new purchasing power, exactly equivalent to the net receipt of goods? The answer of the optimist is that the supply of goods is only increased by the exact proportion that new purchasing power is created either much or little, so that there is really no problem at all. But this equation might be secured on a very low amount of reparations.

If the existing home supply of a given article is not affected adversely, we must assume that the extra supply from German imports is wholly additional, and absorbed at an unreduced price by the reinforced demand. This is the kind of thing that might possibly happen if the imports were, say, wheat or meat or beer, and the added purchasing power were given by the remission of taxes upon the very poor. But it is very unlikely to be the case with German manufactured goods. Even if it were, the home manufacturer, with unused factory capacity, would still feel he had a first claim to meet the new demand. As it is, the general effect will be that the new demand for such an article operates only to a very limited extent at the old price. To give a substantial addition to the demand, some reduction in price is necessary. If German costs are sufficiently low, this reduced price is a natural feature, and so a reduction is quite possible to Germany and affects the whole home industry and supply.

In our report we have laid great stress upon the *price* at which individual demand will take off or absorb the German production. Suppose that in one year an Allied country had sufficient urgent need to buy at current or nominal prices one million articles from Germany. The home currency paid for them by the Allied purchasers would go, via the Transfer Committee, to relieve the home budget and taxpayer. An equivalent in gold marks provided by the German taxpayer would go, via the Transfer Committee, to

pay the German exporter and vendor. Now suppose
that the following year the keen edge of desire for the
article is reduced (owing to many people being
already well supplied), then perhaps a million only
will be sold to those whose desire is *less* urgent and
less effective, at, say, one-half the former home price.
Then this same quantity of goods only results in half
the relief to the home budget, and only half the
amount in gold marks is paid out by the Transfer
Committee to the vendors. Germany is not able to
make her reparation payments effective without a
considerable *increase* in production effort in such a
year.

Fortunately, however, for home industry, the full
effect would not be felt or exhausted in the Allies'
home market; the German exporter, rather than
suffer such a poor return in gold marks, would seek
other world markets or neutral markets. We avoid
the evil of dumping in the home market only by
transferring the difficulty to competition in our export
market. It is by spreading the German supply wider
that the worst evils of price cutting at home can be
avoided. *But we have to pay the price of a disadvantage
for it.*

Even under such a special scheme as the report
outlines, the advantage of relieving domestic markets
is bought at the price of the disadvantage of some
depression of heavy export industries. We should like
to see their present hard times, which are accentuated
by their over development during the war and the
policy of disarmament now being developed, given
a real relief by special stimulus abroad. But this
stimulus is to go mainly into reparation payments.
Can France really get reparations unless she has an
adverse trade balance? Only if it is accompanied by
equal debt payments to her creditors.

4. *Selective tariff policy based on costs.* – One of the
avowed principles of tariff construction in certain
countries – e.g. the United States – is to impose a

duty which will make good the difference between foreign costs and domestic costs.

This either presupposes the highest degree of efficiency in the home industry, or a developing or infant industry, or else it is the negation of the economic principle underlying foreign trade, viz. "the law of comparative costs" – that doctrine so hard to the lay mind, which declares that it may be worth while for a country to import goods which it can make cheaper itself, if its relative advantage for other manufactures is still greater.

I believe it to be true that Germany can only pay her debts by a lower real standard of living than she would have if she had no debts to pay, longer hours than she would otherwise have, and greater efficiency per working hour than other countries – one or all of them together. With a scarcity of home savings, I think the greater efficiency item can only be a small contribution. In so far as she has to rely on a lower real standard of living, the tariff policy abroad designed to rectify this difference is a real obstacle to Germany's reparation payment, as it is to the payment of Inter-Allied debts. *The British Safeguarding of Industries Act* openly includes consideration of comparative wages and costs which operate on similar lines and make transfers more difficult.

The United States, through debt repayment by Britain, France, Italy, and Belgium, and their own interest in reparations, will be the major recipient of the outflow of German wealth production, especially if the full Dawes annuities cannot be transferred. A tariff policy variable at the will of the President on the above principles, though obviously not designed to this end, will make Europe's task and reparation payments progressively more difficult, and thus possibly hinder the real settlement and peace and general disarmament so much desired.

5. *Labour policy and hours of work.* – Workers in other countries who have secured shorter hours find

the employees in Germany working longer hours in similar industries, which, of course, reduces overhead charges there, and makes for prompter deliveries and thus leads direct to loss of contracts by non-Germans. We hear in Britain of an attempt to get international agreement to restrict hours. This, if successful, instead of enabling Germany to make the required margin for reparations by producing *more* and consuming *less* per head than other similarly placed workers, throws the whole burden upon the standard of living. Germans will the *more* easily produce saleable reparation goods in sufficient quantities if no restrictions are put upon the workers.

I do not say for a moment that measures along the above lines are in no circumstances and to no extent permissible or praiseworthy in any country. Obviously that cannot be the case. But I *do* say that if every·one of the above principles is pursued to the full extent desired by individual interests in all countries, then the collective effect must be very great, and the task of securing transfers made very difficult. The desire to get reparation payments in our budgets is a new factor in international trade. Claims for protection or restriction that would have been readily allowable before, must, in the light of this new feature, be scrutinised with greatest care, and their advantages balanced against the disadvantage of their effect on the Reparation Scheme. Let it be realised that, nationally, we are making a choice of mutually exclusive alternatives and cannot have it fully both ways.

It may well be desirable to protect particular fixed capital and skilled labour *at home* from increased competition in imports or lower prices. But a price must be paid, and that is the curtailment or discouragement of some *export* industry, for the German goods must find a market elsewhere in competition with our own exports.

A good part of the new demand liberated at home

by reduced taxation may, indeed, go direct into home industries and stimulate the activity of these producers. But at some point or other new imports have to come into the Allied countries if reparations are to be effectively received, and these will be paid for by such producers from their new resources. These new imports will be, say, foodstuffs from some neutral country exported in return for German manufactures. These may partially displace existing exports from that same Allied country, or, at any rate, prevent the natural expansion of those export industries.

6. *The stimulus and direction of demand.* – I have emphasised in the report that the supply by Germany of a large additional amount of consumption goods that go to individual purchasers and individual homes, where the purchasing power is limited in its range, may show more acutely the effects of reduced prices than the supply of capital goods to collective bodies, corporations, states, municipalities, and the like, where what the economist would call "demand schedule," or the purchasing power, is based on a wider range of view and is not so susceptible to *individual* psychology. You will know that the individual with his shorter range of immediate purchasing power will respond to increased supplies, as his various needs are satisfied, only if there are progressively marked reductions in price. This springs from the nature of individual economic psychology. But the demand of companies and corporations and local authorities is based on a wider range of purchasing power and altogether less personal considerations. I feel that Germany can add to the capital goods of the countries of the world – that is to say, the machinery for future production of which these countries will enjoy the benefit – on a much larger scale, without destroying a reasonable level of price, than she can possibly do on the goods of everyday individual consumption.

Possibly, by some kind of encouragement of *deliveries in kind* to take the form of capital goods for capital development in different parts of the world, we shall greatly help to solve the problem of transfer. This, however, is not going to be done without grave protest and sectional difficulty in different quarters. I take, for example, the following protest from the Chamber of Commerce of Lille, which I got from *Le Temps* of May 4th. The President of the Chamber had just addressed the following letter to the Prime Minister:

"Already, on several occasions, and notably on October 19th, 1921, November 21st, 1923, and January 26th, 1924, the Chamber of Commerce of Lille has cautioned the Government against the danger menacing the national industry, and notably the industry of the regions that were victims of the invasion, on account of the deliveries of manufactured goods made by Germany under the heading of *Deliveries in Kind*.

"As much as it is desirable that Germany should furnish, under that heading, raw materials that France does not possess in sufficient quantity, and of finished products that French industry cannot procure, so also it is perilous for the French national labour that Germany be called upon to deliver products that France is able to manufacture.

"Already, in 1924, the Northern textile industry had sent forth a cry of alarm; to-day it is the whole metallurgic industry that is keenly and legitimately affected by important orders made to Germany of naval and railway material.

"The Chamber of Commerce of Lille estimates that this kind of deliveries is of a nature to favour the German workmanship, and to allow the German industry to work and prosper to the detriment of French industry. It is indispensable to avoid the slowing up of national production; we must above all maintain and save our industry.

"Without a doubt, if the delivery of finished products develops, the French State will be indemnitised in part, but it will bear, in consequence, an under-value of taxes which may become considerable, without reckoning that the slowing up of industrial activity will cause unemployment, so costly to the public treasury, and so abundant in deplorable repercussions of all kind.

"Therefore the Chamber of Commerce of Lille demands that the finished products to be received from Germany be designed limitatively and with judicious prudence, and that in any case orders be not made to Germany until after a preliminary understanding with the interested economic groups."

This is an example of a feeling that is perfectly natural and, up to a point, prudential and praise-worthy. One cannot help thinking, however, that if this attitude becomes representative, and if the receiving countries really take up a restricting atti-tude, we shall make progressively more difficult the problem of successful transfer. If we agree that this class of goods must be carefully excluded from our *own* countries by tariffs or by arrangement, then, unless we are to thwart the Transfer Committee in their labours, we incur at once the severe responsi-bility of blotting out the active, and possibly other-wise premature, development of neutral and more remote parts of the world. *We cannot have it both ways!* We cannot say that we will not have intro-duced into our own country the only goods by which Germany can effectively pay, and at the same time sit with our hands folded and take no part in finding the least harmful outlets in other lands. We cannot leave the German industrialists to find out these outlets for themselves and then talk resentfully of German "*economic penetration*" into countries in

which we have financial interests; nor grumble at
the languishing of our export industries in iron, steel,
shipbuilding, electricity, and the like. Let us face
fairly and squarely up to these antithetical difficulties
and make our choice. If these half-developed areas
are to be irrigated by German reparations, let us all
take a hand in planning that irrigation and entering
into our share of its ultimate advantages on the lines
indicated in the report.

Now let me take a still more recent example,
which I also summarise from *Le Temps* of May
24th:

"The Minister of Public Works has received a
deputation of industrialists who draw attention to the
troublesome reactions on industry which orders for
rolling stock given to Germany will have. An order
of 4,000 railway wagons given to Germany is one of
the finest examples of how one country can be
enriched in its actual possessions at the expense of
the labour of another for capital purposes. This gives
rise to great unrest among the French industrialists,
who naturally do not regard it as proper deliveries in
kind. The Minister undertakes that this sort of thing
shall not happen again until his domestic factories
have had their proper consideration. He concludes
that, in order to conform as closely as possible to
the best interests of the French industry, it will be
unnecessary to secure from Germany, under the
operation of the Dawes Plan, the maximum of raw
materials and products which France normally
lacks."

We could not have a better illustration of the rivalry
between the principles of defending one's home and
one's domestic fixed assets and skill, and the interests
of the national treasury.

Let, however, German coal be exploited *as a raw
material* to the full extent, and we find at once that

the British coal industry, which in its exports aspect forms the vital feature of British economic equilibrium, is depressed. The latest illustration of the tendency to provide for the specific and obvious (imports), without setting out clearly the price paid in the general and the unseen (exports), is the suggestion by the Federation of British Industries that there should be a great national campaign: "Buy British Goods," stated to be in "aid of trade," and the Government are to be asked to subsidise it. Since every import has, in Mr. Higgs's graphic phrase, "an invisible order for an export tied round its neck," the Government are being asked to subsidise a depression in our export trades. If factories making for export are full to overflowing, and factories making for home markets are starved, this would be an intelligible policy reducing the total foreign trade. Apart from restoring such a lack of balance, it does not seem to be advantageous to national trade as a whole. This is the interest of import industries versus export industries. But if the issue becomes "import industries" versus "transfers," then the bearing of this campaign on our reparation policy is obvious. I am not for a moment complaining of the natural instinct of self-preservation in this matter. I am only saying that, to the extent and measure that we indulge this instinct, we incur the responsibility of thinking ahead and of surveying the world where suitable channels for capital irrigation may be found in order to further their natural development, and also the responsibility for taking a hand, through finance and enterprise, in the actual digging out of those channels. Nothing could be politically worse than to allow, for a long period of years, German penetration of all these countries to go on unchecked, and unaccompanied by watchfulness and safeguards on the part of our own industrial and financial interests.

What Are My Conclusions?

First, I have given illustrations of the kind of contest that is going on between sectional or industrial interests and national or financial interests almost before the real problem of reparation payments is begun. It fills me with the gravest misgivings if this kind of thing is to go on for the next twenty or thirty years. *Either we want reparation payments or we don't!* If we do, the duty of continuous constructive, co-operative thought is upon us, and the day of spasmodic, destructive, sectional recrimination should be over. No problem was ever any the worse, but often the better, for such mobilised thinking.

Second, I have tried to show that every restrictive, safeguarding, or protective measure is *anti-reparation and anti-debt-payment* in its tendency, and that such measures on a large scale will either defeat a reparation or debt-payment policy or make it progressively more difficult, so that only the most important of such measures should be put forward if we are serious in such policy. Many people would shudder at *imposing* taxation to support or protect a particular industry, but cannot see how closely allied to it will be a policy of making a possible reduction of taxation impossible in order to protect particular industries. *Let reasoned and conscious* choice between the two aims supersede a petulant alternative grabbing at both. What will be the upshot? The business man's policy may beat the taxpayer, and transfers become so difficult that the reservoir fills and the German effort is relaxed. If so, the next development will probably be a further postponement of the real transfer problem by a widespread holding of investments in Germany held by neutrals or under the direction of some international body.

Third, I have tried to get to grips with principles. Let us no longer say that peoples who are fearless before their enemy's guns cannot face their own facts.

XII

MY LORD MAYOR AND GENTLEMEN, –

I am greatly honoured at being asked to address such a representative institution, and such a full attendance as I see here to-day. I am the more honoured when I observe the distinguished speakers you have had to address you in the past. My subject may not seem a very attractive one, but it is one upon which there is a good deal of sensitiveness amongst individuals and districts. Therefore I will ask you not to take anything I may say as being specially directed at you. If you recognise any of it as fitting your own case you must do the application yourself. I shall be like the Irishman who, when asked by his friend how he had got a black eye, said, "I have been giving Mike O'Flannaghan a hiding." "What for?" "Because he said insulting things about my sister." "But I did not know you had a sister." "No more I have, but it's the principle of the thing." So with rationalisation, in speaking at Bradford, I am dealing with the principle of the thing.

This does not mean that I am going to be theoretical. It is true that subject is mixed up with economics. A schoolboy recently said that "political economy teaches you how to get the most you can with the minimum of honest effort." While I realise that many of us are trying hard, I am going to suggest that the effort might be a little greater, whether it is honest or not. You will answer that you are all working as hard as possible, and I reply, "Very

[1]A speech to the Textile Institute at the City Hall, Bradford, on January 9th, 1930.

likely, but it may be a different *kind* of work that is wanted." No, I shall not be theoretical, and what I shall say will be derived to a considerable extent from personal acquaintance with the problems.

The explosive industry was rationalised under my own eyes before the word was known. The chemical industry I have also seen something of, and something too of the process in the smaller metal industries, while we are continually proceeding with the rationalisation of the railway workshops, and of our locomotive stocks.

But there is no doubt that, if we are to judge by some recent comments on the subject, there is a reaction setting in against the word, and perhaps against what people think it denotes, so that my subject to-day is really rather topical. The other day, in *The Times*, a well-known and distinguished individualist spoke of the lessons of the past fifteen years and especially of 1929. "They surely leave us doubting," he stated, "the wisdom of the mass method." Industry was honeycombed with trade associations limiting production or increasing prices. "Only in a Socialistic world would the follies and fallacies of rationalism be tolerated for a moment. It meant restricted output, less employment, higher prices, and, when the consumer found it out, more rationalisation and more trouble. Let us," he concluded, "dedicate 1930 to the consumer and to the private enterpriser." He was followed by another who said: "Rationalisation, mass production, monopolisation, and trustification are very closely related."

Now, if this is true, then the situation is indeed serious. Let us consider how far these things all mean the same. There is of course much loose description. Various methods of amalgamation are constantly proceeding; they take different forms and are for different purposes, and it is not surprising that, if we do not direct our minds to the differences, we shall get them confused. For example, I pick up one of the financial journals, the *Economist*, for September 7th, and I find the following references. First we get the Linoleum "merger." We find here that the only economic reason given for the amalgamation is the concentration of the purchase of raw material, jute, linseed oil, etc. It is not clear at all what influence this is going to have on prices or economic costs. It may mean that one industry will merely gain at the expense of another. Then in the next paragraph there is a reference to the Margarine-Lever "fusion," and the extension of "influence" that will result, no reasons for the fusion being given. The following paragraph refers to the Automatic-Machines "amalgamation." Here it is said: "The need for amalgamation in the automatic-machine business became obvious some time ago and the fusion of these two leading companies would round off the process." The scheme, it is said, will "eliminate the company's only powerful and serious competitor." The next paragraph refers to the "rationalisation" of the flour-milling industry. We are told there was a redundancy of plant at the end of the war, some of it badly out of date, also that the *per capita* consumption has fallen from 6.10 bushels in the five years before the war to 5.74 bushels in the last quinquennium. The proposal is to form a pool for the purchase of the out-of-date units and to close them down. It is not yet known whether the remainder will need to have any regulations regarding output. Now, note, "the scheme is expected to make possible such improvements in technical organisation that operating costs may be lowered, in which case the consumer may hope to participate in the resulting economics." A still further paragraph deals with the progress of negotiations for amalgamation of the Dorman Long and Bolckow Vaughan companies, on the north-east coast; here we are told: "A *combination* for the economic working between all the raw-steel producers of that area is greatly needed, so that costs can be reduced by the redistribution of work among mills, so as to get continuous running on those best equipped for particular kinds of work, by the scrapping of superfluous plant, the substitution of modern for obsolete machinery, and all the other improvements which large-scale co-operation makes possible. . . . In their present form the separate companies are not in a position to raise the new capital which the industry urgently requires."

Here, then, you have the various terms all in a row: merger, amalgamation, fusion, rationalisation, trustification, and combination. You can see how very different are the things which they cover and how wrong it is to confuse them, if by rationalisation we really mean those constructive changes which are referred to in the references to the flour-milling industry and the North-East Coast amalgamation.

What are the facts that face us? We have a number of industries which for various quite different reasons are in difficulties, but in general they have this in common, that they cannot market a reasonable proportion of their total productive capacity at prices which will recover their total costs. There are two main methods which may be adopted to remedy this position. The first includes the various devices for keeping up the prices, and the second the various methods for reducing the costs, by improved efficiency and the application of capital methods. In my judgment, true rationalisation is always directed towards the latter, i.e. towards reducing the unit costs of manufacture. This may mean by reducing the costs of a particular supply or by getting a larger supply for the existing costs, or by concentrating the aggregate supply under demand into the more efficient plants.

But this is not the first time in history that businesses have been in difficulties. Pure individualism, particularly on a small scale, found its way out of these difficulties by the economic annihilation of the less fit units in the struggle for the means of subsistence. They started to do badly and then to lose money, and they kept on losing money until their capital was gone, when they perforce had to close down. Ultimately they had to go, but in their dying struggles they enfeebled all the others and reduced the whole industry to a precarious position. They were often a long time dying, especially if the people who had come to their support threw good money after bad, or temporised with the inevitable, because they hated facing facts, and would rather write off a bad debt next year than this. Now true rationalisation does not defeat or hold up economic consequences. Let me give you its three main characteristics in relation to economic forces.

1. It ascertains what is in due course inevitable, whether from the technical point of view or otherwise (but not financial), and then it brings that about more quickly by definite action.

2. What it finds necessary to do, it does more humanely, because some of the cost of doing it is spread over the industry in a prescribed and definite and known way. This seems to throw the burden on the healthy units – true, but they will regard it as a good substitute for all that enfeeblement which resulted from un-co-ordinated economic action.

3. What it does, it does with more certainty and on more intelligent lines. For instance, the individual businesses that have gone under in the past were not necessarily the least efficient from a *technical* point of view; they may have been financially weak – unable to obtain financial backing at a critical time. This method of selection was arbitrary. True rationalisation proceeds on the bases of comparative technical efficiency and the greatest potential good for the future, and not upon the accidents of the present financial situation. Note the difference when you compare this process with those which the public mind confuses with rings, quotas, and trusts, and even tariff walls. All these try to prevent true

economic facts from asserting themselves. They delay and try to circumvent them, and, while they may succeed up to a certain point, the social and economic consequences elsewhere must be bad.

If the word "rationalisation" is going to stand in the way of the proper process because the public have been confusing it with other things, then surely let us rather get rid of the word, and find a new one, than stop the good process itself. Industrialists may say "But there are other ways out. We have had depressions before, but our skill and industry have triumphed. It needs only patience and the power to tide over the bad times – not any drastic reorganisation." In my judgment, it is idle to suppose that, in foreign trade, small-scale individualistic units can any longer hold their place against large-scale individualistic units. We may not like it, but it is no good kicking against facts. Even the recent steel rationalisation on the north-east coast to which I have referred does not altogether overcome this difficulty. The two concerns in question have now a capacity of $1\frac{1}{2}$ million tons of pig-iron and $1\frac{1}{2}$ million tons of steel. I may add that the actual total output of the whole north-east coast last year was just under two million tons of each. Now, a corresponding German unit, the Vereinigte Stahlwerke has an output of $6\frac{1}{3}$ million tons of pig-iron and of nearly 7 million tons of steel, while the capacity of the United States Steel Corporation runs into $13\frac{3}{4}$ million tons of pig-iron and $18\frac{1}{2}$ million tons of steel. Now, granted that efficiency or enterprise is the same in two units of different size, then, if there are any technical or financial advantages which pertain to size, by services or through any other economies, then there is a permanent handicap against the smaller unit and no amount of argument can get away from the fact.

But there is another aspect which makes it dangerous to rely upon the methods and ideas of the past. The small-scale individual unit, particularly in

the textile industries, was really the "backbone," so
to speak, of the great Victorian industrial advance,
and it depended for its continued progress upon the
supplies of capital provided by individual owners
who by frugal and abstemious living were able to put
back into their businesses a large proportion of the
profits which they made. Those were the days when
income tax ranged from 2d. to 6d. in the £1 and
death duties were negligible. Modern rates of taxation, up to 10s. in the £1, on the profits, together with
the enormous death duties, have completely altered
the distribution of the supply of capital – the sources
upon which industry must rely. Those supplies of
capital must now come from the small rivulets of the
many little savings of the masses of the people. Can
you get the required flow of capital into the small,
privately owned businesses? It is a very difficult task.
As a rule it is the large and the semi-public corporations which can best command this capital by reputable public issues, with recognised names and a high
degree of negotiability for your debentures and preference capital. The small concern, little known for
its product or its personnel, at the finance market,
finds that it can never have a very active market in its
shares, and its opportunities are limited accordingly.

We may not like this difference of outlook and control. Each of us likes to be his own master, carrying
on business on a small scale. But it is an inevitable
evolution, and therefore we must make friends
with it.

The industries that are in difficulties in different
degrees at the present time or are struggling to regain
their former prestige may be roughly classified into
three groups. At any rate, this classification will help
us to place them in relation to their economic conditions.

In the first place we have those in which he total
output capacity is a completely uneconomic conception because it can only be marketed if the prices

are so low as not to return net costs for that output. This can happen even where there is no *great* difference in efficiency between the different units. It may be impossible to bring costs, in any case, within what economists would call the "schedule of demand." Now, in this case, merging or combination may be true rationalisation if it saves selling and advertising costs, and if it concentrates like production in particular units instead of splitting it up amongst the many. This may at any rate achieve some reduction in costs, but the natural method upon which they rely in such cases seems to be quotas and price fixing. Arrangements of this kind do not force lower costs, but merely preserve the relative *status quo* of the people in the industry, disregarding the question of their relative efficiency in the future. It makes no contribution to the national problem or to the problem of costs in the export industries which may rely upon them. It is a method which suits industries made up of jealous or rather selfish proprietors, with no great difference in average capacity or enterprise. But by common action in rationalisation they would not greatly disturb the relations between themselves, although they might get the same aggregate profit at a lower rate from a larger and cheaper production.

In the second class, total output capacity is still an unreal conception because, with the *wide* differences in efficiency, a section of that total must be made by some units which have costs very much higher than the others, and these can only be kept in existence at prices which would lose the whole trade. Now, no merger or fusion whatever which maintains these units in production can possibly be real rationalisation, for the better units would not be producing to full capacity. I would even go so far as to say that the passion for quotas and for output restriction in such industries is a national menace. There is now a paradoxical situation in the steel industry. Highly capitalised units are capable of very low costs, but only if they are fully occupied. If they are half occupied their costs may be higher than those of an inferior factory also only half occupied. The drag of the quota for other less efficient units, therefore, prevents a really first-class plant from giving to the community its real benefits, and results in keeping up costs all round. I have known, myself, a price ring in an industry where one unit has found itself, by improved methods of production, so much in advance of the others that, with the prices as fixed by the ring, it has been distinctly alarmed at the rate of profit it was making. All its representations for a, reduction of prices and more extensive markets have been met by protests from the least efficient units, which have only just been able to make ends meet at the fixed prices. Fortunately there was the possibility of breaking away and making a new equilibrium of lower costs and larger supplies. But it is often a long time before this can be done, and it would certainly be a long time if there were any tariff walls to protect the markets.

In the third class we must put those industries which are sharing a reduced world-demand at common world-prices and which are not relatively different from the corresponding industries in other countries either in their level of efficiency or of costs. Such, for example, is the artificial-silk industry, where the plants are all modern enough for us not to be able to suggest scrapping them. It is quite probable that temporary limitation of output and fixing of prices is superior as a method to tide over a period of depression to any general scheme of rationalisation. But the evil is that so many industries think that this is their real position. They hug to themselves the notion that trade will come back, and they therefore hide from themselves the truth – i.e. that there is a general loss of their position in world trade, on account of their high costs, and that they have a

large percentage of obsolete units which are an
obstacle to a larger and more cheaply produced
output. It is industries that are really in this third
class, but think they are not, about which I am most
worried, because they are adopting the wrong remedy
or else none at all. There are lots of people who are
dead and do not know it. These are the people who
expect to play to-day's cricket by the runs that were
made yesterday.

What are the chief reasons for the "stickiness" in
rationalisation in particular industries? First of all,
there is the disinclination to believe there is a permanent change and that other people have now definite
advantages which they did not previously possess.
We say to ourselves, "There are such things as trade
cycles. We are now in the trough of the cycle, and
there is no compelling evidence that we shall not be
on the crest again before long by a sudden change in
the fashion or an increased demand." We are like the
old man who, when congratulated on his health, said,
"Yes, I always notice that, if I live through April, I
live to the end of the year." So long as we have this
conviction, of course, there is no compelling incentive to unite or to take drastic action.

In the second case, we may feel bad or wretched,
but we lack the precipitating agent, what I think
chemists call the "catalyst," to start the action
working, particularly if the financial supporters
behind the different units are rival banking interests,
none of which want to be "let in" for giving up their
prior claims in any combination or merger. I think
that in many cases the absence of a person trusted by
a group of jealous individuals who might bring them
together and start things moving is a really important
factor.

In the third place there is the natural desire to
preserve the ancient status in any financial merger
without regard to differences in technical equipment
and the potentialities of the future. This may lead to

a merger so capitalised that it is unable to afford to break up the *status quo* and to close the least efficient units. If so, it must be doomed to failure from the very start, because it is merely a change in name and not in form. On the other hand, if it is so heavily capitalised that it attempts to save potential losers from any capital losses at all – to enable them to keep their nominal capital intact – then again it is hopeless.

In the fourth case there is our traditional British secrecy and conservatism. This keeps anyone from knowing what the true position of an industry really is, or the relative positions of its constituent parts, in efficiency and financial strength. I will say, without any fear whatever of effective contradiction, that mergers arranged on a purely financial basis, without some preliminary technical examination to guide and rule the decisions of the relative financial interests in their capitalisation, are very unlikely to be successful.

The preliminaries to the merger must be followed, after becoming effective, by closer technical comparisons aided by strictly comparable process costing.

Let us look at the Lancashire Cotton Corporation. In the course of nine months this has now gone a long way towards concluding the preliminaries of rationalisation. Two hundred concerns have been examined, twenty-five of them have been refused as impossible to make efficient. There have been 135 capital offers of absorption, of which twenty have gone no further; seventy-one are definite; forty are negotiating. There are soon to be ten million spindles controlled by the corporation, and arrangements are also under way for single purchasing and selling and for economic distribution and transport. If, from a technical point of view, the right units have been chosen for inclusion and the right units for exclusion, and the units excluded have no further hope, then it is a case of rationalisation within my definition.

I should like to say something at this juncture of

what has been done, and is still going on, in Germany. There is the greatest confusion between the virtues of the old cartel system and genuine rationalisation. The United States have used large-scale organisation mainly to cheapen costs by mass production and common services, but the past history of Germany has been to allow all production to share in the market and to maintain prices without any special reference to the matter of giving the most efficient units the best chance. But the worst abuses of the cartel system that raised prices and limited output have been prevented by the power to break away. (In this country the recent proposals of the Coal Bill have the vices of cartelisation with few of the virtues of rationalisation. There can be no real rationalisation unless the economic process of pushing out the marginal mines is quickened instead of being retarded. The methods of quickening may, indeed, be made humane financially, but they must certainly be put into operation. Cartelisation from a technical point of view so frequently means merely preserving the *status quo*.)

What I have to say about recent events in Germany is derived partly from my own knowledge of certain industries and partly from Mr. W. Meakin's book, *The New Industrial Revolution*, which every industrialist in this country should read, and also partly from a new book by Professor Angell on *The Recovery of Germany*, which makes a thorough and impartial examination from the American viewpoint. It appears that, in the process of recovery, rationalisation is a most important element, first in particular industries, and secondly in a very comprehensive national machinery to promote industrial efficiency. This machinery works by local committees, and is so devised in form and spirit that no industry can escape its influence, or, indeed, the mere obligation to live up to what is expected of it. Following on the war-pressure and the 1921 conditions, this National

Efficiency Board, though highly centralised, began to cover the whole country. It is impossible to say how much of Germany's recovery is due to it, but it appears that the only industry that has escaped much impression is agriculture. In Germany they have looked very much to the United States for a model, first for the standardisation and simplification of the products, and secondly in scientific management, by such methods as time studies, simplification in machinery, the flow of production, planning of the works, and vocational training; and thirdly in the elimination of duplication, cross freights, and sales.

In my opinion, there is no defence needed for what has been done, but it is possible that over-organisation has taken place. There is now a catch-phrase that they have to rationalise the rationalisers, but, of course, Germany had to get capital to do it. They have borrowed abroad very extensively, and they have made the mistake of carrying the process too far. They have a smaller average volume of production than America, and also a much lower wage level than the Americans, and Americans can afford, or are forced, to make substitutions where they cannot. It therefore does not pay Germany to mechanise to the extent that is profitable in the States. In the coal industry there has been a large-scale physical re-organisation. Shutting down mines has been very costly, and the owners complain they have so far had no benefits because of the fact that the remaining units are burdened with those heavy capital charges, and because there has been a great increase in wages. It will be some time before they can expect to feel the beneficial effects of this process. Sometimes the scrapping has been overdone, and plant which was quite up to date three or four years ago, when it was installed, has been taken out. In the case of one particular Ruhr concern, fifty-six ovens, of sixteen tons capacity, turn out 1,200 tons per day, and the entire process from raw coal to graded coke requires only eighteen men per shift.

There is no doubt, however, that rationalisation has made an important but adverse contribution to the unemployment problem. Men have been pushed out by machinery far more quickly than they have been absorbed elsewhere. This aspect of rationalisation, however, is too great a problem for me to deal with on this occasion. But it does not obscure the fact that a surgical operation may be necessary before we can be really well, and that a temporary increase of unemployment – through rationalisation, followed by an eventual revival in purchasing power in other directions which lower costs can achieve – is far better than permanent unemployment handed on to trades permanently dispossessed of their markets by permanently high costs.

.   .   .   .

If I may quote the theologian Bengel, as I have done before, "Tranquillity is a good thing, but it lies very near to danger." We can do no good work of reconstruction if we are in a panic or an overwrought state, but it is up to us all to give the new movement towards rationalisation the most careful consideration, and, above all, to examine our own state of affairs in order to see that we are applying so much of it as the circumstances of our industries, dispassionately considered, really justify. It is for you to say whether the textile industries of the West Riding are to be exempted altogether from a process which has proved so imperative elsewhere.

XIII

MR. CHAIRMAN AND GENTLEMEN, –

In thanking you very sincerely for those extra-ordinarily interesting and illuminating opening remarks, I should like to say that, as a Londoner, if I were not acquainted with Lancashire, I should be filled with very great nervousness at having to address people of such a mentality that a Londoner might easily fail to reach their standard. But I have had the good fortune to live amongst you in Lanca-shire for a time, and it is years now since I made my first acquaintance with the coal and cotton industries, not very many miles from here. I got an introduction to those industries as a young and indefatigable member of the Revenue Department, and, in regard to the cotton trade, I remember being engaged in looking over your balance sheets in the days when the automatic sprinklers were being widely installed in cotton mills, and I know that the expense of in-stalling them used to nestle away in the most modest way possible in your Revenue accounts, and it was my duty to pick it out and add it to the profit. And, also, it was my duty to explain the process to you, if it really needed an explanation. Still, I had to do it. And I remember my first experience, too, of the coal mining industry, in this neighbourhood. I was going down in the cage with a mine manager, and it hap-pened that this particular gentleman had had with me, if not an acrimonious, at all events a decidedly difficult correspondence about his own personal

[1]Speech at the Bolton luncheon of the Economic League, October 31st, 1928.

237

liability to tax. He discovered my identity, and, as we were going down, he said, "You are Mr. Stamp, I am Mr.-So-and-So; now, about this correspondence of ours"; and I said, of course, "Oh, it is not finished yet; you will get another letter." "Oh, very well," he replied, "but remember that, unless I am going to get the one I want, you don't come out of this place alive." The obvious reply was, "Unless I come out, you will never get what you want."

Well, I am very delighted to visit this flourishing branch of the Economic League. I know that it is one of the brightest jewels in the crown of Mr. Crawford, and I know something of the fine and faithful work done by some of the people round me here, including Mr. Mabbott, who is behind all good things.

I was particularly interested in what you, Mr. Chairman, said, because, when I was looking through the objects of this league, I seemed to see, as I have done in the objects of other associations, placed there in invisible printing a thing one daren't put down clearly in black and white, or none of you would join. The *first* item on such a list of objects should be: "I myself, must have a better knowledge of what I am talking about, and be, myself, a better economist day by day," and, only secondly, "I must convey those views to others." Whether you can really subscribe to those objects, thus stated, is hidden at the bottom of the hearts of each one of you, but you won't pretend to yourselves, at any rate. You may, however, be saying to yourselves, "Well, I understand my own business thoroughly, and I've common sense for the rest of the world, and that's that, and that's all I need." But I want to say to you that in this complex world of to-day it is not all you need. If you have not a knowledge of underlying forces at work all over the world, and if you cannot apply your brains to the general problems that arise, with the same zest as to the problems of your own business, your knowledge won't carry you beyond your nose. I will not ask you to confess to me how many of you have recently read a solid book on economic problems, by a competent author dealing with current phenomena, and have mastered it; but at least I may say that, if you set out to teach economics to others, to the "proletariat," and at the same time are not educating yourselves in these problems, you are false to your own ideals. I have spent twenty to twenty-five years studying these problems, and the great thing I notice about them is that they are constantly changing. The solutions of years ago are not the solutions of to-day. You have never done studying. Of many of these problems I do not know the solution. You may know it or not; perhaps *both* you and I are ignorant. But there is a worse kind of ignorance than mine – indeed, it is the only kind of ignorance that matters. The harm is not that you don't know a thing, but that you don't know that you don't know it. That is the real crime. The first job of the Economic League is to quicken in our minds the sense of the necessity for a *closer study* of all the problems, as well as this combative and excellent programme of conveying these economic truths that we ourselves have mastered to others, who, perhaps, have not had the same advantages of experience and education as we have had. Of course, one of the things we need is a sense of proportion. We know that the thing we live with is biggest and clearest in our own eyes, and we, perhaps, do not see something else in necessary relation to it, equally big and clear. And so we get those insular and local jealousies of trade and trade, and place and place, and time and time; and these three classes of antagonisms are things that prevent us getting a clear vision of the whole thing. We need a real sense of proportion. In looking at these objects of the Economic League, I am struck, of course, with the extraordinary activity that is going on in furtherance of the mass of objects that you desire to achieve, but I read in your headquarters circular a sentence which set me thinking. It is a sentence in which modern industry is described as "a growing organism in its early stage of development." Why "growing organism" and not "growing organisation"? The whole trend of modern thought and its successful application to modern problems is going to depend on whether you use the word "organism" or the word "organisation" in that connection.

The ordinary man says his own beliefs in these matters are "economics," while the beliefs of the other fellow are "politics," but we know in our hearts that the particular views that we have, unless they have been reasoned out, down to first principles, and checked up against hard facts, are only "politics" after all, and if our beliefs are merely our wishes they are only politics too, and unless we can verify them as principles they are not economics. These words about the "growing organism" or the "growing organisation" of industry contain in each of them two whole streams of thought which lead right away from the one centre, one of them in one direction and one in another. One of these is in a wrong direction and it is for us to decide which.

Let us take the case of industrial disputes, which figure so largely in all economic literature of the league, because we see quite readily how important the subject is. This statement of aims reminds me of the story of the mayor of a town in Yorkshire who had risen from humble circumstances and done fine service for his town and reached this most eminent position. Everybody admired him; he was in great demand, and it was difficult for him to hold the position because he had to preside at all kinds of functions. But he had an indefatigable town clerk who used to help him by writing his speeches. On one particularly difficult occasion he did not know in the least what it was all about, but he ploughed right through the speech that the town clerk had written for him, and then he said: "Well, I agree with every word of that." So I have read this literature of yours, and I say I agree with every word of it about industrial disputes. But, I want to ask you, have we any clear measure of what is the loss due to industrial disputes – I do not mean only statistically, but also functionally? We can here only look at this question very briefly and superficially. The common way of expressing it, particularly if you are talking to a working man, is to say, "How foolish it is to have a squabble like this. The loss has been so much in wages." And we often measure the loss in time and wages as loss of purchasing power, and treat that as the loss to industry resulting from the dispute. But look at this way of stating it for a moment: if a community consisted merely of a man making something for himself, and if he were to have a dispute with himself and went on strike with himself, the clear loss to him would be the loss of his own production for the period when he had a bilious attack, or whatever it was. But, suppose it were the more complicated case, where the man was associated with somebody else, as master and servant, and they were working together on the job and one of them refused to work. The loss now is not merely the production due to the one who has initiated the dispute or the man who goes on strike, but also that of the other one, also kept from functioning, because we are, by hypothesis, talking about a *joint product*. It is a loss that would belong to the two of them, and therefore the loss is not merely the wages, but it comprises also the loss in interest and profits, and all that share of the common production which goes on to the other partner. Therefore it is the total value of the unborn production which is lost purchasing power, not merely the share that goes in wages.

That is the first measure of the result due to an industrial dispute, and we may think that that is a very short, simple, and efficient way of stating the real loss that industrial disputes bring about. But it is not, and for this reason: we have not to deal with the simple case in a simple community of two people working for themselves as producers, and consumers of their production. We to-day are living in a very complicated community, and joint production is very rarely completed from beginning to end on any particular product. The joint production between capital and labour in any one industry is only part of the total process. We have to deal with more than the loss in what that industry is responsible for – what I may call the *added value*, – because the added value is added to a total. Let it be supposed that their loss in that industry in case of a stoppage due to a dispute is represented by £10 in profits and £20 in wages. But those sums have to be added to £100 spent in buying materials and all the different services in transport and the like, and the fact that one factory drops out of production stops not only the £20 and the £10 from being made, but it stops a whole chain of production worth £130 for the finished product. If one department of a factory went out of action there would very soon be nothing for the others to function on. Their partial contributions to the total would not be wanted, and therefore the loss would not be merely the loss of the one stopped department, but also the stoppage of the whole factory. You see all that plainly enough in the case of a factory, but when it is divided up between all the different factors of industry – all the people supplying from far away – it is not so easy to visualise that it is the whole £130 of the final value of the finished product upon which production has been stopped. All industry is so complicated that you cannot take out one particular section of it without affecting the whole range of action, so that, if there is a stoppage in an industry – we will call it A – which is in the habit of paying £100 for goods and services to all the other industries around, and of adding £30 value by the work it does upon the goods, then the loss in unproduced goods when there is dispute is measured by £130, as far as itself and the others it buys from are concerned. The others have to go on short time or suffer a period of slackness. The loss may not be so striking in the case of the particular business which is stopped but it is bound to affect the total productivity of all the people who are fixed up in that particular sequence of productivity, and you will see that the figure of £130 is a very different figure from the £20 loss in wages with which we started. And the figures I am using are not fantastic. Here we have to pull ourselves up and see the cumulative effect of this trouble. What happens to this £130 worth of goods? If they were consumed entirely by the producers and wage earners and the capitalists and debenture holders in the industry itself, that would be the total loss to them. But industry is so organised and so minutely sub-divided to-day that that £130 worth of final product is simply something that is exchanged against somebody else's £130 worth of product of another kind. Production of goods is both production and also a purchase of other goods. Supply and demand are demand and supply. Goods have to be produced, and then that amount of goods is used as a purchasing power for an equal amount of somebody else's goods. If the original £130 worth are not forthcoming, then by and by those other goods also do not come into existence. In the process of complicated exchange that goes on in a nation, A and B are not the sole exchangers, but A and B, as we have seen, are mutually dependent, and, if A stops, the whole range of £130 value stops, and B has to stop his range of exchanging £130 too. It is no good his producing something to be exchanged for A's goods, there is nothing to be exchanged against. All this is bound to affect the purchasing power of that industry which has been partially destroyed, and, if so, the people in that industry have nothing, or so much less, to enjoy in consumption, and the other people who normally exchange goods with them are equally affected. So that to the £130 worth of unborn production must now be added £130 worth of potential production in industry B. B also has to slow down, and therefore, instead of £20 wages, or £30 of loss in wages and profits to industry A, or even £130 in the chain associated with industry A, you have now got up to £260 of value ceasing to be brought into existence because of a loss of £20 in wages due to stoppage in one industrial dispute. But we cannot stop there. B is not the sole exchanger with A in actual practice. There are also C, D, E, and F, and others right down to the end of the long row of members, each and every one waiting to take a share in the manufacture of £130 worth of goods to be exchanged. The dispute therefore spreads its counter effects over the whole community, and it is very difficult to see exactly where the process stops. It depends on the kind of product whose production is interrupted, but the fact remains that it spreads. It is just as though you had a whole team in a line working for a particular object, and one man's contribution was x. If that one man is struck down, the real effect of x getting stopped is that $10x$ are stopped. And it is that kind, that class, of dislocation of industry to which the particular trade dispute we began with leads. The slowing down does not confine itself to the industries in direct exchange; it affects every industry from which they buy. If C, D, E, or F were each making the whole of the product value £130 with which each of them entered into the transaction, the loss might stop there, but in many cases they are only making added portions, value £10 or £20 towards the representation of the £130, and the effect therefore goes back to the people who are supplying them with raw materials and accessories, and in certain cases the stoppage, therefore, may be represented by a figure of even more than £260, all called

forth by the original stoppage over £20 in wages.
You will understand, of course, that I am using small
figures so as not to bother you with millions, but you
know the thing is true when expressed in millions.
You in Lancashire never think in anything less than
millions. It reminds me of the story of the astronomer
who came down to Lancashire to lecture to a popular
audience about the sun. He talked on the wonderful
activity of the sun in radiating energy away, and he
told them how it was gradually spending its force,
and that in a hundred million years it would be
all burnt out to a cinder, and all the solar system
would be cold and dead. At the end of the lecture a
questioner appeared, a poor worried-looking working
man who asked the lecturer if he would mind repeating what he had said about the length of time the sun
would last. "Oh, yes," replied the astronomer, "it
will all be over in a hundred million years." "Oh,"
replied the questioner, with evident relief, "I thought
you said a million."

Well, I have been talking so far only about the static,
or photographic snap-shot, loss inflicted upon the
community; but I now want to speak of the dynamic
tendencies set up by this process of stoppage which
are more far-reaching than this static loss.

Suppose, in a business, everybody went off for the
afternoon, so cutting off an afternoon's production.
If everybody started work again next morning the
loss would stop there, and you would know the extent
of it. Something depends on the way the afternoon
off has been spent as to whether everybody can start
again next morning. If next morning you and everybody else felt like nothing on earth, and with all of
you it was a case of the morning after the night
before, then very likely the next day the production
of your business will be affected, and you will realise
that that afternoon off will have had a very strong
dynamic effect. Suppose, for instance, that when you
got there next morning everything about the place

had been moved and changed, and you had to spend time in finding your tools or your books, and your partners or your neighbours at the bench had to do the same. You will realise that the effects of all that on the next day's work might be very important indeed. You must look at the dynamic effects of a stoppage.

There is the extensive static interruption in production to reckon with, and it is more far-reaching, perhaps, than we sometimes see, as I have tried to show you; but, after all, that is but the smaller part of the real effects of the stoppage. You set up by this stoppage a dynamic process of dislocation as well. The shortage in the exchanging industries due to this dislocation is not wholly borne by labour. It is fairly obvious that in many businesses men are kept on who are not fully employed. Staffs must be kept on, and there are overhead expenses going on all the time, as you cannot immediately reduce the whole of your expenses in accordance with the reduction in the exchange or purchasing value of your goods. A dislocation in another trade may easily affect you in that way. It is not buying as rapidly from you as it was, but meanwhile your overhead charges are going on, you cannot cut wages and your labour bills keep up, but your profits are affected and the interest earned on your capital is less. We all know that one's "overheads" are relatively constant, and there is less elasticity about the elements other than labour than we would like for the purposes of adjustment to the new conditions. All this means that the business owner may have to bear the thick end of the stick, in a purely financial sense. Now the fall in the profits and interest earned in an industry means that that industry is unattractive to new capital, and therefore the natural expansion that it would otherwise undergo by the buying of new machinery and equipping itself with new kinds of plant is obviously checked. If an industry is not showing good results, you hesitate to borrow large sums at perhaps ruinous rates of interest, and there is a general slowing down in the progressive aspect of the industry. It ceases to grow and to keep up with its competitors in some foreign country. The first effect of all that, when observed by people outside the business, is to increase the rates of interest because of the added risk. The value of the industry to lenders is lowered on the actual return, and also the incentive to people to take new *risks* in connection with that industry is lowered. People say, "I don't think much of this industry; it is going down. I won't put my money in it, the risk is too great." It is more expensive to get new capital for that industry. People are less willing to take the kind of risk your industry holds out. All this means that you have seriously disturbed the proportions in which the shares of the total production are distributed to the different factors in the industry. The profits have shrunk. The total product is now being divided, let us say, in the proportions of 80 and 20 instead of 60 and 40 as formerly, owing to the reduced value of production. You necessarily begin to look round for ways of economising, and perhaps you want to reduce the wages bill. Generally speaking, this sets up a feeling of unrest. You have destroyed the natural equilibrium, which was regarded as fair by all the agents in this particular industry. You rather tend to resist claims for increases in wages, or you yourself put forward the idea that costs are too high to enable you to meet your competitors in foreign markets. Some of these difficulties you may stand up to and weather, and come out all right, but some of the risks of industrial trouble must materialise. That is the first kind of dynamic loss we have to reckon with.

The second kind of dynamic influence is that one trade dispute tends so to spread itself and to dislocate the proportions of the elements in other businesses as to lead to the risk of trade disputes in those other industries far enough removed from the one in which it started. You may very easily start the process afresh from a new angle, and you can see then at this particular point that our credit system begins to be more stringent just when it would be most convenient to industry if it were less stringent. Of course, we are all familiar with that process. Enlarge the risk and credit contracts. On the other hand nothing succeeds like success; if the business is booming and flourishing you can get any amount of money you need. A drawing in of activity on the productive side means a drawing in on the financial side. There is always a series of cumulative effects. Compare the position of the railways with a vastly decreased volume of traffic owing to the kind of trade depression we are all experiencing. Reductions of staff cannot be made equal all at once to the fall in work to be done, and the burden of the reduction falls to a very considerable extent on profits. Railways become a less attractive industry to which to get new capital; new developments and new outlay become more and more difficult. Effects tend to be cumulative in that direction, and one could give abundant illustrations of the fact that these dynamic effects of interference or interruption with production are as important as the static effects, or more so. There is not only loss of production, but loss of balance and the effect of the cumulative series of risks.

Well, what has all this to do with "organism" and "organisation"? When we speak of an "organism" we are thinking unconsciously of a physiological conception. You know that in medical practice the doctors rely a good deal on what they call the *vis medicatrix naturæ* – the natural tendency of the body to heal itself. The doctor gives a little medicine, perhaps, but he prescribes the patient a week's rest and thinks that nature will effect its own cure. If there is a wound he brings the broken tissues together, but cannot do more; it must be nature's work to join them again. And so, in the physiological sense of this word "organism," we tend to rely on natural forces to do the main part of the whole work. That is a very simple thing. We say, "Let us put the thing in the right shape to heal itself, and nature will do the rest."

Is that how we look upon industry? Has it *within itself* some kind of natural healing power, so that, with the optimism of our minds, we say, "It will come right," as we might to a wounded boy when he is bruised? Do we think industry is bruised and will be worked on by natural forces and that it will come out all right in the end?

Or do we look at economic society, not as an "organism," but as an "organisation"? – a piece of mechanism, elaborate, large, with huge productivity when going effectively and smoothly, but a hopeless ruin when it gets out of order? What happens when a portion of the mechanism goes wrong? Do you just let it go wrong, trusting it will somehow come right of itself? I think not. We generally agree that it will get worse if we leave it alone. Worn bearings will get worse, other parts will be out of true, and, if you do not attend to the portion that has gone wrong, the whole machine will go wrong and stop. There is no natural restorative there. It is not like the case of a horse that has met with a bit of an accident; you can bind up or treat that with oil or an ointment, and nature will heal the wound and it will be quite right in a week. Suppose that, instead of a horse, it was a locomotive to which the accident happened. You cannot put the locomotive in a field and leave it there to get better after giving it a little more oil or a new coat of paint, and expect it will be all right when you go back for it in a week. Well, do you not now see the enormous difference there is between the social conception of an "organism" and an "organisation"? With an "organisation," if anything goes wrong you need the highest engineering skill to get quickly to the root of the trouble, but, if it is an "organism" you are dealing with, well then, as I say, you can just give a little relief for the pain and in a day or two it will come all right. You see how fundamentally different these two conceptions of economic society really are, how vital is the question whether you think of it as an "organism" or as an "organisation." If it is an organisation, a machine, a piece of mechanism, there must be somewhere outside of it a controlling brain that understands it and can get to the bottom of its disorders.

Where is that brain? I *hope* it is in the Economic League. What are our economic destinies? Can we control them, or are they in the lap of the gods? What is your fundamental belief about the economic destinies of the country? Do you think that what is going to be will be? Do you think it is fate? Do you think that by taking thought you can add a little to your stature, but not very much? Or do you say, "This is a thing made by man; he hardly knew how he did it, but it must be controlled and mended by men." If it must be mended by men it is no good our relying upon the doctor's *vis medicatrix naturæ*.

I should like now to discuss a figure or two with you, if I may. Between the years 1919 and 1926, trade disputes in this country affected 11,000,000 workers, and 357 million working-days were lost. When we look at those figures to consider if they were cumulative in their effects upon the organism or organisation – which ever way we regard economic society as a whole – what do we find? We find that 117,000,000 tons less coal were mined, and 80,000,000 tons less of that total were upon the railways in the way of transport. Six million tons less iron ore were produced and carried, and $7\frac{1}{2}$ million tons less of iron products, pig-iron and castings and the like. The effect upon the railways in 1926, with its huge drain upon their reserves, was a thing that was not lost with the year, but continues for many years to

come. You cannot take seven or eight millions out of
reserves without affecting the outlook of the future in
regard to the acceptability of the railways as an
investing centre with outsiders, and without producing upon the outsiders the kind of outlook that
does not favour new enterprise or the expenditure of
money on problematical extensions. Therefore you
are less able to give general relief or assistance to
subsequent production. That is what I mean by the
dynamic effect of a stoppage of the kind we are
discussing.

The upshot of all this, as it seems to me, if I may
sum up without giving the arguments leading to it,
is that from an economic point of view a natural
equilibrium *will* come to restore the body politic and
economic, and will arrest all these harmful tendencies,
unless there is a repetition of the shocks, but, if there
is a repetition of shocks of a similar character, then
you get the full cumulative effect until the displace-
ment carries the system too far over its centre of
gravity and the whole machine topples over. But fortunately the balance of supply and demand does
tend to bring things back over their centre before the
system has been pushed too far in one direction and
there is a swing back. The danger is that the system
should get a second, third, or fourth push in the one
direction, so that it travels too far outside its own
base. If it does that, then over it goes. Fortunately
the reverse is true, and every tendency to put things
right, every correct thought that is put into action in
the body politic and economic is likewise cumulative
in its effects to bring the system back again. It means
that economic society should avoid like the plague
every disturbance of an unnecessary character in the
way of industrial disputes, and that it should help
every kind of movement towards greater harmony and
fuller understanding.

You see, as production becomes less, due to the
occurrence of these disputes, then disputes are more

individually likely in the disturbed trades, and this very likelihood is the thing that prevents the aggregate possessed by an industry from growing greater. We want to ensure that the cake to be shared out should be a bigger one, and it is no use people asking for a larger slice from a smaller cake. We must secure that the cake is a larger one, and this can only be brought about by having complete harmony among all the agents of production. Therefore let us welcome every individual experiment for securing better industrial co-operation, and let us follow it eagerly and closely. I am not going to enlarge upon my own efforts in this direction. As you know, we have tried to get a fresh start in the London, Midland, and Scottish Railway, by getting everybody to realise the actual facts on which the welfare of the organisation depends and that sound functioning of the whole on which the existence of the system must rely. The thing itself is only there in being if you are working *with* it. The sooner we get that home upon men's minds the greater the chance of co-operation. Then there are the steps that are being taken in the larger field of industry as a whole, and on the more general questions. Here, while we realise that success attends many of the efforts that are being made, we need not be discouraged if some others are failures; we can argue as well from the particular to the general as from the general to the particular. Let us not be sniffy and sceptical and hostile when we see what idealistic people are doing in their own businesses, and then try later on to get all the advantage of the pioneer work of those who succeed. Let us put our *own* shoulders to the wheel, and try to arrive as quickly as possible on the true and direct line upon which these things should be done.

Before sitting down I should like to deal briefly with another aspect of the same subject. I mean the need for taking long-sighted views of what constitute economic costs. We have, for instance, at present, two rival systems of transport, rail and road, both of them highly useful, both absolutely necessary to industry, and the thing we have to do is to find their true economic equilibrium. If we look at real current individual costs peculiar to ourselves, we get one standpoint; but if we ask ourselves what are the total costs to the community of one system of transport or the other, we may get quite another standpoint for judgment. There is a kind of problem that I want you to give your minds to in the formative discussions of the next three or four years. Try to arrive at the far-sighted view. Nobody asks that the railways shall be subsidised or bolstered up in an uneconomic position; but, in considering both systems of transport, we must try to see whether the true economic costs in both cases are brought out. I cannot deal at any length with the economics of this question of road versus rail, it would absorb the time of a whole sitting, but I do say that I find many people have got a short-sighted view. A man thinks it is going to be cheaper for him to transfer his traffic from the rail to the road, but I ask him to reflect what will happen to the heavy industries if the whole of the revenue derived by the railways from the more valuable forms of traffic are going to be abstracted permanently from the standard revenues of the railway companies. It means that the railways will only have the heavier basic industries to depend upon for freight traffic revenue, with serious consequences to those industries. If you want to retain a railway system at all, to let it get into a position of that kind is bound to come back upon you from another direction. Although you may gain in one direction, depriving the railways of their revenue from the carriage of the lighter and more valuable goods, the whole community must suffer if the railway system is unduly starved or is destroyed. The problem is to find equilibrium, taking a long-distance view as between the two. It is for you gentlemen of the Economic League to put it to the

traders that if they can get down to the true economic
costs they can help the railways by giving them the
maximum support, not only as actual, but as potential users. You can get the traders to assist in
making the conveyance of their traffic less costly.
Consider the tremendous cost of discharging wagons
at private sidings, of wharves without proper equip-
ments. Consider also the question of taking delivery
of goods from, and of tendering goods to, the railway
carmen, and of using *to the full* the elaborate organisation of collection and delivery vehicles maintained by
the railways. There are all kinds of problems relating
to despatch, and if the traders apply their minds to
those questions they might make it simpler for the
railways to master them in practice, and the benefit
would come back to themselves. After all, railways
are regulated industries with regulated profits, and
anything that traders can do to help them will in the
end go back to themselves, and not to provide a fat
living for more railway officials or exorbitant profits
for railway shareholders. My final appeal to you as
business men would be this, that I, speaking for my
own railway, am most anxious that we should learn
with you to know and to satisfy the real requirements
of the community, and my officers have instructions
wherever possible to get into direct touch with you
in your representative capacities to learn your problem, and then fit our machine, as closely as it can be
fitted, to the problems you have to solve.

Well, gentlemen, I have now only to thank you for
listening to me on a subject after my own heart,
industrial unrest and its static and dynamic effects.
I never make any speech on this subject without a
deep consciousness that, behind all these things I
have been talking about, there lies the greatest cause
of all, the problem which, unless it is solved, will in
ten years bring this country into the position of a
second-rate industrial nation. I mean the problem of
a stabilised unit of currency and purchasing power,

the problem, in short, of price level. Until that is settled, these industrial questions will continue, and all the goodwill and all the Christian sentiment in the world will avail little with a changing price level. That is the root trouble behind all national and international loss, and the rest of our problems can never be solved until that is solved.

This was followed by a letter in The Times *of November 14th, 1928, on the subject of "The Stability of Price Levels."*

Sir, – In a speech to industrialists at Bolton I suggested that the root problem of our economic future was stability in the price level, and that if it could not be satisfactorily solved we might find ourselves reduced to a second-rate economic position in a space of ten years. I have had so many expressions of surprise at such a statement that I am tempted to ask your permission to state briefly some of the considerations that were in my mind.

The problem of maintaining a stable world-value of gold (in its effect on prices) is an international one. No one European country can do it by itself, although the United States is approximating to the position of being able to do it alone, because it is rich enough to stand the racket when it is necessary to hold a mass of idle gold off the world and treat it as non-existent.

Opinion is hardening in the direction that most forces now at work will make gold more valuable. There is a growing national sentiment in America against "losing more gold to Europe," as if it reflected on the power and prestige of her people. There is a growing desire, with economic recovery on the part of many countries, to acquire gold. Trade policies continue to be based on the idea that exports should exceed imports, for, all countries taken together, this position cannot be settled by an increase in foreign investments; it tends, therefore, to a struggle for gold. If the civilised world cannot during the next decade find a way of securing the stable purchasing power of gold, and if gold continues to rise in value on the scale of the last few years, this country stands to suffer more than the other chief economic Powers.

1. Under the influence of a continually falling price level we cannot expect this country to expand materially in production and business, or to recover very much from its present unbalanced position. In this, the proportion of foreign trade to total trade is an important factor. America has been rich enough in natural resources, etc., to secure industrial prosperity, even at a time of falling prices, but this is an exception to general experience.

2. The National Debt expressed in fixed gold terms is a higher proportion of our total production than in the case of our competitors. In the event of the falling price level referred to above, it will become a progressively higher proportion, to the point of being, compared with to-day, really an absolutely crippling burden in the service of interest and repayment. We shall also compare with America, with virtually no debt, and other countries, with devaluation of the unit in which their debts were incurred.

3. Germany's gold obligations abroad for reparations will be scaled down, under the Dawes Plan, with increases in the value of gold. Our obligations to America will not be. The gap may become important between what we receive and what we pay. Even with the principle of the Balfour Note secured at the outset, no arrangement can secure it for the whole period of our debt.

4. Apart from the rigidity of the above division of the product of industry between different classes of capital, we have very poor peaceful means at present for deflating costs, with the downward changes in

price level, other than through unemployment. In this respect the several elements of valuation of services in our industrial life are much less mobile than those to be found in America, France, and Germany. In these circumstances, *inter alia*, our position with a given change in gold values is worse than that of the others.

The best results of industrial co-operation and religious sentiment in securing fair settlements in 1929 can be destroyed under such devastating financial redistribution as a considerable change in price level would bring about. The problem of the long run stability of the price level is therefore fundamental to all other problems of the day; unemployment, foreign trade, industrial co-operation and peace, and this burden of taxation. The short period stability has been fairly secured.

XIV

THE ECONOMIC VALUE OF ARBITRATION [1]

I confess that before I received an invitation to be present I had no clear knowledge that there was such an Institute, but I have had a very lively sense of it since investigating your labours, and those present come up to that standard of wisdom in appearance and judicial character which my perusal of your *Journal* has led me to expect. I am reminded of some words about Sir Oliver Lodge: that "no man has a right to be so wise as he always looks." I cannot understand why you have invited me to your dinner, unless it is that the whole *raison d'être* of the Institute is to educate each other, which you have now so far done that it would be very difficult to find amongst yourselves anyone who can teach the rest. Therefore you looked outside, and have given me the opportunity of showing my qualified ignorance of the whole matter. I have enjoyed the benefits of the services of arbitrators, in the various businesses I have been connected with, to a great extent, and have myself been asked to arbitrate in one or two important matters in the City. I was the arbitrator in the matter of the panel fee payable to the panel doctors under the Insurance Act, which was no small task to adjudicate, but my greatest flight of imagination in this field was "arbitrating" between the Governments of England and Northern Ireland in the matter of the financial contribution towards Imperial expenditure, which was indeed something to revel in. However, the arbitration or

[1]Speech at the annual dinner of the Institute of Arbitrators, January 9th, 1929.

judgment has stood so far, and I have not heard that anything has gone wrong with it, so that I feel I can rest a short time with my laurels still green upon me as an arbitrator. I think many of you have experienced, when reading your papers and journals, a certain amount of irritation at the growth of modern knowledge, when you see that some subject has been "recognised" and there has been a Chair created at one of the universities—say, for chemico-psychology—and you have rather rebelled against this continual subdivision of modern life and science, as though people were making little nests for themselves and hatching out for themselves instead of joining in the general movement and co-operation. There is nothing more fascinating than the construction of a new science, then making a new terminology and wallowing in it. So you rather resent this continual contribution to new "branches" of knowledge, with new Institutes growing around every thought of man, and, if a new institute arises, to protect each as a necessity, and generally to boost its advocates and its interests, you are inclined to say that it is going too far! After all, is not the great secret of modern progress rationalisation and consolidation? Should we not be putting things together and putting them under one hat instead of making a lot of new little heads? When one looks at it broadly, that may appear to be wisdom, but the mere application of principles like that cannot condemn, out of hand, movements towards differentiation of functions, until one has examined precisely what it is intended to do and how it is proposed to set about it. Before I made up my mind to come and propose your health with great gusto, I was in some doubt as to the wisdom of your separate existence. I canvassed in my mind what was the real function that arbitration could perform in the furtherance of economic progress. I asked my Solicitors' Department: "What is the difference between a judge and an arbitrator?" and the answer was that a judge can go to sleep, but an arbitrator cannot. So I said: "Yes, but judges never go to sleep without some very good reason, and no counsel has ever succeeded in getting any benefit; for the judge always seems to know more about the case, when he wakes up, than the counsel." Then I had the question put to me: "But what about rabbit hutches?" and was told about a certain judge who was hearing a case, and the learned counsel was expounding wisely on rabbit hutches. Presently this learned judge went to sleep. The case came to an end, and the next case came on, in which the same counsel was engaged, and he was in the middle of his exposition when the learned judge woke up and listened for a time with great intentness, and then, interrupting, said: "Yes, this is all very interesting and very good indeed; but are we not getting rather a long way away from the rabbit hutches?" It seemed to me at that stage that I was not getting an answer to my question, so I went to another member of the department and asked whether he could give me any information as to the difference between a judge and an arbitrator, and he said: "After all, an arbitrator can be removed, but a judge cannot be shifted without constitutional dynamite."

The Elements of Wealth

I will apply as a test the contribution to be made to the economic welfare of the country. Merely that the process of arbitration happens to be cheaper than the existing agency of the law courts, is not enough.

The competitive process is not a sufficient reason, because the truth may be that the existing process could be made more effective, and that might be better for us than to defeat it. When a price is brought lower by a little competition, one competitor ought to fade out, unless there is to be a kind of uneconomic waste in duplicating the function. So it is not enough for the time being, or even finally, to do it cheaper; it needs further economic justification. Economic wealth and economic advance consist first of natural resources and accumulated capital; and the second great element of economic wealth and economic advance is skill in leadership, without which none of these, in a modern complex world, can come to anything at all. There must be not only skill in leadership and organisation, but also in the average level of the great masses of people who now are to work the economic machine. There is the question of their general education, first on the elementary plane and then on the secondary plane. It is because of that we believe we are going to have a better economic people – by reason of levelling up the masses. And then, thirdly, there are the scientific men and their capacity for the raising of the general level. Our scientists must take their part, and industrialists must apply their results to industry. Fourth, there are institutions for human relationship, which I will divide into two classes, the financial and the non-financial. I will not dwell on the financial aspect, because you all realise that a complex community cannot carry on the life of interrelationship without a proper system of currency, of credit, and a standard of value. Capital now is so far flung, not merely in space, but in time, and there is a vast sum to-day that reaches over a long period of time – say, forty, or even sixty, years. Its utility is in going far forward, and the standard worth of £1 sterling ought to be the same then as now. On payment of our debt to America in forty or fifty years' time it should be worth the same then as now, and not one halfpenny more in human effort. This is a fundamental problem of the age, and, unless we solve it, civilisation as we know it cannot persist.

Human Institutions are Wealth

I must now take the other institutions for human relationship, which are also an important feature in economic advance. Where should we be as an industrial and financial nation if we had not a developed system of accountancy, and no developed system of insurance for risk, no good law of contract, no administration of such a law, and no means of clearing up disputes? All would be chaos and disbelief and fraud, and every rogue would have his day, while even the honest would not know whether they were using the same accountancy. If we had no proper system of accountancy, all our industrial wealth would be in deadlock, incapable of moving on with its full power; and, in the same way, if we had no developed institutions for insurance of risk, it would act as a tremendous drag on our economic machine, and the country that had it not would fall behind others that had it. And then, if we had no good law of contract, I could conceive a highly complex industrial system collapsing; that would happen too if we had no good administration of that law of contract, for it is one thing to have a theoretical law, and another thing to have the machine to adjudicate on it. If these things were not in existence; or if we had no means of clearing up differences of opinion or disputes, we could not imagine how those vast contracts on which our civilisation depends could be carried on. That, again, is institutionally a method of lubricating the machine, and in itself a definite part of economic wealth. All these things are economic wealth in the same way as transport is wealth. What does it do? It puts the things, from where they are not wanted, into the spot where they are required, and so they reach the places where they can satisfy human desire, and we turn potential value into actual value. These are all valuable aspects of economic wealth without which wealth cannot come together in complex and abundant forms to satisfy the community. The more complex the mechanism the more important is the lubrication, and lubrication in itself begins to be a separate subject of study, a separate science, for it is no use having that very elaborate machine, highly adjusted in its parts and most effective when running well, if it is not thoroughly understood by those who are running it. If the system of lubrication is at fault, it will bring the whole to a standstill, and the product is nil. It is all vastly different from the days when machinery was simple, so that when it went wrong the village blacksmith would put it right. Lubrication, which is so simple a thing, becomes of increasing importance with the increasing complexity of the mechanism of society. As society advances, I think we are right in saying it becomes necessarily more moral and law abiding. If that is so, differences of opinion and disputes ought to be less and less about things which are right or wrong in a moral sense or in a legal sense, and those differences of opinion must be more and more on questions of degree, of a technical character about performance or quality. Consequently the weight of the legal aspect of modern differences of opinion should become less and less. With the complexity of the law, because of the complexity of society, new problems are created; but, in general, the question whether a thing is right or wrong in a moral or a legal sense is becoming less important in relation to the differences of opinion in regard to quality and degree. So there is more and more room for an impartial judgment on expert lines, which is not a matter of law in itself.

Industrial Arbitration

The second field is the question of relations in the matter of contracts for wages between wage earners and capital, which is becoming increasingly "solidified" and of vast importance. It is becoming increasingly important not to make mistakes, and it is becoming increasingly difficult to judge the wide variety of facts. We learn that economic product is not the greatest where the solution is brute force or conflict. Where cordial relations exist in the field of industry they have proved to be most valuable, for there we have relied on brute force as the last remedy and not the first. Where both sides mean well, each side sees it has no cause for a quarrel, but each of them knows where the shoe pinches, and the capitalist knows where the shoe pinches his profit and loss account when he says he can pay no more wages. Each knows his own case so much better than he can see the others, and therefore that difference of degree, that psychology, is the very reason why we want the impartial and wise person to come in and judge the facts for both of them. After all, the world would be a strange place if we all judged ourselves finally. It was this way with the little girl who, coming home from school one day, said: "Mummie, mummie, what do you think; I am the best girl in the class!" "I am so glad," said the mother; "who told you that – the teacher?" The little child replied: "Oh, no, I found it out myself." Society will not bear running on that principle, neither will it run on the principle of the fond mother who was looking out of the window as the troops were marching past her house, when she turned round and said: "Look, they are all out of step except Jock." We have to be frank with ourselves and bring frank subconsciousness to the top and make it a working part of our lives. *Punch* last week had a story of the mother who asked her little girl whether she had made any New Year resolutions, and the little girl replied: " No, I have thought and thought and thought, and I cannot think of anything that would be an improvement." Well, there is a place for such judgment of a non-legal character, which seems to me in the economic world to be increasing. That is the field of arbitration. If the exponents of the art are good, and give better service than the strike-leader or the lawyer in the long run, then this field will justify itself as a field of separate science, of separate study, of separate constitution. It will then succeed. That is the field to be covered.

Intensive Study of Principles

Who are the people who claim it, and how do they propose to cover it? That, I take it, is the task of the Institute of Arbitrators. Now, there are two methods I have observed of advance in science. The first – going back to the first point of the institution of a new science – is to "hive off" a hitherto undifferentiated sphere of knowledge and practice; and so we are going to treat this as a separate subject of study. You know what happens with something that lies between two things on which attention is concentrated – we concentrate on the centres, and the edges are not in focus. Now let us abandon those two centres of focus, and where the two edges meet treat that as the centre of interest. It is astonishing by that process in science what remarkable advances have been made, and how extraordinarily fruitful the process· has been. Think of Graham Wallas concentrating on the meeting place of politics and psychology. Think of the specialising in accountancy, what it has done, abstracting principles applicable to this account and that account and bringing them together, putting them into a common scheme. We know what an immense advance the accountancy profession has made in the last fifty years, yet, seventy or eighty years ago, who would have thought of starting the idea of a separate Institute of Accountancy or a separate science of accountancy? It would have struck us as particularly odd, and the same with the Corporation of Insurance Brokers, and Institutes of Actuaries, of Cost Accountants, and even of

Industrial Welfare. In practically every aspect of life, you will now find the specialist. Then we have the Institute of Industrial Psychology, which has entered into an exceedingly rich field of study. When reports are made by them we say that that "really was what the general manager should have found out for himself." But the general manager has many functions, of which this is only one, and by specialising on one of them it has been made a really new subject. In those valuable subjects will be found bio-chemistry, social biology, economic geography, all brought about by this method of new division, a new focus. See what a new subject has been made of social psychology. So that what we really achieve is getting the new focus and the new picture or field, with a much closer observation of the old fringes; we get a new and *ad hoc* analysis of that particular field. In specialised journals we get special experiments applied to a particular point, and a new drive to explore it; we invent a specialised machinery for dealing with the problem. When this is applied by new institutions we have the possibility of extending human knowledge and human activity actually to its highest point, and what happens? First of all we maximise the general knowledge everybody has and make it common property. It is only when we bring all these things together that we can really maximise knowledge – say, about arbitration – and then, of course, by comparisons we get the latest methods, and they too are made common property and we find the best standards. I am not suggesting that we can make all arbitrations uniform, or that we should be certain of getting the same award and the same set of facts from every member of the Institute. I recall that there was a certain learned counsel who was preparing a case for arbitration, and someone said to him: "What do you think the arbitrator will say about this?" and he replied: "How the devil do I know what the arbitrator will say about this until

I know who the arbitrator is?" The Institute evolves its code of honour and right practice, which is a standing guide to those who may not always discern it for themselves. If we look at the high position of the Council of the Institute of Chartered Accountants, or the Society of Incorporated Accountants, we can see what kind of body they are, and it is on such bodies as these that people focus attention, for they know they can obtain from them the best experience and advice. If the Government wish to consult a professional body on any particular subject, they will go to the board or society which deals with that subject. They have the means of gathering information quickly and of expressing it quickly. Take any great Institute, far older than your own, and you will find every one of those stages I have mentioned verified by concrete experience. The second way in which science has progressed has not been merely the "hiving off" of knowledge, but also by abstraction. If we get a wide range of common activity away from concrete manifestation, we can do great things with it. Take arithmetic, which is a thing we learned independently of its application. We all remember the story of a boy who took a note to his teacher from his father: "Please do not give Tommy any more sums to do in beer, as we wasted five and a half gallons last night." You all know that sums in beer can be done just as well in water. (I did not say "on" water.) Take statistical science, which is the hand-maiden of every science. It helps the science of medicine, of public health, finance, and other vital problems, and all those problems have to be handled in a statistical way. Many may not like statistics, but they are the first to fly to them, and generalise from them, wildly and improperly. We have to realise that statistical method is the method of approach to a vast number of subjects, and, much as we may dislike it, we have to make friends with that method. Statistical science has made a striking advance in the last hundred years by abstracting itself from its concrete application, in the science of sampling, the science of correlation. That can be expressed in a definite figure, and is applicable to all branches of knowledge to which statistics are applied, and so we make a powerful use of the method of abstraction by taking away from the general applications of the thing all the common properties of that particular function and specialising upon them. Here we have it, in a high form, in arbitration, arbitration in every kind of field and subject, and yet having its principle and its highest methods expressed, and then re-applying them in practice. And so with the method of abstraction we are exemplifying to-day – that is the most important engine of economic advance, and I am prepared to propose your health with genuine sincerity because you seem to me to be extending progress in a very real way.

Legal Procedure versus Arbitration

May I say that you have a field of new activity of this kind with certain qualifications? Form and order are highly important in your field, and therefore you need to have certain legal framing and procedure, but my view is that you will never justify your existence as a separate profession of arbitration unless you keep that legal framework and procedure resting lightly upon you. The more you allow it to absorb your attention the more you will allow it to grow on you. The more you ape being a law court the less efficient you will be. I read in your *Journal* that you claim that arbitration is an economical boon because it eliminates waste, reduces costs, and promotes goodwill. I believe these things are true. Certainly there is no shame in a professional man, any architect or accountant, belonging to both his own profession and to this as a specialist in that particular field. I believe it does you good and is all to your advantage.

I read again in the *Journal* of your Institute that people like, not merely a legal, but a human, helpful award. The arbitrator wants more than anything else a technical knowledge in the field in which he has to arbitrate, but he must not be a crank in that field, he must have a judicial mind. The judicial mind does not mean an extraordinary aptitude for splitting the difference. That is sheer laziness. In my early days when I was in the Inland Revenue in the provinces, a surveyor of taxes was before the chairman, before whom he had to plead. This chairman was very aged and deaf and very tenacious – so much so that he would not give up his position as chairman. His method was to allow the proceedings to go on – quite unheard by himself – by both sides, and then he would become impatient and say: "Gentlemen, this cannot go on longer; what does the appellant say the amount is?" The clerk: "Three hundred pounds, sir." The chairman: "And what does the Inland Revenue say the amount should be?" The clerk: "Five hundred pounds, sir." The chairman: "Well, I think the case will be properly met by four hundred pounds." You could settle all your appeals in two minutes if you went about it in that way. Anyone thinking that arbitration is splitting a difference is merely relying on laziness or deafness. Arbitration must proceed lightly touched by judicial forms. There are two kinds of proof. In the law courts you have the legal proof, which, as I see it, is not quite the same thing as scientific or technical proof, and you have to use one lightly and rely in the main on the other. That will give you your right place, otherwise you are but a faint copy of another institution. You have to justify your existence by strictness and economy, and have this great advantage over the procedure of the law: the law does not get altered quickly, and we find that at times it is even lagging half a generation behind. So there is a continual strain on the judicial framework to meet modern requirements. That is not necessary in arbitration, and, moreover, there is sometimes an inherent vice in the law to be administered because of the ignorance or the haste with which the law was passed, but that is not a matter which necessarily, if at all, binds arbitration. I have convinced myself, even if I have failed to convince you, that you deserve well of the community, and I have the greatest pleasure in proposing your health, coupled with the name of your president, Mr. Gillbee Scott.

XV

THE SOCIAL VALUE OF THE BUILDING-SOCIETY MOVEMENT: HOME OWNERSHIP AND NATIONAL SAVINGS [1]

1925

I count it a great honour that the first occasion of my occupying the presidential chair of this society, with which I have had such long family associations, is one invested with such historical interest as the Jubilee meeting. I am quite sure that no one would be more astonished at the present state of affairs than those men of humble position and simple ideals who, fifty years ago, with little idea of the magnitude of the movement they were starting, met weekly and paid in their monies for the secretary to take home in a bag. This is something upon which any student of human institutions and their development may well ponder. Many have been begun with brilliant publicity and great circumstance, which have long since ceased to be, while this grows from strength to strength.

I desire to make a few remarks upon the general position occupied by saving, as promoted and assisted by such societies as this, in relation to the general economic position of the country. Students of the economic history of the nineteenth century, to whom the past is not a mere succession of dates, but like a landscape that one has traversed, stretching out behind, will remember that 1874 stands out as a turning-point in many ways. As nearly as may be,

[1] Annual meetings of the Abbey Road Building Society at the Queen's Hall – the largest "business" meeting in the country.

that date coincided with an important change in the economic conditions of the country.

Twenty years of most remarkable progress, on a rising tide of prices, largely resulting from the new gold supplies, came to an end, and was succeeded by twenty years of comparative stagnation, with occasional smaller revivals; a stagnation due to the gradual diminution in the supply of that same potent metal. If you want interesting reading in these days I suggest you should get the evidence of the Royal Commission on depression in trade in 1886, which is quite remarkable in the sidelights it throws upon our new outlook. In the first period of twenty years, from 1854–74, the national income more than doubled; in the second period it increased, but by only twenty per cent. The year 1874 marked the turning of agricultural land values and of rates of money wages. There was, of course, progress afterwards in many ways, but it was largely masked, in so far as it was expressed in money values. The early days of this society must have often been in difficult and depressing times.

The building-society movement in 1876 had barely £21,000,000 of assets, and it remained comparatively stationary for many years after 1880, with assets round about £50,000,000. It was not until in 1894 that, with rising gold prices, outward signs of prosperity again set in. During the whole of this period, but particularly the earlier part, the accumulation of capital was extraordinary. The age was quite unique; there had been nothing like it in the history of the world. We are apt to regard the saving habits and the success of them during that period as natural, whereas they were largely exceptional. They were for the most part built upon a foundation of a considerable inequality of wealth; the unrecognised understanding being that those who had the incentive to produce, and had profited by it to the extent of great riches, did not consume their wealth, but turned it again into production, thereby raising the standard of living of all classes in an almost incredible way measured by the total output of commodities. It had been remarked that "saving had assumed all the virtues of a religion." Although inequality was the basis of such saving, society acquiesced because of the immense general advantage. Despite this fact, the general slope of the distribution of wealth was not made steeper, and there was an improvement throughout in which the working classes even gained relatively in the later period. Savings at this earlier period had been probably round about 100 to 120 million pounds a year. The national capital rose at a much greater rate up to 1875 than before or since. Nevertheless, before the war the national savings were 350 to 400 million pounds, of which some half accumulated abroad through compound interest without actually being enjoyed by the owners. This was essentially an unstable state of affairs, and the immense budgetary responsibilities of modern times, and the high progressive taxation that they entail, are now taking the top layers off those large incomes which become taxes instead of savings. Upon what fund are we then relying for an increase in our national accumulations ?

The question before us as a community is: If we no longer tacitly agree to the freedom of those large surpluses on the understanding that they become productive capital, and if it is a matter of importance that capital accumulations should be maintained with a growing population in order that the capital employed per head, and therefore the product per head, shall not fall, who is to take over the responsibility of making those accumulations? Are those classes lower in the scale of distribution taking over the duty of putting aside for national accumulation? If they are not, the whole rate of progress of the country must be retarded. If £500 was formerly saved by a person with £2,500 per annum, and he now pays this in taxes, will fifty people with £250 per annum save £10 each to make up this deficiency? We are quite in the dark as to the effect of the process of redistribution on society, but there are two important indications. One is that National Savings Certificates purchased in the last four years approached £50,000,000 a year. It is true that £30,000,000 per annum is cashed, but it does not follow that these are not, to a great extent, maintained as savings.

The second indication is the building-society figures. These are quite remarkable. There is an increase in the assets in five years of over £10,000,000 a year, which, in itself, is only a limited test of the amount of savings flowing through the building-society movement and being re-lent as they are released. The receipts in 1923 were £69,000,000. This is a most important contribution to the total capital accumulation problem. Moreover, the movement is not merely a channel for saving that would exist in any case. It is a dynamic that creates saving that might otherwise never be made. Many of the young men who join the society would, if they were faced with a fixed mortgage obtained in the ordinary course, through a solicitor, have no incentive and, indeed, no convenience for gradually reducing it. In this case, however, they have an incentive, and form a habit which will last even after the house is paid for. It is an amazingly good thing for the country that organisations with years of experience and practice stood ready for the great national emergency that had arisen. Without them, hastily contrived schemes and organisations might have led to grave abuses and a reaction to thrift. Thrift calls for as much proper organisation as production. Cicero said, "Men do not realise how great a revenue thrift is." The aspect of the ownership of the home is, from a political point of view, one of incalculable importance.

Coleridge remarked that there are three ends which a statesman ought to propose to himself in the government of a nation. First, security to possessors; second, facility to acquirers; and third, hope to all.

*   *   *   *

1926

The growth of the movement reminds me of the incident in H. G. Wells's *The Food of the Gods*, where the growth of the inventor's baby amazed even its parents.

"The friends were equally impressed. 'Very big indeed,' said Bensington; 'I don't seem able to imagine – even with this – just how big things are going to be.' . . .

"Meanwhile, quietly taking their time as children must, the children of the food, growing into a world that changed to receive them, gathered strength and knowledge, became individual and purposeful, rose slowly towards the dimensions of destiny. Presently they seemed a natural part of the world, all the stirrings of bigness seemed a natural part of the world and men wondered how things had been before their time."

This is how one feels with romance of a little thrift organisation growing into the dimensions of a great public institution. Romantic they may be, but these are cold facts, showing that the society has coped in an extraordinary way with a situation altogether remarkable in our social history. The fact is, we are witnessing a complete change of economic habit in the transition from tenancy to ownership. I well remember my surprise some years ago, when Professor Plehn remarked, in dealing with the problem of valuation in the United States, that not five per cent. of the assessors and valuers had any mental conception at all of annual or rental value. Their minds worked in terms of capital values thereon, because houses and property passed, except in a few areas in the States, from person to person by outright ownership. If they were asked to produce an annual value, they could only get at it via capital value, and then the ordinary investment rate of interest. It was incomprehensible to them how our minds worked by thinking in the opposite direction: first of what a house would let for by the year, and then arriving at a suitable capital consideration therefrom if we wished to buy it. All that was before the war. We are now only too clearly aware that letting values are a much less important factor in our mental attitude towards property values. We have not yet any statistics showing what proportion of residential property is owner-occupied compared with pre-war days. It may still not be a large or very high percentage of total property, but it must be an extraordinarily high percentage of new property, at any rate, over a certain minimum level. The question I ask myself is, Has the building-society expansion merely hung on to the skirts of an·inevitable economic change, so that this expansion is a simple effect, from an overwhelming cause, or has the potentiality of expansion, which sound and reputable building-society work provides, been the actual predisposing influence in the change; that is, has it been partly the effect and partly the cause of the change? These are questions I leave you to answer. But I am quite clear that such a change must have meant suffering, privation, and anxiety in the minds of thousands, which the ready expansibility of the building-society movement has contributed to relieve or to allay. I suppose, while we are in the middle of it, it is yet too early to gauge the final economic effects of so important a change, I will not say in the habits of the individual, but in his strategic position. We can see that the influence upon his character will be all to the good in the pride of home, in the way he spends his money, in the habits of thrift that have been fostered in its acquisition, and in a score of social ways.

Sidney Smith put it very high when he wrote to Lord Murray that "a comfortable house is a great source of happiness. It ranks immediately after health and a good conscience." There must be something fundamental to the best spirit of man in this sense of personal ownership, when we find such ancient proverbs as the Spanish, "The smoke of a man's own house is better than the fire of another's," and the Latin, "Your own house is the best of all houses." At any rate, personal ownership to most is good business if they feel they personally enjoy all betterment and improvement. An old English proverb said: "He that buys a house ready wrought, hath many a pin and nail for naught." But apart from effects on human motive and human happiness, there are other economic aspects.

Exactly how this change will affect the average man or worker in his mobility in relation to the forces of production and distribution of the labour market we cannot say. We do not even know whether it is in the best economic interests that the average individual should actually be as mobile as he used to be. It made for characteristics in him and his employer which perhaps were not for the best. At the present time, at any rate, there is not the slightest difficulty in selling his house if he wants to better his position, to move to another locality, or has a disagreement with his employer. Nobody can say that it is yet operating to give the *status quo* of industry a tyrannous hold over him, or to subject him, through economic friction, to the disability of being kept below his market level of remuneration rather than be uprooted. If a man has to sell his house to preserve his mobility of employment and improve his position, I imagine that his chances won't be any worse because his house has passed the building-society requirements. That alone ought to be something like a certificate to help him; unlike Swift's man who "had a mind to sell his house and carried a piece of brick in his pocket, which he showed as a pattern to encourage purchasers." Except for our incurable habit of grumbling at everything, we cannot honestly deplore what are called sometimes "the evils of land-lordism" in the past, and then *also* be afraid of the prospects of owner-occuppiership in the future. But, that an economic change is going on in our midst, in the economic framework within which all our activities lie, is perfectly clear.

*   *   *   *

So far, I have been thinking only of the destination of the society's money; that is, what it does with it; but one of the most important features of its work is where all the money comes from; and here you will all be amazed, as I was, to know the enormous proportion of subscriptions to share capital that are coming from young people under twenty-one. We have not been told whether any of these are in joint names, and whether it is going to be a feature of courtship in future to make joint contributions on account of impending events. I believe the lawyers have in contracts what is known as the "break" clause. I am wondering what provision is made in this connection. The question is whether surreptitious visits in the inspection of house property will rank in any way as compromising incidents, or will merely take place as incidents without any implications in the course of an afternoon stroll. I think we shall be saying that the development of the society is romantic in more senses than one!

The year 1925 has done nothing to alter my views that accumulation is the key to advancing civilisation; that this denying of oneself for the future is one of the most important features in the development of individual character, and that it will be an unmixed blessing if, instead of allowing the necessity for accumulation to devolve upon a few lucky and dyspeptic individuals, its duties and its privileges and its

movement is ultimately based on certain human qualities – first, character; and second, psychology. The individual is committed to a standard of saving which he creates the habit of maintaining, and which he certainly would not have attained, if left to the whim and counter-attractions of day-to-day life. He is also given the stimulus to possess, and the fact that he has· estimated his capacity to save rather higher than he might by later experience have desired – the fact, indeed, that his goal is set – means that more is saved in this way than could possibly be put by if left to personal volition. This is almost the only old Puritan virtue that is really left to us to admire, or shall I say it is the only Puritan severity that now proves to be virtuous. You can run into debt, but you have to crawl out. The house purchaser is different, for it becomes part of the routine budget. Remember that "peace of mind is better than things you cannot afford." You may have to pitch the regular demand a bit high for your weaker moments, but it is worth it in the long run if the plan is carefully made in the first place. Sir Arthur Helps gave some good advice about giving advice: "You should not look about for the wisest thing which can be said, but for that which your friend has the heart to understand and the ability to accomplish." Now what "ability to accomplish" an original undertaking do our borrowers possess? A few months ago the directors met specially to review the cases of all borrowers in arrear. The then total of 8,100 mortgage accounts were reported on, and out of these only 61 were placed on the arrears list – a percentage of .75. This is a wonderful testimony to the excellent personal covenant of the borrowers, particularly as the review followed a period of unprecedented industrial depression.

The economic effect upon the borrower does not cease with this saving; there is a greater care in the use of one's own property, and this must produce

certain improvements in habit. So the public virtues
of ownership in that most personal of life's associations – one's home – are well and truly based upon
the cultivation of the private virtues. It is not always
the case that the best avenue for public good is
secured by the best development of the private. So
far, in the great social transition that is going on
under our very eyes from the system of tenancy to
that of ownership in the middle classes, and in an
important section of the working classes, no one has
yet discovered an anti-social or anti-economic
element or drawback. Once £100 has been saved and
put into this movement, it does its work again and
again. For it goes into a house for a borrower, who
gradually passes it back, and, as it comes back into
the society, it passes out again into a new advance
and circulates in its task, like a boy scout doing his
good deed every day. A saving which provides one
fixed mortgage advance, and stays there, has nothing
like such social virtue, for it does not create new·and
compulsory savings. Do we need savings to-day? The
Colwyn report just published concludes its remarks as
follows: "Generally we conclude that the falling off
in the national savings, equal to 150 million or 200
million pounds at present-day prices, gives ground
for anxiety, but not for pessimism. It would be un-
reasonable to expect that in a period of severe trade
depression, due to deep and world-wide causes, there
should be an abundant flow of savings. It is not clear
from the general trend of the evidence before us that
the diminished flow has been inadequate to meet
current trade demands. When those demands increase, we do not doubt that savings will answer to
the stimulus; but the need for capital may be very
great, and it would be unwise to assume that there
will be no shortage."

*   *   *   *

1928

The building-society movement just seems to have the potentiality to expand to an unlimited degree to meet the public need, and grows automatically with that need at the same time that it creates it, for it seems to grow by what it feeds on. The larger the thing gets in the ordinary way the more easily you can detect its deformities and defects. You will remember that the ladies of Brobdingnag in *Gulliver's Travels* were beautiful indeed to the gentlemen of that land, but to Gulliver their complexions were far from attractive. He was able to detect many blemishes, owing to their great size, that were hidden from their own swains. We look anxiously, then, at this beauty in her great expansion, but fail to find any drawbacks or imperfections so revealed.

Someone may object that when money comes in and out again as it does in the case of a building society, size is significant of nothing. Rather like the Aberdonian with the very large family who, instructed by his wife to get a steak for dinner, bought a piece which proved to be rather small, and as a result of the wife's cooking process it became very much smaller; so much so that she brought it to him with some concern before the meal. "All right," he said, "leave that to me." When they were all assembled, he said, "Now then, who will have a piece of steak and who will have a penny?" True to their race, they nearly all chose the penny, and the father and mother had quite a good meal. Then in came a substantial pudding. "Now then, children," said the father, "who will have a pennyworth of pudding?" Is there, in fact, any advantage in belonging to a big society?

The position of the country in regard to housing is righting itself more rapidly than at one time seemed possible. Apart from those types in which public-fund subsidy has been an important element, the general provision of homes has been greatly aided by the lubrication of accessible finance, regular protective methods and procedure. It is an epoch-making event in most simple lives, the choice of a home and its purchase, and to have a well-trodden path down which smiling and successful friends have passed is to rob this procedure of half its doubts and fears.

The crying public question is to lower the basis of the national credit; that alone could make our annual debt charge less; and without this most conversion schemes are mere juggling with figures, giving no material relief to the annual burden of taxation.

The Colwyn report is a clear evidence of the narrow range of budget saving possible if there is no change in the general money-rates. The most essential element in this change is an abundant supply of new capital for all purposes, and our present supply per head of population is obviously not abundant enough. Do not be deceived by over-subscription for new issues which you read of in the papers. In themselves these are no token of abundant supply or new saving, or better Government credit. The Stock Exchange habit of "stagging" alone can make an issue of a million into a subscription of ten millions, where there is neither willingness nor real ability to subscribe ten millions. For the mere knowledge that an over-subscription is likely can lead people to apply for vastly more than they can take, with the certain knowledge that they will only get allotment within their powers. Again, a flotation of a company with a big share-capital is no evidence of new national saving at all. If A originally spent £100,000 on a factory, and, on its success, it is refloated for £500,000, there is not necessarily any new saving at all. A lot of people may sell out securities, etc., and with the proceeds subscribe for this new company. Mr. A, who takes the money, can and does buy the securities thus sold. Not quite so simple as this, perhaps, but the process is this in essence. Never forget that the only real saving that counts must find its way into *objective* forms, visible and real, new factories, houses, machinery, and ships. All other savings are mere appearances and complications of modern finance. But even objective new forms are not necessarily new savings and additions to the national wealth – for wealth may change its forms, and, instead of £100,000 existing in a business in circulating capital and stocks, it may reduce these to £50,000, and put up a new building co ting £50,000.

Now a building-society saving is always a saving – even judged by these tests; in the case of a new house it is obvious. But, in the case of an old house purchased through the building society, the purchase price is used by its recipient in some form which finds its way, via bank deposits or building-society deposits or company share capital, into new and productive enterprise. Your house purchase is not a little isolated transaction – it forms part of the national flow of capital.

I repeat, this flow is deficient for our best national advance, and but for the building-society contribution would be more seriously so. The housing shortage has had its salutary and valuable side, for it has been a prime inducing cause in setting up first a necessity, and then, shall I say, a custom of home ownership, for this has compelled a restriction of current spending of income which would otherwise not have existed, and has thus created a special habit of great value. So, like heavy taxation for the Sinking Fund, it has had its bright side, and been a means of making the individual contributions of the humbler incomes far greater than mere high rates of gilt-edged interest would ever have tempted them to be.

We cannot exaggerate the individual value of the effort made, and I hope the poet will not say of us:

> Ill fares the land to hastening ills a prey,
> Where wealth accumulates and men decay.

*　　*　　*　　*

1929

People outside are very often interested in our activities and our addresses from the platform, but say they cannot understand how we continue to get such a spirit of uplift out of plain business transactions. There are, of course, certain types of business which are definitely of more utility and are more socially beneficial than others. In this movement we are serving worthy ideals and conferring social benefits. While we are following business methods we are furthering public good. Ours is a movement we know we can stand for on every occasion without reserve.

We believe, whatever our creed or party, that the home is the foundation of our national life. There is an old proverb which says, "A hearth of your own and a good wife are worth gold and pearls." I do not know which is which. I don't know whether this society will ever choose a coat of arms, but, if it does, it could not have a better motto than the old tag of Cicero, "Your own house is the best of all houses."

When the great strain came, the building-society movement was ready; that is to say, it had its methods and its approved traditions, and it had not to fumble about with improvised ideas. Without any change, it was able to adapt itself to a condition of things which it had never thought of in its wildest dreams. May this be true of the building-society attitude towards its task in future economic unity. It has inculcated foresight and it believes in the individual, and building-society management must exhibit that same kind of forward-looking attitude and sagacity. Cobden said that the only way to get anything done at all was by constant repetition, and that anybody with a good thing should never be afraid of repeating himself — that the only possible way was to continue to hammer home simple truths. One might say that with great force about the building-society message on the question of personal thrift and the value of home ownership. It may seem trite to those who have heard it many times, but we are wont to look at it from the point of view of the masses of the people who still have not this priceless asset of the forward outlook, which this particular institution does so much to engender. It has been said by an American writer – and it is certainly true – that we have practically completed the task of democracy in its quantitative expansion. Now we have the much more difficult task in connection with its qualitative expansion. Having given everybody a voice in the government of their own country and the formation of their own destiny, it is now our task to make it qualitatively valuable, to raise the standard of judgment of the democracy until it is really what we intended it to be. First of all we should place a higher standard on individual education, by which I mean, not so much the mastery of facts, as the ability to judge of great public questions; and, secondly, we should have that great biological factor, the ability to look forward. Biologists tell us that what distinguished man from the lower animal kingdom was his ability, not to think merely of to-day, but to think of to-morrow; and what will distinguish the greater democracy of the future will be to think of next year, and, in fact, the whole plan of life. Since in the animal kingdom this power to look forward has been a biological differential which has given it a survival value, so in this great and unknown mysterious outlook for humanity, with contending races at conflicting stages of their development, if we project that particular idea forward, we shall find the ability to plan life as a whole as with individuals of a great people is going to be a factor of survival value of immense importance. Those nations will survive, in the great struggle of civilisation, which cultivate the particular factors of looking forward and planning life as a whole. The building-society movement takes this particular idea in its infancy, and it is very often the first real looking-forward experience of many a workaday family. We are not finishing a great movement, but starting something on a much bigger scale than has ever been contemplated, giving our people content and stability. If it is a biological factor in a long-distance view to racial supremacy it is for us to see that England does not fall behind other lands in these qualities. In this qualitative uplift of the mass of the people it is not merely the habit of thrift that we inculcate. There are a dozen ways in which a movement like this must be a new window for many lives. They will come in contact, perhaps for the first time, with the real meaning of capital, and that would be a priceless outlook for twenty millions of voters. They come in contact with the real meaning of interest, and value as a function of time. The whole machinery upon which this simple transaction rests will teach them the three of the most important factors in modern civilised life.

XVI

I. The Obstacles of History

At the Brotherhood Congress at Prague five years ago, General Smuts, one of the greatest men of vision of our time, said that "from the ruins of the Roman Empire arose the great ideal of Christian brotherhood, binding together serf and nobleman, Jew and Gentile, Roman and barbarian, which became the basis of our European civilisation – so from the ruins of our time should arise a new spirit of human brotherhood."

The failure of the first great impulse was largely due to the gradual inability of this spirit to force itself on a universal scale through human institutions ill-adapted for it. The essential dangers of conflict and unbrotherliness in the relations between lord and serf, autocratic monarchical ambition and subject loyalties, privileged knowledge and widespread illiteracy, could only be kept at a distance so long as every man in an acquired or inherited position of power or superiority over his fellows was a fully converted spirit. Christianity did not come upon a world full of institutional relationships which were helpful to its spirit, for where it triumphed it had to do so in spite of those institutions. A few persons in high places with great powers, falling short of the minimum qualities of the Christian spirit of brotherhood, could effectually block its general progress. How could two neighbouring peoples cultivate a spirit of brotherhood if those who could preach and

[1]Address delivered at the World Brotherhood Conference at Prague, September 12th, 1926. (Interpreted for the Czech audience by Dr. Kaspar.)

teach and lead them, from whom their main stream of ideas was derived, fostered hatred, even as a part of religious belief itself? Even suppose this handicap to be surmounted, and the peoples themselves to feel brotherly toward each other, of what avail if two ambitious monarchs whom they were compelled to serve, acting in personal aggrandisement, called and led the peoples to combat, and nursed and legalised racial hatred? Once the combat had been joined, on whatever issue, how difficult to reintroduce a spirit of brotherhood through generations of vendetta and national antagonism! Christianity did not, and could not, at once give the world new political institutions. It was a spiritual force, not a constitutional device. The intense localisation of peoples, their age-long distrust of strangers, their ignorance of each other – the natural fighting animal in them all – completed the factors which, with the institutional forms of semi-civilised life, made an uphill course for the spirit of brotherhood. Where brotherhood existed it was the localised union of men sworn to a common purpose and moved to a collective opposition thereon to the rest of the world.

II. The Change in the Outlook

But to-day the institutional and constitutional difficulties are vanishing. We have democratic control in nearly all lands. Even in the monarchies no single individual personal cupidity can prevail to lead a whole people astray, if they themselves are watchful and exercise the ultimate control they possess. If the spirit of brotherhood is in the people and is potent in control, no autocrat can thwart it by compulsory call to arms. Misunderstanding, a defective focusing of the popular will, an inability to throw up or choose wise statesmen and leaders, any or all of them, may bring about a catastrophe. But if the brotherhood spirit is properly backed by responsive constitutional methods, by individual intelligence and knowledge, it can no longer be thwarted and defeated by its old enemies. One man cannot hold up a nation in defiance of its ideals. Brotherhood may have, and certainly actually has, its perils, but they are not the old perils. They will be the problems of the new times. Nations are no longer going to war upon each other at the bidding of despotic monarchs; nor for territorial aggrandisement by rulers; nor for mere collective lust of booty; nor for a difference of two vowels in a religious formula; nor for an historic vendetta. They might still wage war on each other for a point of national honour or insult, or by suspicion or distrust, or misinformation, especially if no institutional device exists for a patient examination of the cause of the trouble and the obtaining and promulgation of full intelligence. However well disposed we may be to others, a fear that they are ill-disposed to us – seeing a thief in every bush – may embroil us in troubles, but if the slow moral education of peoples raises the tone of individual thought amongst them to regard national enmity and war as a disgrace, the League of Nations, the powerful instrument now set up to prevent it and resolve its causes, will be a welcomed friend to every citizen. "To know all is to forgive all" runs the proverb, and, if there is a *desire* to know more, in the firm belief that the best intentions may be proved (which is the brotherhood spirit), then the institutions now exist which enable this spirit to flow freely to the fullness of its mighty possibilities. Ease of travel and the mingling of leaders, international news through the Press and wireless, the constant meeting in international congresses of all kinds, these ought to make international misunderstanding through sheer ignorance and lack of information yearly more impossible. The number of solvents to-day is greater than ever. Science has no national barriers and its language is international. Art and literature have national schools and native beauties, but in their higher aspects they are the world's property. Shakespeare belongs to the world, and you rejoice in the trenchancy of George Bernard Shaw. Kubelik, Emma Destinn, Karel Capek, Dvořák may be yours, and great must be your pride in them, but their art is international in its scope, and appeals to all of us and makes us all kin. Sport and athleticism in various forms are becoming more international, and keen rivalry combined with the spirit and rules of the game issue into mutual respect and understanding. Commerce is daily more world-wide and interdependent. All the countries of the globe play their several parts, complementary and mutual, and not inevitably rival and antagonistic. The world is channelled over with international grooves for irrigation and common fruitfulness as never before. The spirit of brotherhood, if copious enough, if inexhaustible, has an opportunity for its mighty work as never before.

III. *The Motive for the Brotherhood Solution*

The peoples of to-day have been down into the abyss. They have learnt the peril of final oblivion that awaits any civilisation that is based upon force and material ideals—the more glittering and advanced the civilisation the greater the peril. They have been sick unto death. If some generations of armed and ruinous peace had lulled them into a sense of security through the shortness of men's memories and the comparative unreality and remoteness of the historical message, to-day they are fully alive. They have every incentive to try a new and a better way. But old forms of thought and modes of expression cannot be changed in a moment, and we are in danger of slipping back into them from time to time. Now, though some are cynical, and some are sceptical and some are fearfully hopeful, most are willing to give the new spirit a trial – it cannot lead to worse results than the old; it may lead to better. But these are not the stuff of which a glorious advance is made. There must be in every country a band of men of thought, of speech, of action, who are really *convinced* of the conquering and sufficient power of the spirit of brotherhood. These will rally the fearful, the cynical, the sceptical, and, in time, make a spiritual army of them. We used to talk of creating troops of morale from raw and undisciplined material. Just as surely must spiritual morale be created in any forces which are armed with the spirit in a spiritual conflict against the forces of evil, hatred, and all uncharitableness. The world *must* be saved from itself, the world *must* be sent spinning once again in the grooves of a higher destiny. The impulse to try the spirit of brotherhood to-day should be at full tide.

IV. The Wider Race: Nationality and Internationalism

It comes to all of us at times to ponder in a wider way than our daily custom, detached from our age and place, upon the destiny of the human race. The age-long, slow development of human relationships and ideas, and speculation as to their future development, is a fascinating study. We think of little groups of men tied down physically and mentally to small areas of the world, regarding the communities even in their immediate neighbourhood with suspicion and distrust; moved by animal passions to attack and defend, with no larger ideals than mere physical existence demands. We see these tribal groups develop into the larger communities of race, with rudimentary forms of government and some small economic dealings with others, but divided by the great barriers of language and misunderstanding and lack of free communication. Time adds to these a race consciousness intensified by the sentiments of historical development, by deep religious convictions, by clear economic differences of interest, and leads us into the modern world, with all its risks that these elements will explode into physical warfare.

Now we have a passionate desire to emerge into the *next* stage where the higher ideals of greater intelligence and a spirit of common humanity call for a clear advance. The peoples who share a common idea and a common faith have tended to become larger. Does this mean that nationality is a passing transitional stage in the history of the race, just a step on towards a complete internationalism? If ideal conceptions of human well-being in this now tiny planet can only be realised by a dead level of internationalism, are we to understand that great outbursts of patriotism and the spirit of nationality are a setback in the human development, something not to be encouraged or emphasised – something to be waived as soon as the frail human spirit can rise superior to it? No one can reflect upon the need for a more international view, and the sudden intensity of re-birth of the nationalised spirit to-day, without asking this question in all seriousness. In my own feeling, the answer is both "yes" and "no." I can conceive some forms of the new nationalism – and indeed see them in some quarters – which are going to be a drag upon the best development of human ideas of international well-being. But, fortunately, I can discern other ways in which the power of patriotism and of national feeling, pride and history of country, will not be antagonistic to, but will even further, international relationships. Each man, and each group of men, small as the world now is, cannot be expected to be as interested in, or as passionately fond of, the hills and valleys of the competitor, and the history and bravery and the achievements of distant peoples whom they only rarely hear and see, as they are of those of which they form part. I count it no bad thing that we are more intensely interested in our own kith and kin, in our own beloved scenery and haunts, in our own development of literature, in our own chosen form of government and leadership, in our own industrial pursuits and economic success. You cannot water these things out into a flat level of accomplishment and enjoyment and interest for all peoples alike. Nationality and patriotism have a sound basis in human sentiment, make life a precious and worthy thing, and they need not be in conflict with international ideals, provided certain essential factors are present. If we maintain the principle that a man, because he is a stranger; or a race, because it is distant; or people, because they are competitors – can all of them be treated on lower moral standards than our own immediate kinsfolk and compatriots; if we have a lower standard for them and no particular desire to understand their point of view and to give them justice, then, of course, patriotism and nationality are ill-conceived and mischievous. It is the glory of the whole Czech record in history that, despite their intense national self-consciousness, which was able to burst out into a full and wonderful life after every effort for 300 years to destroy its very germ, it has always had the wider field of human well-being at heart. "Its own cause was always bound up with the cause of humanity in general." The spirit of the race has indeed valued bravery and great warriorship, but has valued it less, perhaps, than wisdom and statesmanship. Dr. Kaspar has very well said that the development of Czech ideals, from the time of John Hus, has intertwined the individual ideal with the larger conception of nationality as an indispensable condition to a better future for mankind – nationality that is not merely for itself, but leading to humanity.

Now the hearts and passions of men, and particularly the group moved by intense race consciousness, are not going to work for internationalism, and a universal concord and understanding, unless certain important spiritual principles are present, and these "solvents," as I like to call them, will do nothing to *belittle* the value of the love of country, and of its national institutions, but at the same time they will harness these great forces into the development of human destiny on its noblest side. For this development to proceed and make good every step of its way, we depend upon (1) the right institutional forms being there, and (2) the active spiritual elements being there also. I have spoken already of the past lack of the right *form* of institution. To-day we have the institution of democratic government which prevents the popular will being set at naught; the League of Nations and various types of international conferences; a higher level of education which enables other ideals to be appreciated and does much to remedy the barrier of language. These are all-powerful if they are informed by the right spirit. *A wide conception of brotherhood, and a deep realisation of its significance, is the greatest of all solvents.* It belittles no patriot and no nation; it ennobles all nations and institutions. No man is less brave and less of a man because he is fair, gentle, and considerate. Brotherhood is a solvent within the nation itself, between its class interests, and can be, and I hope will rapidly become, a solvent between the nations themselves. If it is cultivated in the heart of every subject of two different nations, it will no longer be possible for statesmen to convince their peoples that interests are irreconcilable or ambitions are antagonistic. Such a statement will not be accepted without examination. One people that knows that the other is informed with the spirit of brotherhood will not be ready to accept a statement by its politicians or its Press that the designs of the other are nefarious and dangerous. The constitution of soul and attitude towards suspicion and panic, decision and action based thereon, will be unfavourable to the growth of those rank, obnoxious weeds. If the same spirit informs the leaders and politicians and Press, the position will be impregnable. Even if the peoples themselves were inclined to give way to passions stirred by past history, they would be held in check by the enlightenment of such leadership. Our duty clearly, then, is to stand firm in support of all international institutions, and all constitutional expedients which will help the spirit of brotherhood not to be stampeded by the coarser vices of collective communities. The cynics who see nothing before us but history and baser humanity repeating itself, and the sceptics with no belief in progress, even in progress as a spiral sometimes returning upon itself, sneer at all these ideal efforts and believe that they are made but to break down. Maybe. But, in the onward march *some day*, the edifice will stand. Perhaps this is that day.

I consider, therefore, that that recrudescence of the spirit of nationality which stops short in being a feeling of race consciousness in isolation and independence will be a drag upon advancing civilisation. It has all but the *one* thing which is lacking. Give it the spirit of world brotherhood, and it at once becomes the mightiest civilising force we can conceive.

If all that were needed was an intense nationalism, then it existed in the nineteenth century. But "a nationality can be as ambitious and despotic as a dynastic ruler." Place or group consciousness has provided some of the bitterest conflicts in history. It became a real obstacle to any realisation of general world peace. But fill it with a corporate brotherliness, and the twentieth century may change it all. I do not belittle it, for I think a strong pride of country and history and firm central constitution is an immediate necessity; nationality is an essential preliminary to internationalism. You can get no stable brotherly relations between nations, unless the nations are in themselves well governed, with central ideals and a common pride and purpose. The great apostle of

Chinese unity, the ex-premier Dr. Tang Shas Yi, who is a progressive advocate of Chinese nationalism based on enlightened democracy, recognises this. He says "localism, provincialism, centrifugalism, are strong now, because we have not yet a consciousness of the unity of national interests – our dispersed and divided multitudes are unacquainted with one another and ignorant of their interdependence and brotherhood." He draws on the parallels of history. "All nations – there is not an exception – have had their periods of internal blindness, disunion, and strife. America only found herself after she had fought one of the bloodiest civil wars in the history of mankind."

V. Brotherhood – Its Counterfeits and Rivals

I have said something about brotherhood being a spirit or motive and not in itself a *form*. It is essentially an idea which cannot be engendered by mere form, but must spring from spiritual motive. There are certain movements in modern life which look as though they should be informed by the same spirit. They are counterfeits. They may be appearing to treat men as equals, to relieve them from autocratic control, to give them in particular an economic millennium; but upon examination they fail at every point which is essential to the true spirit of brotherhood. Communism, of all constitutional and social forms, would appear at first sight to be in its basis identical with brotherhood, and may base itself on humanity and equality and even fraternity. But if you wish to distinguish it, and see how really different it is, you must ask it some questions. First, does it spring from, and is it based upon, a materialistic conception of life, or does it believe that moral and spiritual forces must ultimately prevail? Does it base itself upon the mere *forms* of equity and distribution of wealth while hatred may exist in the heart? Does it treat lightly or encourage immorality of life, or does it condemn it?

Having set up or suggested its forms of government and institutions, is it intolerant of all human views which may differ from it, so intolerant that it seeks to suppress by main force, if necessary, every enquiring thought, every critical faculty, playing round the edifice that it has erected? Is it literally *afraid* of thought and the expression of thought, as are some forms of religious belief and Church government that are still prevalent in our midst? Is the spirit that informs it one of suspicion, or of trust in our fellow-men? Does it call, in defending itself, for a service of secrecy and spying and intrigue? Does it fear the light of day and shun the truth? Does its leadership work in the dark and cover up its mistakes and make "the worse appear the better reason"? Are its leadership and selection private and uncontrolled? Does every humble participant in the system really preserve liberty of selection and a share, however tiny, in unbiased and unfrightened action and selection? Does it induce the ordinary man to feel that he holds his view by terrorism or by liberty? Is it informed by love and human dignity? These tests will enable you to distinguish between brotherhood and the counterfeits of brotherhood.

Must a religious or political institution, by its mere form or governance, be inside or outside the pale of brotherhood? By no means. If the tenets of Romanism – or any Church that you like to name – about the facts of the future life and the supernatural are honestly held by people free to make a choice, people under no kind of compulsion, people not kept in enforced ignorance, then what those people may feel towards others can be consistent with the spirit of brotherhood. But, if when they feel others are mistaken or wrong in their views, they must also deny those others political justice or equality; if they must try to coerce them into the form of agreement; if they differentiate against them in life's activities – then they are inconsistent with the spirit of brotherhood. I would rule out no set of ordinary religious beliefs from its scope; but, if the only official touch that such an institution has with the rest of the world is expressed entirely through interference with liberty of thought and generosity and tolerance of action, then I would say that it is barred from sharing fully in the brotherhood movement. Brotherhood does not demand identity in intellectual belief or creed, but it does represent the highest common factor of spiritual feeling on the part of free peoples.

In the same way the forms of monarchy or republicanism, of individualism or socialism, are all compatible with a brotherhood spirit, though its expression may be found to be facilitated by the institutions of one more than the other. Let us scrutinise them in every social form, particularly that of communism, to see whether, though theoretically it acts in the name of freedom, in practice it enslaves men, dominates and coerces them and makes them, not more, but less definitely brothers in spirit. And, if we find such movements anti-brotherhood in spirit, let us oppose them with all our force in the name of world brotherhood.

VI. *The Practical Expression of World Brotherhood*

Men are so constituted, and women still more so, that, taken as an average, they are not capable of thinking and feeling deeply in the *abstract* for sustained periods. Some objective or concrete representation to embody that abstract conception is the greatest aid, not only to thought, but to conviction. Few women can think for long of an abstract quality and discuss it and analyse it without, in secret at any rate, attaching it in their minds to some individual they have known, and, however broadly they may try to generalise, they are nearly always reasoning in particular. Some men – by no means all – have a greater power of detachment, but taking our races as they stand to-day, if we want a thing to become an effective force, concrete presentations or individualised conceptions are of immense value in practice. It is of the utmost value to talk continually of brotherhood as an abstract conception, but we shall fail to sustain it if we never have any occasion upon which it forms the subject of definite, collective, objective deliberation. What kind of occasion do I mean? Annual conferences between Churches and societies consecrated to its ideals. A journal devoted to regular illustration of brotherhood requirements and promulgation of brotherhood idealism picked out for emphasis, as it were, from the other activities of those Churches or political groups. Local meetings and institutions designed to give day to day manifestations of its underlying spirit. All these are focuses of the idea, in which new drive, new power, new illumination are given to the idea itself. As between two peoples, one of them paying mere mental service to the idea of brotherhood, and another having some concrete celebration or representation of it, I feel convinced that the life of brotherhood as a force will be more full of vigour where it is given an opportunity of objective expression. Let it give each person something to do, which is a brotherhood action. The Brotherhood weekly meeting, supported by members of all Churches or no Churches, of all classes of political belief, is the method which fits the requirements in Great Britain. I do not wish to be dogmatic as to the way a nation will express its ideas – it will depend upon its own development and its own genius. There are some nations, such as the United States, which have an insatiable appetite for the spoken word, and can listen to speeches and lectures when many other peoples would be tired or unresponsive. Others, perhaps, may prefer a steady sustained literature and are more impressed by study in the home; others need some common form of conference, of periodic celebration. But some practical outlet, some focus, some determined space of consecrated effort, I am convinced there must be.

It is in such a conference as this that we can study the forms that have been developed in different countries and adopt or adapt those most suited to our own. One thing I would emphasise. Brotherhood must not be limited merely to the purpose of common betterment of a community select by territory, or by belief, or by class; it must be an internal bond to perform deeds that will go beyond the group, and carry external influence. It is not mere charity from rich to poor, mere succour from the able to the hurt, though it must include these things. It is an attitude of mind to the views and lives of others, and a determination to fasten upon and develop what we have in common rather than upon our differences. Far be it from me, in a land which has known the word "brethren" and "brotherhood" as an intense conviction long before other countries had any conception of it, to dogmatise upon what world brotherhood literally means, but in the field which I have made my study – that of industry and trade between nations – may I give the merest hint. Partly through general ignorance of economic truth amongst our people, and partly through the habit of reasoning from individual interest and imagining that a collection of industrial interests aggregates to the common interest (which is not true), we still have the most barbarous views about foreign trade. We use the terms of warfare, invasion, attack, defence, as though countries trading with each other were mortal enemies. Let us realise that international trade is international barter, and barter benefits both sides, and there is the widest scope for the language of the great family to replace the language of the battlefield in the common purposes of life. International economics needs to be taught and understood, and then permeated with the spiritual elements of brotherhood.

In President Masaryk's *The New Europe*, where he summarises the meaning of democratic peace, he says: "Democracy . . . rests on the humanitarian principle; no man shall use another nation as an instrument for its own aims. That is the moral purport of the political principle of equality, of equal rights. Everywhere his sense of free nationality has been to raise the internal culture and moral spirit of the people." Everywhere success in so doing is to bode, not ill to other nations, but well. This distinguishes the glorification of nationality from economic aggrandisement and military domination and conquest that have so often been nationalistic aims.

The secretary of the League of Nations Union, speaking to the British Association at Oxford on the psychology of patriotism, said that group sentiments and loyalties, as we now know them, tended to resist, instead of promote, the perfect integration and free working of all mankind. There were too often differentiations, rather than integrations, of the world-wide society of mankind. Patriotism, the sentiment for the nation, which was only the lowest common multiple of all the other groups to which a man belonged, was strengthened by all the other group sentiments, and tended to be of paramount importance. It was made stronger still by common land, language, race, religion, government, economic interests, and, most important of all, a common tradition, a memory of great personalities that seemed to embody in themselves the character and ideals of the nation. An overbalanced patriotism tended to prevent allegiance to truth and fair play, and tended to override international justice. There was more individual freedom to be got from international co-operation than from a single cosmopolitan world state. The first thing a patriotic statesman had nowadays to consider about any measure he proposed was its effect on the world as a whole. If it was harmful, the public opinion of the world might say so through the Assembly of the League of Nations. Whatever advantages it might seem to have had would then be outweighed. To serve first the interests of the whole world-wide society of mankind had come to be the first maxim of practical statesmanship.

I rejoice, then, in every community that has conscious pride of race and country. It is becoming ready for the ideals of world brotherhood, and could not realise them until it had first realised itself. There is no inevitable antagonism between nationality and internationalism.

Delisle Burns says: "To arrive at a world policy for every State that will not be a mere contending with other States may not be possible until more men can think sanely of different and distant other men and women." Discussing the implications of nationality, he insists on co-operation in definite tasks as best calculated to develop its nobler side. "There is nothing in its nature which proves intractable to the finer suggestions of civilised thought, and there is no reason to suppose that distinctions of nationality, even if they now cause hostility and suspicion, should always and inevitably do so. A more imaginative appeal might easily and rapidly transform the relations between States." He leaves quite vague what this appeal may be. I declare it to be Christian brotherhood.

XVII

Anyone who has the privilege of talking on free and intimate terms with American, French, and Italian friends, to learn their respective viewpoints upon the subject of inter-Allied debts, may get an idea of the irreconcilable elements in the problem quite different from that formed merely by reading the published word. When using the term "Americans," I necessarily make a distinction between those in the New England States, and especially New York, and those from the Middle West; for between our friends in the former, who come most into *actual* contact with European questions, and the rest of the States, there is often a wider gulf in opinion than exists between those friends and ourselves. Indeed, one may get quite false notions of *effective* American opinion, if one accepts the broad-minded and far-sighted views of the East as operative in practice against the inert insularity of the majority of the other States.

I have, on a recent occasion, touched upon the strange results that emerge when one pursues high-sounding "principles" to their logical or statistical conclusion, in an article which one distinguished writer regarded as a *humorous* effort on my part. I found that, (*a*) if the existing debts were pooled and paid according to average wealth, the United States would have to receive 1,461 million dollars from her four chief debtors in place of over 11,000 million

[1] The *Observer*, June 28th, 1925. (Written before the Council for Foreign Bondholders had made their effective case on the subject of the Mississippi default).

now due; (*b*) if the different nations contributed towards the war cost as a whole, according to their respective "abilities," the United States would have to receive 1,479 millions; (*c*) but, if the war costs were pooled as a whole, and not merely from the dates when the different nations came into the war, the United States, on the "capacity-to-pay" basis, would have to give up her present debts and pay out a further 10 million odd dollars!

To establish abstract moral principles, and then expect to be able to hammer international facts and conditions to fit them, is too idealistic for the real world of to-day. Democratic nations can rarely be, in practice, more idealistic than their less noble or imaginative elements, and in economic relations least of all. Establish the limited circle of your facts and figures, and then extract the highest common factor of moral principle you can – that is a practical maxim for this age, however cynical it may appear to a better!

An Italian friend recently reminded me that a loan had been made to one of our English kings of early days by Italian lenders, and had never been repaid. At compound interest the debt had accumulated until it certainly offset the present debt of Italy to us. Since £1 lent say, four to five hundred years ago would accumulate to-day to £500,000,000, this may well be arithmetically accurate. In a similar way we often hear it loosely stated in club talk that, by the repudiation of State debts in America, England lost a sum which up to date exceeds her debt to the United States. Assuming for the moment that the one matter is even distantly relevant when the other is under discussion, what are the facts? Twelve States at different times during the fifty years 1830–80 repudiated their obligations. If we take the face total of the capital and accumulated interest at the date of formal repudiation in each case, and from that date work it out at a fair rate of interest up to the

present time, and then assume that a liberal proportion was subscribed by British investors, I do not
think the American "debt" to this country would
exceed £250,000,000. (If we were to take also the
host of minor authorities, cities, etc., that repudiated
their debts, and also adopted, for the accumulating
compound interest, the actual rates of interest
promised, we might reach a figure of perhaps
£500,000,000.) It is probably those States, the old-
established and financial centres, which were also
affected as investors, and expressed most indignation
at the time, that to-day are most lenient in their ideas,
and whose policy is most open to appeals on the
ground of sentiment. That area which is least open to
sentiment, or to any other than a purely contractual
view, includes many of the repudiating States. The
situation presented a pretty problem for "national"
honour at the time. Either the Federal power was
one with its constituent area, the State, in its
attitude to the outside world, or it was not. If
Greece or China had defaulted, a European nation
might bring diplomatic, or even military, pressure to
bear upon it. But would the Federal power look
quietly on while a repudiating State was pressed in
like manner? The great John Quincy Adams, early
in the history of repudiation, had put forward a plan
which is not without its amusing side in the light of
later history:

(*a*) that a State by repudiation violated the
constitution;
(*b*) that, if such State, in consequence, involved
herself in war with a foreign Power, other States,
or the United States, should not be involved in such
war; and
(*c*) the peccant State should cease to be in the Union.

Of course, the real remedy in the long run was, as
Professor Scott, the American historian of this
financial episode, has shown, that the credit of such

a State fell so low that it could borrow no more
money. But the disgust of its neighbours and the
Federal power, whose credit was also influenced, was
also a powerful corrective. A Commissioner negotiating in London reported:

> In my intercourse with gentlemen of the highest integrity in
> the money circles of London, whose names are familiar to the
> American public, I did not long remain in ignorance of the
> prevailing sentiments with regard to the object of my solicitude.
> The defalcation of the several States in the payment of interest,
> and the apprehension that the doctrine of repudiation, as it is
> termed, may prevail in others, has, as they say, produced a preju-
> dice so deep and wide that, until the doctrine has been abandoned
> throughout the land, American securities must remain without a
> market on the other side of the Atlantic. I was told that no house,
> however strong and influential in the money market of Europe,
> "dare venture" to present an American loan to the British public
> with the slightest hope that any portion of it would be taken off
> their hands. And, although they professed to understand the
> nature of our confederacy, and entertain full confidence in its
> resources and fidelity, yet they could not, they said, undertake to
> explain satisfactorily to their friends, on whom they relied for a
> market, the distinction between State securities and those of the
> general Government; and hence, should they have the temerity to
> take up the loan, instead of being able to diffuse it among their
> pecuniary constituents, as was customary in such cases, they
> would be compelled to retire it as inactive investment on their
> bureaus.

It is now forty years since the public commotion
died down in such final gasps as "Are we a Nation of
Rascals?" (*North American Review*, 1884). In four
years the twelve States, which owned a quarter of the
national wealth, added to their wealth sufficient to
pay twice over every dollar of the defaulted debt,
but they showed no disposition to do it! Forty years
is indeed well within the length of time over which
repayment of our present debts will extend. But
comparative national psychology is important. In
American development, thought, and memory, 1880

might as well be as far back as the Flood – the doings
of another age. In the longer perspective of Britain
it is not much more than yesterday. The proper view
for us to take is that the episode is one of the ironies
of history. There are innumerable reasons why
chatter on the subject, so far as we are concerned, is
idle. In the first place, we have settled the terms of
our debt and ought to cease to fuss over it! That
settlement has no *necessary* relation to our attitude
to our own debtors. Second, if there were a "counter-
claim," it is quite indeterminate in amount, but it is
clearly only a fraction of our present obligation, and
it ought obviously to have been mentioned at the time
of the new borrowing. Third, individual losses in
financial speculations with impecunious subordinate
Governments cannot be brought into line with
collective and non-speculative transactions between
sovereign bodies. Finally, the best elements in the
eastern States, though powerless to mobilise full
American opinion, are our close friends who, by their
very affection for us, are the more sensitive on such
an issue, and hurt by our resuscitation of it. If we are
a proud people, and wish to pay any claim which
our creditor has designated a debt, let us also be
uncomplaining, and free from triviality. The people
who *ought* to be affected by such an issue as a
"counter-claim" are those least sympathetic with our
difficulties, and the idea of such a claim leaves them
quite cold. Moreover, the real question for the future
is the position of the French debt, upon which this
historical curiosity has hardly the slightest bearing.

XVIII

It is pleasant – and therefore, to some extent, useful – to be retrospective in any field of knowledge or art in which there has been quiet study and useful collective work done over a long period. While we have been participants in the work year by year we have been hardly conscious of advancing steps, so trivial, halting, or temporary has each seemed. It is only over a long view that we can see the evidence of material progress and change. Such change over a period of forty years in the realm of accountancy is too obvious to need emphasis; indeed, it is now almost a hackneyed topic. A wider range of application and recognition has brought about a steadily rising sense of responsibility, guild consciousness, and – partly in self protection, and partly to meet outside expectations – a steadily rising standard of professional skill.

Was it not possible a few years ago for a practising accountant, with only a suspicion of exaggeration, to tell this story of his younger days relating to a test through which an aspirant to the profession was then put? On being asked for a definition of a debtor, the young man replied: "Somebody who owes someone something." This was so far satisfactory that it brought the inevitable corollary in the request for corresponding information as to a creditor. The examinee, feeling clear that it must be the complete opposite of his previous reply, answered: "Somebody who doesn't owe nobody nothing." In those not very far off days, when, after all, England's trading supremacy reached its height, the accountants' touch

---

[1] *Incorporated Accountants' Journal*, October 1925.

was by no means firm or universal. I can remember only twenty odd years ago, when a young Revenue official, that profit and loss accounts for taxpayers were confined almost entirely to the larger cases on the occasions of appeal, and I was the proud inheritor of a small black book of traditional wisdom from my elders in which I learned how to make an assessment upon a butcher from the number of beasts he killed; on a baker from the number of sacks he baked – with a little bit on for the confectionery – and, marvel of marvels, that an aerated-water manufacturer should make £100 per lorry, and be grievously suspect if he didn't! In those days balance-sheets were looked upon rather as encumbrances than as of assistance in the analysis of profit and loss accounts, and they were very rarely rendered and still more rarely used. It need not be thought that these limitations in accountancy, as applied to taxation, existed only amongst officials, for I remember one of the most eminent accountants of his class who had the task of rendering the returns of a number of large taxpayers in the Midlands, and who regarded it as a reflection on his professional competence if any question were asked about his cases. I dared to penetrate this barrier, and established him as wrong in his computations for one return on sixteen points of principle!

Retrospect like this tempts one to look forward for thirty or forty years and to ask: "What then?" It is human nature to think that there is unlikely to be such a change in the future as there has been in the past, and that further scope for improvement or extension is relatively limited. This, however, may be a mere habit of mind or personal prejudice. Is it possible for us, Wells-like, to take a "leap forward," even at the risk of being preposterous? Some years ago Lord Rosebery described accountants as the "financial conscience" of the community. We can only be intelligent prophets or seers if we take the accountant separately in relation to the chief social activities of our day and consider each.

1. We must consider him as an impartial promoter of sound business in its internal aspects, *i.e.* as standing inside the business.

2. The exercise of industry itself and the provision of capital for it are two entirely separate functions. Accountancy stands between them as one of the most important go-betweens or essential links.

3. The accountant in relation to the fiscal system is in a position of profound importance.

4. The accountant's part in social and industrial relations is of growing importance.

5. The accountant may be the promoter of exact economic knowledge.

Many people would add a sixth, viz. the accountant's part in public life as a member of committees and commissions. He makes such a useful cross-section of all industry and business life that he is able to supply a unique and needed ingredient in collective wisdom, and his recent participation was very well brought out in a recent conference, when the position of the accountant in public life was discussed. I do not propose, therefore, to elaborate it especially, because I think that all his worth in this capacity is really derived from his experience under the five heads to which I have referred.

Great as the position of the accountant has become in the first capacity, viz. as an indispensable and integral feature in the conduct of business, it seems to me insignificant to what it may be, for scientific costing in businesses of an average size is still in its infancy. I know a manufacturing business of considerable magnitude in the neighbourhood of Birmingham, employing a large number of hands, where the administrative head never has a document or paper of any kind, and keeps no records and needs no desk. He "administers" simply by walking round the factory and – looking. Figures of prices are carried in his head. Costs are non-existent. I believe that in forty years' time it will be next to impossible for such businesses to survive, save in most exceptional cases. There will be such a network of responsibility in each industry as between employers and employed, the State as tax-gatherer and the State as public watchman, that all businesses will require other numerical guides and tests than an annual balance-sheet and profit and loss account. Accountants will be very short-sighted if they do not keep a very firm grip upon these internal departments. Not only will accurate accounting extend further down into the scale of general business, but the present tentative efforts that are being made to bring it into our greatest industry, agriculture, will, I believe, with the rise of a new generation of agriculturists and the scientific missionaries from the agricultural colleges, bear full fruit, and we may expect to find reasonably kept accounts, audited in most cases, kept by all the larger farmers in the next generation.

As to his second capacity, we have found that the spread of large-scale businesses and amalgamations has increasingly divorced the conduct of business from the supply of capital. The signature of the chartered or incorporated accountant to the statement upon the prospectus is now the real solid point in the whole shifting sea of promotion methods, and we have evolved a conventional system to meet our present needs. But it is doubtful whether the function he is at present allowed to perform is as exhaustive as it might well be, and there are many aspects of the business in which future development of economic society may make publicity desirable. It is at least possible that the development of the social conscience will require the customary certificate of the amount of profit made over a period of three or four years to be supplemented by information as to the conditions of the industry in regard to its workers,

its competitive position in the whole supply, and its
part in foreign trade, with more exact details of the
actual hard capital invested than are at present
thought necessary. If selective or directional saving
increases, such guides will be essential.

In his third capacity – his relation to the fiscal
system – immense strides have, of course, been made
in the past twenty-five years. The success of an
emergency tax, like the excess profits duty, would
have been almost unthinkable without taking into
account the peculiar position of trust which the
accountant occupies. In my opinion, the reason why
it is much more difficult in Germany to secure real
efficiency in tax administration, even with an elaborate
differentiation of functions in the staff, is that the
position of professional accountancy in the community has not advanced to anything like the same
extent. I have seen in a typical revenue district in
Germany that in only a small proportion of cases has
a professional accountant come between the taxpayer
and the Revenue to the advantage of both. Their
elaborate system involves frequently sending out a
Revenue official to examine books, and it needs but
little reflection to realise that it is a poor substitute.
The prescription of a commercial code is also a very
doubtful substitute for recognised professional assistance. It seems to me that whatever elaborations
come into our taxation system in future years – complications of double taxation adjustment, sales taxes,
Rignano estate duties, capital levies, or what not –
the accountant is now so well entrenched in its day-to-
day working, and the solicitor so completely ousted,
that the prospects of accountancy remaining in the
field for all new developments are of the brightest.
The essential standard of probity is already very
high; in the future it may need to be even higher,
expressed in practice more precisely, and its obligations generally and clearly understood by all.

The vexed question as to the real duty of the

accountant when he becomes aware of points in which there is at least a doubt in favour of the Revenue, and the extent to which he may be purely passive and await investigation or official initiation, does not lend itself to public discussion. There is every *degree* of obligation towards the Revenue, and a good many degrees of recognition of such obligation. The question will have been settled by a common understanding in the next generation.

We are at the beginning of the accountant's experience of his fourth capacity, that of the independent referee or "conscience" in industrial relations. The complicated arrangements affecting the whole of the coal industry in the last three or four years under the agreement would have been quite impracticable without the assistance of the professional accountant. Whatever measure of social or industrial control comes into the conduct of industry – and it will probably be large in the next three decades – the accountant will be in it all. His presence will not necessarily be an index of continued bad faith and suspicion existing between the employing interests and the employed, for even the utmost goodwill in business relations does not dispense with accurate records and elaborate principles adjusted by disinterested skill. But he will be accepted as a natural part of all machinery for profit-sharing and variable rewards, whatever form they may take, as well as for all control in the interest of outside parties. Those developments which are presaged by the possible operations of the Food Council – the necessity for knowledge of and control of price-fixing in essential industries, the cost and distribution of food and so forth, every kind of prevention of profiteering, or of the abuse of a particularly advantageous economic position – are all hopeless without his aid.

In the fifth place, my readers will smile and say I am "barking up the old tree" when I speak of the accountant as the door-keeper of the new economic knowledge. But this is not a dream – it is an awakening truth. There is a precision of knowledge of the conditions of the whole coal industry in the last three or four years, such as has never existed in the history of industry, and without which the present controversies would be sheer Bedlam. It is not necessarily to be supposed that more precise knowledge clears up all points of difficulty and difference. On the contrary, it may provide new ones by putting into cold fact what was previously only suspicion or theory. But principles clearly seen, and no longer confused with disputed facts, can be readily discussed. This economic knowledge has come to stay. I read only recently that, in America, 143 concerns in the retail meat business were regularly supplying an economic organisation with periodical information in a standard form, and similar information is becoming available for other industries, and that, from this collective view, new light is already being thrown upon the theory and nature of profits and the relation of marginal returns to the total volume of business. The United States are well ahead of us here, but we have a habit, when they have shown the way for a few years, of "weighing in" really in earnest. I dare to prophesy that in forty years we shall have a precision of economic knowledge, due to aggregated accountancy throwing light on underlying economic theory, which is beyond the dreams (or nightmares) of ninety-nine per cent. of our present professional community.

What does all this looking forward demand from us in attitude of mind? Professional competence, of course, and the unselfish dissemination, for general use, of the best methods and solutions without loss of time. These are sufficiently encouraged by the existence of established and respected organs of publicity in our present accountancy journals. Only the individual willingness to profit thereby has to be improved. To a much greater extent we have to ensure a "forward-looking" attitude of mind, rather than a reluctant relinquishing of past conceptions, on the part of all writers, lecturers, and governing councils in the profession; a readiness to recognise that, while personal profit and status are indeed engulfed, they are engulfed in an extraordinary opportunity for the vital service of the community. If we suspect there is to be a modification of our social and economic structure, profound if not radical, then economic guidance is imperative. We may not call it progress, but, instead of dragging pettishly at its heels, let us live in its brain-pan.

XIX

You have referred to me as an expert, Mr. Chairman, and you all know the definition of an expert as "A man who knows more and more about less and less."

I was frankly puzzled to know in what possible way I could be of any help, or enjoyment, or amusement to you, because you represent a class to which we have no exact parallel in Great Britain, discharging a function in the body politic that is discharged in other ways in Great Britain, and it seemed impossible that I could talk to you on any subject as an expert, which would be of value to you. But I was told that you represented the men – the young men in the main – who knew exactly what ought to be done, but who are not yet in a position to do it. Some day – say in ten years time – you will be in a position to do it, but unfortunately there will then be another race, younger than you, who will know something different, so that what you will then do as having superior ideas may not receive that ready response that you feel you would be entitled to credit yourselves with to-day.

Well, it had been my intention, having regard to your special functions and knowledge, to say something about conditions in Great Britain, over the relatively narrow field of the supply of capital to-day, and the movement of the capital market. There are great changes coming over the whole of that problem of supply, it is coming from a different quarter, it is being secured on a different basis, and that has, of

[1] Speech at a luncheon of the Bond Club of New York, June 5th, 1930.

course, important industrial and economic consequences.

It was suggested to me, however, that I might be rather wider in my field of thought with you than that, and give you a very informal talk upon the general economic outlook in Great Britain, and so I am forgoing, in the main, the narrower topic of the supply of capital, and shall try to cover some other fields, and perhaps, therefore, risk an inadequate outline of some of the chief problems that are affecting Great Britain to-day. If they affect Great Britain, you know they will have some effect upon you, because we are so inter-linked now internationally that no industry or country can prosper or be in the doldrums without the general business world being affected in some way. You know, at any rate, that important European consequences follow from movements in values in New York. Now, I have to do this broadly and on bold lines, and I must make a rough classification. So I want to speak of three aspects: first, capital equipment and supply; second, labour conditions and supply; and, third, the thinking machine for our adequate guidance at the present. But possibly time will fail me for all three. I am reminded of the story of the man who was canvassing in a British election. He called at one house and the lady met him at the door with two children hiding behind her. Of course, at election times, children are much in evidence and invariably beautiful. After passing the usual pleasantries, the candidate got into conversation with one of the little girls, and said, "What is your name?" "Oh, Agatha." To the other: "What is your name?" "Maude." "How old are you Agatha?" "Five, sir!" "And you, Maude?" "Five, sir!" "Oh, twins, then?" "No, sir." "But you are sisters?" "Yes, sir." "But how is this – sisters, both five, and not twins?" "No, we are all that is left of triplets."

It may well be that of my triplets one may get

slaughtered. But the third one, the thinking machine, to me, at any rate, seems the most important in the group, not only in our own country, but every industrial country, and I shall deal with that first, so that it shall not be the one left out. There is a tremendous amount of mental activity going on in all of these problems. Times, I think, have never been so difficult to read so as to yield the right solutions, though a great amount of discussion is being done. I think it was Lord Oxford who referred to somebody's mind as being "a very active mind, always in motion." He said, "That is, the motion of being on hinges, not on wheels." One fears a great deal of the intellectual activity that is going on to-day is the kind that is on hinges. We have, too, a great many people with open minds, so open that nearly everything falls out. I would much rather have a few people whose minds were more retentive and close, and who did not forget that their talk one day was different from their talk of the day before. One day we are discussing the financial aspects and come to one conclusion, and the next day we discuss the aspects of foreign trade and arrive at new ones, and the third, or fiscal, question gives yet more. They are all irreconcilable, but all parts of the same problem. It is, in my judgment, of highest importance that whatever thinking is being done should be in the right direction. There is a story told of an Aberdonian who, true to his tradition, was running alongside a tram-car, and he called out to the conductor, "How much to the Town Hall?" The conductor yelled back, "Four cents." (They don't say "cents" in Aberdeen, but that is for you.) He said, "Four cents." The man did not jump on, but kept on running for about five more minutes, and he then called out to the conductor, "How much is it now to the Town Hall?" He said, "Six cents; you are running the wrong way." I think my meaning is clear, that merely to run fast is not much good unless we are running in the right direction, and my judgment is that, in the thinking now to be done, it is of first importance that the direction should be right.

There are plenty of facts – we have immense volumes of facts about large questions that ten years ago did not exist – but sometimes, when knowledge comes, wisdom lingers, and the power to interpret those facts, and the ability to see where they really lead, is the thing that demands public education. I have been impressed in America with the immense amount of knowledge the average business executive keeps on his desk. He has the latest graphs, curves and tables and devices, telling him about everything, but I have yet to learn he has to the same extent increased his mental equipment for applying them to practical affairs. It is not enough to have the material, unless you have the technique of application for each man to use in his own case. If that is true about the business executives in America, I am quite sure it is true of Australia, and of economic questions in Great Britain. We have vast masses of facts. We have sometimes been told that, if we only had the facts impartially recorded upon any industry, we should have broken the back of all industrial unrest, which arises from the possibility of that misconception that makes trouble as between capital and labour.

Well, I will only say that in the coal industry in England, in the last seven or eight years, every fact about every district, about every ton of coal, has been meticulously known in the most accurate way – every carload of it, nothing whatever left to be disputed. From the point of view of facts, the story has been complete, and yet I am afraid it has not brought that peace and understanding that have been expected. No industry in any part of the world, in any time in history, has been more fully and accurately documented than the coal industry, but unfortunately the psychological conditions behind it, and the long, painful, disastrous history of relations in the past, still have their influence on it.

Nearly everything that is happening in the economic machine is the concern of government, and most disputed questions are largely economic to-day, though they are racial too. There are very great imperial problems, all become so heavy that the governmental machine is inadequate to control or judge them. When I look at the letters I possess written by Gladstone as Chancellor of the Exchequer, two generations ago, on Budget matters, and then consider what the Chancellor has to cover to-day, the difference seems to be, not only years, but centuries in time. The whole machinery of government is overwhelmed. Parliament cannot deal adequately with one-tenth of the economic problems that are brought before it to-day.

The great problem, then, is how real thinking can be done about all these matters. It is not enough to have official staffs to make suggestions. The pressure is at the point of taking final responsibility, and leaders have to "get their heads" around every problem, and time fails them. That is the great problem of the "thinking machine." After all, the political machine, the House of Commons, is not well adapted for dealing with problems that are essentially economic, where "the wish being father to the thought" cannot be the real solution of economics, though there is a temptation always to think that the most palatable solution is the advisable one.

Economics seems to be the science in which you can hold opinions with the minimum intellectual effort. The man who would hesitate to give you an opinion on physics or chemistry, because he has had no training, will give you an opinion on an economic subject, absolutely off-hand, without any hesitation. He is ready with the proper solution, and does not for a moment consider it to be a subject in which that kind of discipline is necessary which he finds in the other sciences. The consequence is that, in

In the second place, on the capital side, the causes of our trouble are both mental and physical. There are physical causes, for, with the long suspension of normal action during the war, and with the financial difficulties since, many of our industries are not in an up-to-date condition in regard to their machinery. The industries are in individual concerns whose size and outlook are those proper to the conditions of the Victorian era, in the stage of semi-individualism.

For example, the textile and woollen industry in Yorkshire is a representative case – an industry carried on by, say, fifteen hundred firms, of small size, and many individuals. In the opinion of many, there ought to be a wholesale programme of amalgamation, involving an improvement in machinery, and new devices. But so impoverished are the individuals through crippling taxation that the old Victorian practice of "turning in" all of the surplus profits no longer supplies the capital necessary for the individual business. There are physical factors in competition with America and with Germany, which are against British progress in any case. But the recent currency difficulties bring out weaknesses that would otherwise, perhaps, not be sufficient to break the structure down. The mental difficulty is, therefore, national and internal. The international one I refer to quite broadly, as depending on price levels and the sensitiveness nowadays of the money market. I hope the day will come when the psychology of bank-rate changes, devoted to equalising supplies of capital between different money centres, will not be taken so seriously by industry as it is under the present state of affairs. Newspapers and writers often teach people, when a change is made, that it is going to have a profound effect on employment. I am thinking, not so much of the mechanics of the situation, as its psychology, and we greatly desire that, in the course of time, industry will be more philosophical about changes made for non-industrial

relations between politics and economics, "what I think is economics and what you think is politics." Well, the House of Commons is not a well-adapted machine for threshing out either the effects of economics or economic principles. It often touches but one aspect and ignores all of the other consequential changes.

To give you some notion of the devices that have been introduced to help the government machine, there has been recently set up what is called the Economic Advisory Council. It advises the Government of the day, just as the Committee of Imperial Defence might do, but it is a great experiment, and nobody knows how it is going to succeed. It has certain great political perils. For instance, take the Minister of the day bringing in a new Bill with certain economic presumptions and consequences. A member gets up and says, "Will the Prime Minister tell us whether he consulted his Economic Council on the Bill?" The answer is either "Yes" or "No." If it is "No," his position is exposed. "You have an Economic Advisory Council and you are afraid to consult them." But, if he says, "Yes," then the position is double-barrelled, for this member will then say, "What did the Economic Council say?" If they said, "No," then the Prime Minister would at once be condemned for having brought in a Bill against the advice of an entirely independent and highly experienced force of experts. If he said, "Yes," then you see at once the position of the committee would be exposed. Any member of that committee being attacked in the public Press might say, "I voted against it," and the disruption of that committee, if turned into politics, is obvious. It has been built up on the principle of representing a large number of interests, such as labour and finance and industry, with the academic people forming a sort of seasoning. What one finds, therefore, is a representative number of interests, and one cannot conceive that on any subject, other than its own supreme competence, that body must ever be unanimous. It has been meeting once a month with the Prime Minister, for some months, but it is too early to say yet whether it will be actually a body of thinkers to help the Government get through its task.

Then we have had a committee to consider industry and trade in all of its bearings, known as the Balfour Committee. It sat four or five years, and published a number of volumes, a magnificent record of achievements and failures, but now so out of date that people are despondent of finding a guidance for the developing situation. A committee has since been set up called the Macmillan Committee, to determine such questions as how far currency and finance affect industry, and how far industry is hurt by the practice of banking; whether the control of the machine is wisely administered in the Bank of England; whether, as it is so frequently alleged, for example, those in control of that machine have their minds upon the international money market and put the bank rate up without considering its effect on employment and industry. In fact, the whole question of the central control of the credit machine, especially in relation to the day-to-day conduct of industry, is under investigation to-day by that committee. Some people go so far as to say that the unemployment situation is almost exactly related to the bank rate. It is a very acute problem. A second problem for this committee is the exact connection between the London loan market for foreign issues and exports. Both theory and practice have shown in the past that, when a big loan is floated in London, it has had an immediate and stimulating effect on exports and must find its way out ultimately through the export trade. But what happens when the total issues of loans in London are great and when the price of exports is too high, so that, instead of the loan finding its outlet in exports, it must find its exit otherwise? The loan

is made; nobody knows at this time whether it is in excess of the true savings of the country. If it is not represented in exports, what happens? Either the country borrows short what it lends long or else gold flows out. There is no other intermediate course in the long run, and so this continual tussle between the interests of the City of London, independently considered as a great loan market for the Dominions and for Europe, this tussle with the real export possibilities of the country, and also related to the total savings, is continually going on. The Macmillan Committee is considering that problem too. It is also dealing with the relation between unemployment and the price level, and on that point, of course, we are all greatly exercised, in Great Britain, owing to the tremendous drop in the price levels throughout the world. It has exposed our export position very acutely. It has added one thousand five hundred millions of real burden to the National Debt. You can translate that into seven and one half billion dollars – about a quarter of the National Debt additional. This fall has made acute difficulties in the situation, and altogether we are very despondent about the position of England, if we are to be exposed to a continual falling price level. That gold problem is being looked at closely by the Bank of England, and also by such people as the "gold group" of the Institute of International Affairs. The Bank of England is being alternately praised and blamed for doing all kinds of things it has never done before, "entering the field of industry," and touching things it has been supposed to know nothing about. Criticism, heretofore, has been that it has not taken sufficient notice of industry, but now the criticism may be in the opposite direction. All the rest of the thinking is done by a few isolated thinkers, writing articles, with their haphazard effect upon public policy. Frankly, we realise we are living in unprecedented times.

reasons. Our internal position, when we resumed the gold standard, was foreseen by only a few people – it involved a much more difficult step than then appeared likely, having regard to the levels indicated by the foreign exchanges, whereas the change of real levels was at least a jump of ten per cent. We have never really recovered from the ten per cent. adjustment that was required at the time the gold standard was resumed, while on top of it we have had the general international fall which is bothering everybody.

In 1920 and 1921, when we were coming down from our paper levels in that great slump, to new levels of wages and contractual relationships altogether, if we had only deflated by another ten or fifteen per cent. at that time, we should probably have got rid of the worst of our troubles. But, as from that time, the economic mechanism tended to get set at that stage; and, following the great strike in 1926, there has been since the greatest reluctance to touch the money wage levels, and the best industrialists have said, "You must not talk about touching wages; they must stand, and industry must accommodate itself." Obviously, if the whole price structure changes, and the most important item in that price structure is absolutely a fixed quantity, then all of the margins which go to the business man, and other factors, are in danger. With high taxation, and the growing proportion which the money wage level has to the total money price of an article, that margin is to-day in some industries non-existent. People, in talking about the unemployment in the country, often lose sight of the fact that employment results wherever a man, by bringing together capital and labour, estimates he can make profit. Therefore, that profit margin is still the mainspring of the whole economic machine. If you tinker with it too much, either by taxation or the non-adjustability of the factors that enter into the total cost of production, then that

particular element disappears, and the motive force
for the mechanism is gone. That is the situation we
are reaching in England to-day, owing to changes in
price level.

In the coal industry we now have a Bill passing
through the House of Commons which has been
highly disputed, which will tend to force amalgamations in a conservative branch of industry where they
are perhaps the most difficult to give effect to
properly, but where, particularly on the distribution
side, they are most grievously wanted, if we are to get
prices to anything like a reasonably competitive basis.
The cost of coal at the pit is one thing, the cost of
coal to the consumer is a totally different thing, and
between the two there are all kinds of economic
wastes going on, and if they can, through amalgamation, achieve economies and rationalise, I think we
are going to have better times in the coal industry.
But, of course, it does involve that great question of
liberty – not as great, perhaps, as the one that is
perhaps agitating you all here – whether a business
man is going to be coerced into an amalgamation he
does not want.

In cotton we undoubtedly have a very serious
situation. I suppose the great prosperity of the textile-
machinery exporting industry some twenty or thirty
years ago was bought at the expense of a later generation, for it is quite possible to have an industry at any
given moment buying success at the misfortune of
another later on. If you get great prosperity by
vigorously exporting textile and similar machinery,
the day must come when the products of that
machinery will enter into competition with your
own. That kind of situation is the one we are face to
face with in cotton. Of course, cotton has its other
troubles too. I heard this story – I must not vouch
for it as true, although it seems sufficiently good to
be true – of a cotton employer, whose employees,
the girls, all went on strike for higher wages. He

called them all together, and said: "Very well, you shall have higher wages on one condition," and they all listened very carefully. "I am going to have you each personally examined by a committee of matrons, and any one of you who is wearing any cotton at all, and is not entirely clothed in artificial silk shall have the rise." Not one of them got it. They were all absolutely devoid of any cotton garments, and so the employer, knowing well what he was doing, dealt with that situation in the psychological, not to say physiological, manner.

In the woollen industry, the trouble is that its machinery is to the extent of perhaps seventy-five or eighty per cent. built mainly on the lines of manufacturing stuffs which, as you know, have been dispossessed in favour of the lighter and more diaphanous materials. What is more, the quantity of those materials that is being used is so much less than was in the minds of those who built those factories that, pending some reversal of feminine opinion on the subject, it does not seem as if the output of the woollen-textile industry can be anything like it used to be. They also are suffering from self-generated competition and small units.

In the steel industry we have a specially peculiar situation: A modern steel plant involves and employs so much capital that it is economic only if it is full. When half full, its costs are probably higher than those of a relatively inefficient and obsolete plant, and the only way in which one can get the real advantage of a modern plant is to have it well occupied; but, as long as you have got the obsolete and smaller plants in operation, they prevent output being focused in the modern plants, and all costs are unnecessarily high. The steel people are quite right when they say, "If you would give us the output and shut up these other plants, we could produce at prices which would bear comparison with those of other countries." The rationalisation of the steel industry is presenting extraordinary difficulty, but until it is put in four or five large territorial groups, I do not think the English steel competition will be effective, except in specialties.

In the shipbuilding industry we have enormous capacity, much greater than we can now possibly picture being fully employed even with our great predominance in the world's tonnage of shipbuilding. Therefore, under the auspices of the Bank of England, a new concern is to be set up, to be controlled by shipbuilders as a whole, to build up an annual fund charged on contracts which will produce the interest on the debentures of capital now being solicited. That capital is to be used for buying up shipyards and closing them, as the best device to bring that industry into its proper scope and form, for building the kind of tonnage we expect to need.

In transport we have been going through a very considerable revolution. I dare not let myself go on that, or I shall take up too much time. I will say, having, through prejudice on the part of many people, failed to get legal powers to enjoy the possibilities of road transport in 1922, immediately after the railroads emerged from Government ownership, a period elapsed during which public opinion had to be changed, and during that period the railroads had to subscribe large sums to public expenditure on building bridges and roads to compete with them. They had to do it, too, under our system of taxation, but public opinion realised that matters had become too acute, so two years ago, after a prolonged struggle, legal powers were given, and now the railroads have secured throughout the length of the land a fifty-fifty interest in the chief passenger transport agencies in each district, and real co-ordination has now begun. It has enabled the railways to look more closely at the branch lines, which were built in the early Victorian era, at the time when landowners and other people refused to allow the railways to run anywhere near the villages they were supposed to serve. Immediately the motor-'bus appears, it is clear that a particular line of railway no longer serves a useful purpose. Nevertheless, the company has to keep the line open for passenger traffic as feeders to its main line; but, now that the railroads have an interest in the road transport, they are able to consider rapidly the closing of uneconomic branches and the substitution of road services for them.

The introduction of the container as a means of taking goods from the top floor of a factory and discharging its contents on the top floor of a factory at the destination is going a long way toward restoring the possibilities and prestige of the railway as against the mobility and rapidity of the motor-lorry. The same kind of struggle is going on as you have in your own country. We have not perhaps, anything quite so drastic as the way goods have been moved on the Boston and Maine or between New York and Philadelphia, but we have lost an average length of haul to the road similar to yours. You have in reserve your much greater lengths, which you are still operating by rail, and which have their effect upon your railway prosperity – that long haul to the coast and to the big towns, which in our small island we do not possess – so that what to us is a crippling blow, to you is something you have been able to offset by extending the use of your remaining assets.

In this whole question of rationalisation, there are two or three very important obstacles. There is the natural conservatism of the most practical and hard-headed northern English industrialist, who says, "My grandfather built this business; my father had it; he went through bad times, and did not die out; things will be all right, without any monkeying by Government." He lives on the thought of what his training has been, and now his disposition is to consider the trade has not finally changed. He thinks rather that spring will bring it all back again than that there is a definite alteration in direction of demand. Until you get that attitude changed, such men will not attempt to consider a better unit for the purpose of amalgamation with their rivals and neighbours. In most of these industries the proprietors are of much the same standing, there is no dominant personality who can "knock their heads together" and say they have "got to come in," until they actually hit the bottom. Many of them have the banks behind them to varying extents. I cannot say the banking system is working well in this respect. What is wanting in many of these industries is for the banks to waive their particular obligations, which they are so anxious to keep intact and at full value in their balance-sheets. They are reluctant to allow a few healthy bankruptcies – until that happens, and until there is a way of cleaning the situation out through financial action, there is a kind of riveting of the *status quo*, each bank feeling that it must come out, on amalgamation, on the front line, and, until the banks are ready to change their present manner of doing business, I am afraid we need not look to them to get the real push and incentive. Is the Government, then, to do it? They say, "God forbid! because that means bureaucratic influence; the situation will be worse." The Bank of England has said in effect, "It is not actually our business, but rather than that the wrong people should do it, or that the whole situation should go by default, let us have a look at it." They do not desire to be in industry permanently, but if they can precipitate action as a catalyst, partly by prestige, and, if need be, by using a little money to help other people – a sort of decoy duck like a dollar stuck in the bottom of a collection plate – if they can do that, it is their bounden duty to try it. So the Bank of England is departing somewhat from that tradition of aloofness from industry which has been so sacred to them, and are going out into

the field, meeting the groups of people and trying to
pursue this kind of rationalising action. They have
formed a new company, called the Bankers' Industrial Development Company, where the Bank of
England has a share-holding with the other large
financial institutions, so that in doing this job they
can act as a kind of precipitant to bring it about.

My time fails for me to say what I desired about the
changes in the "capital supply." But I have told you
already that the effect of the general strike, and the
coal stoppage after it, was to make people feel that
money wages must not be touched, though it is quite
obvious to everybody that there is an anomalous
relation in wages between the two classes of industry –
those which are sheltered, corporation employ-
ments and public utilities and the like, each with a
relative monopoly in its own area – and wages that
have to meet with direct competition in export
against Continental levels. The difference is important. Is there any reason why a skilled engineer
should come out of his works with a wage of 57s. 6d.
a week, and ride to and from his work in a tram-car,
the driver in front of which, for much less skilled
work, is getting £4? That is the kind of difference
found between the sheltered and unsheltered
industries.

The first thing to be put right is that the total wage
fund should be redistributed between the two classes.
When the price level changes materially in a product
of which eighty or ninety per cent. is wages, if the
money wage level is sacred and cannot be touched –
mark, I say the money wage, for I am anxious to
maintain the real wage intact – if the money wage
is to remain intact, the margin is gone unless there is
a change in individual output. If you regard the whole
of our products and service as being one great heap
produced by the nation, and we all come to it for our
real subsistence, then if any individual group is entitled to a larger amount of commodities from that

heap, through a stationary money wage and a fall in prices, the strongest and earliest get there, and take away the larger quantity that their money entitles to, so that the weaker come along later and find it is all gone. That is unemployment. If you have a certain quantity to be distributed in a certain way, and the next minute somebody can come along and take more than that agreed amount, then somebody else goes short. There has been the closest relationship between the level of real wage per hour and unemployment. If you work out the money wage and express it in terms of real wage through the price index and you correlate that to the amount of unemployment, the relationship between the two for some years was close and striking.

But only one man here and there can be got to realise it, and price level exponents are still regarded by the business man as academic. If his part is in the daily conduct of running a business, it seems as if he will think of any other cause but that. Fortunately, I think recent events are so striking that he is coming to believe there is something in price level questions after all.

This unemployment problem has been accentuated by two things. The dole system, while it has been often abused, of course has been highly essential on a humanitarian ground, but has had several other unfortunate consequences. It started as a *bona-fide* insurance scheme, and for a long time the men were being paid back the money that they had contributed, but, when unemployment had lasted much longer than had ever been contemplated, and the State had to continue to add to it from State funds, of course it took on a new aspect, and the recent efforts of the Labour Government have been unfortunately to make it easier to secure. Instead of that economic pressure which in all history has been the means of getting away from depression, so that the man unemployed will take the next best job, in the next best place, at the next best wage, rather than stop altogether, now he can sit down where he is and continue to call himself a "miner" or other calling. The temptation for him to think that things cannot get better until he gets the same wage as he always did before is overwhelming. It, therefore, certainly needs policies that did not previously exist. If you have anything here in the way of a commission for dealing with the future of unemployment, bear those particular lessons in mind, and make the eligibility of unemployment insurance on much stiffer ground than we in England have it. There is one ideal that must not be forgotten. British industry, despite all handicaps that it has had, has succeeded in employing till recently a million more men than it employed ten years ago. Emigration to the Dominions and other parts of the world has been less, and we have had a matter of one hundred and fifty to two hundred thousand men more coming into industry than are going out each year. We have succeeded in absorbing all of those men, but have not succeeded in getting rid of the original block of a million unemployed at the end of the war; or you can say we have employed that relative million, but have not employed the hundred and fifty thousand new people each year. But the fact remains till lately we have employed the larger number, despite this unemployment problem. The surplus is a result of the change in the birth rate in the later 'seventies, and also a change in the number of people born during the war, so that, after a year or two, we are entering into a new state of industrial population, in which the numbers going into industry will be about the same as the numbers going out; and we shall reach a relatively stable industrial population, which may have very important consequences upon the absorbing power of industry. At any rate, it is sufficient of a statistical change in the problem for us to look forward to better times.

It is quite easy for a business man, for a financial

man, to realise that this or that ought to be done, and what kinds of readjustment ought to be made – I myself would do three things if I were Mussolini or had the power to act, but they are all of them politically impracticable. They simply could not be got through any political council. (We have not of course to deal with the United States Senate, but that may be another story later!) But the three things essential are the proper adjustment of the present wage fund between sheltered and unsheltered industries; the second, a proper resiliency of the real wage with the total production of the country, and money wage with price level; and the third thing is a proper and immediately sound way of central international control of gold supplies and credit, and you know what a long, long, painful journey that is going to prove before it becomes effective. These steps are "impracticable," because in economics you can only go as fast as the people will let you, and, when they themselves are intending to fight for their own welfare, they can only fight to the extent to which they can realise the interdependence of these problems. Therefore, the willingness to face solemn and bitter facts is the crying need to-day. We shall all have a job to do ourselves in connection with it.

XX

FINANCIAL ASPECTS OF INTERNATIONAL RELATIONS[1]

Without our realising the change that has taken place, certain aspects of international relations have recently come into prominence which are of financial origin. Quite different have been the causes that have divided men in past centuries. At one time, religious differences were the main cause of political trouble. Then followed dynastic allegiances and alliances. Such alignments seem entirely out of date. Later, came questions concerning the extension of the franchise to those elements in the community which should be allowed to participate in self-government. That, too, is a matter of history, a battle that has been won.

When we look at politics to-day, however, we find that, at bottom, practically all political questions are economic, and now we are coming to the point where we can perceive that most economic questions have to be handled, if we are to get to the root of them, by severe statistical methods.

I went some years ago into an embassy – you will readily identify it if I add that I have forgotten the country it was in, and I must not say the country it was for, and the time is unspecified – but, anyway, a member of the embassy looked up from his papers and said, in a rather despairing tone of voice, "This diplomacy business has all gone to the dogs. When I was trained for it, I thought I knew my job. I knew the history of these people and their politics and their

[1] An address delivered at a luncheon given by the Academy of Political Science at the Hotel Astor, New York City, June 2nd, 1930.

balance of power and all that business. But now what do we have to do? We are given all this black magic of finance and economics and currency. Here I am asked to say whether I think this Government is going to get hold of the currency successfully, or whether they will get thrown out in the process, because that will make a difference in their foreign relations. I really don't know the top from the bottom of the subject. I was never trained in this filthy science." He was quite petulant about it. But he did express a very great truth. He did bring out the point that the problems of international relations to-day are in their most difficult aspects mainly financial.

The other aspects are still with us, but very successful provision has been made for dealing with them on a large scale on an institutional or organisational basis. We have a world court which is ready to handle problems and disputes about international law, boundaries, and the like. We have the representatives of the nations meeting at Geneva regularly for common action and common discussion, and we are able to bring together quite quickly – as quickly, at any rate, as diplomatic action will allow – special conferences to deal with major problems like naval and military disarmament. Thus most of the elements of difficulty in international relations have been provided for satisfactorily.

There is, however, at present no organisation for dealing systematically and scientifically with the financial strains that come upon the world's economic social organism, and we have not even improvised one yet, except for something that I shall refer to at the end of my remarks. If these economic questions are to be dealt with in the same spirit, in the same way as the others, new qualities of thinking are wanted on the part of those who take part in international discussions, who regulate international relationships, and particularly those who interpret them, through the Press and otherwise, to the people.

Have you reflected – I do not doubt you have – that
in the history of every branch of knowledge, particularly in its process of becoming an exact science,
there has come a crisis, a period when tremendous
advances have been made, and when it has seemed
worth while for all brilliant energies and super-
abundant wealth to be poured into one particular
field in order to achieve great things in a short space
of time? One can pick out the golden age, the real
drive, in each of the different sciences like chemistry
and physics, electricity, and so on. To-day is the day
when of all times the drive is wanted in economics.
We want to realise that we cannot have too many hard
and brilliant thinkers in that field, too much money
poured into research, and too much patient, self-
denying effort to advance the science; for this reason:
the advances along other lines of progress and invention and the like have been so enormous that the
machine, the complication, has completely outgrown
our old mechanism for thinking about it and handling
it from the economic standpoint. You often hear it
from the pulpit, and I have no doubt it is perfectly
true, that we have made such immense advances in
our control of nature, and of material things and
their production, that science has outrun moral
progress, until man is not equal to the task of controlling what he himself has created.

However true this may be of the moral nature, I am
quite certain that from the point of view of economic
thinking it is absolutely true. Things have become so
rapidly complicated, and differentiated to a degree
that we never knew before, that the existing machine
of economic thinking is neither fine enough nor does
it embrace a wide enough range of people to tackle
the job properly.

There is, however, an immense, but less obvious,
difference between the problem confronting economic science and the problem facing the other
sciences. Chemistry, physics, and the like will make

immense progress, provided that you have great inventive genius making discoveries and launching them upon the world. It does not require any special effort to accommodate yourselves to the new discoveries, to assimilate them and to use them. You do that without becoming an expert in any way or adjusting your method of thought. You may have to accustom yourself to the speeding up of the motor (and the way in which we can accommodate ourselves within a generation is really marvellous), but this adjustment does not require any new intellectual equipment.

In the case of economics, progress has to have two wings before it can fly. First of all, an immense advance is, wanted on the side of the inventor, the thinker, the man who reasons out the new solution. But he is absolutely powerless unless there is a general raising of the standard of appreciation of economic matters on the part of the multitude, unless there is a much higher degree of public appreciation of economic truth. The best inventions, the best schemes, can never work, except through the will and the wishes and the powers of hundreds of thousands and even of millions of people. In no other way can new economic advances really achieve their object. There is, therefore, an immense distinction between economics and other fields of knowledge. It means, of course, that we need to have the power to subdue our prejudices and to realise that, in the long run, things may be different from their immediate aspects, either pleasurable or disagreeable.

Nothing has an uglier look to us than reason, when it is not on our side. We all like to feel that we have right on our side, but we are always predisposed to think that the thing that is pleasant and immediately profitable is the thing that is right. We all of us go a long way in our prejudices before we drop them. I am not pretending, of course, that in economics, any more than in anything else, we can expect the world to be free from prejudice. We might just as well ask for the moon. All that we can ask is that we shall know how to handle people's prejudices and to have as few as possible ourselves.

Hazlitt, I think it was, said that no wise man can have a contempt for the prejudices of others, and he should always stand in a certain awe of his own. The truth of the matter is that economists particularly are apt to think that the data of economic or financial science are really things and facts as they are. That is true; but, equally, what people think about the facts, however wrong and however misguided, is very often to be included in economic data, and is very often more important in the short run than the study of the things as they actually are. People will run just as fast from a dog, if they think it is a wolf, as they would if it were actually a wolf, and if people have a misconceived notion of economic facts, that is just as important in the data of economics as the facts themselves.

There is no field in which the facts are more difficult to realise, not from time to time and from moment to moment, when our attention is drawn to them, but all the time, as part and parcel of the furniture of our minds. We can all see a fact when it is pointed out as a piece of analysis or theory at the moment, but to go into our office the next day and have it as part of the actual working mechanism of our minds is unusual, even to-day.

The fact of the matter is we tend to treat financial operations as though they were self-contained and independent, as though they were an end in themselves. That is partly due, of course, to the fact that men are in finance by itself, or they are in industry by itself, and do not necessarily connect up the two all through. When a man has completed a financial operation, the payment of a debt, the floating of a bond, whatever it may be, the thing is done so far as he is concerned. But that method of thinking, if we carry it into our politics and international relationships, will lead us very, very far astray, because in the last resort (and this I believe to be indubitably true) finance is only a mode of speech. It is only a method of moving goods and services and changing their ownership. It has no meaning whatever in itself. You can sign many pieces of paper and pass them over in exchange for other pieces of paper and make entries in ledgers, and that in itself means nothing. Behind it all is something physical; objects of human enjoyment and necessity are being moved or created, or their ownership is being changed.

If we reflect, therefore, that an apparently complete financial transaction is very often only the beginning of an intricate chain of economic consequences, then we shall realise that the financial aspects of international relations have an immense importance. We have only just begun to study them. We have to get behind the figures that are in the international ledgers; we have to consider the work that is behind them, the leisure that is behind them, the millions of men who are set in motion by the things that have been financially done.

Until about twenty years ago, international finance could be likened to a kind of viscous fluid that moved according to the particular laws of comparative cost in the flux of goods and international trade. But something very important has happened in the last twenty years. In many respects rigidity has increased because of the construction of very deep channels of international finance in which we force large currents of trade to flow. On the other hand, accompanying this greater rigidity, there is a much greater fluidity. Forces act with much greater suddenness and thoroughness and are much more disconcerting than they were, in the field of finance, carrying with them all the while consequential elements in the real work and actions of men. That means, therefore, that all old thinking upon these subjects may just as well be scrapped. We have to rethink them all from first principles, which is always difficult, particularly for second-rate minds that are in first-rate positions. It is singularly difficult for the practical man, especially if he is proud of being a practical man, because, as you know, the practical man is the man who practises the theories of thirty years ago. To most men, experience, as Coleridge says, is like the stern lights of a ship, which illumine only the track it has passed.

We want, therefore, a new world of ideas. Now, "it is only the wise who possess ideas. The greater part of mankind are possessed by them." Every age has the advantages of what has gone before in material possessions. We wish that every age could start where the other left off in its moral attainments, but every age has to learn its Garden of Eden all over again. Every age has to have its own failings and learn the old lessons over and over again. Very often, too, in so far as economic thinking is based upon prejudice, every age has to do its own re-learning. I say this because there lies before us the duty of rather disagreeable hard thinking, and – what is more, and worse than that – the subduing of a good deal of prejudice and preconception.

Now, what are the elements that I have referred to as making the whole question of international relations more difficult to consider along the old lines? The elements of rigidity? We have a number of fixed international obligations of a very extensive kind, not only extensive in time, therefore setting up a fairly permanent state of consequential economic effects, but also extensive in amount in relation to the resources of the countries affected. These fixed international obligations are the result of reparations, war debts, and repayment of war debts. They are the result, also, of commercial loans made to foreign countries on a very large scale. Oh, but you say, there is nothing new in that! Great Britain was a great creditor country before the war. But, indeed, there is something very new about it. Between Great Britain, in the nineteenth century, and the Dominions and America there was the relationship between a relatively advanced industrial country and a developing country. They were in complementary stages. But, to-day, vast commercial obligations are being fixed as between countries that are to a great extent on an equal industrial plane, that is to say, nations which are making the same type of goods in the same way for the same kind of markets. Loans assume a completely new aspect when a country, by its financial operations, is immediately equipping another country to be competitive with it in the world's markets and not merely complementary. Nor is payment expected in classes of goods and materials which are quite different from those the lender produces.

These are new elements, and they force large currents of foreign trade, of work, and of capital, into particular channels, very deep and very permanent.

I said, however, that there was greater fluidity. Finance was formerly viscous. It did not move quickly or sensitively. Now it is extremely sensitive and fluid. There is to-day available on the desk of every business man an international knowledge of stock markets that would never have been dreamed of before the war. Time was when the Yorkshire textile woollen manufacturer, having made so much in profits during the year, thought of nothing but turning it back into his business or perhaps putting it into some neighbouring enterprise. To-day he has on his desk a list of stocks in New York, in Paris, in Berlin, and estimates and all kinds of analyses of these stocks by experts, so that he is able to appreciate that the yield in one country is greater than the yield in some other place; and what money he has left after paying his taxes can more quickly, and does more quickly, by these agencies, find its way into the market which can give the biggest return.

There is, too, a process of economic attraction or valuation entirely different from any that existed before. In the old days, a man would invest money in a concern or a stock according to what he imagined was the capital value of the dividends received, and he would compare that with some other dividend; but after a while he got beyond that stage. He looked, not at the dividend, but at the earnings, and to-day in your papers one finds the earnings regularly quoted per share as a matter of course. That was not so in the former years. Men knew little about earnings and cared less, but to-day they buy far less on dividends, and far more on earnings.

Then the third stage was reached when the prospective investor – with such financial omniscience as was granted to him by an unrelenting Providence – looked, not at the valuation of earnings to-day, but at the valuation of earnings as they might be in years to come.

Then came a fourth stage, and a very important one, of which you had considerable knowledge in New York last year. The third stage was where the investor bought the stock because he thought that satisfactory earnings would accrue to him in due course if he held the stock up to a certain time. He was prepared to hold it until then. Now, however, has come a form of valuation which is based, not on the expectation of holding stock over a long period, but on a much more poker-playing kind of valuation in which nobody supposes anybody is going to hold for that time. It is only a question of who can clear out at the right moment with the largest profit. I am not saying this in jest; it is an absolute psychological fact that economists must take into account. In a developing country, if this particular psychology is very prominent, it has the effect of creating a tremendous magnet or market for quick and ready money all over the world. Consequently international relations are complicated by the flow of funds to the markets which at particular times exhibit this particular attraction to the greatest extent.

A third fluid factor is the fact that there are large short-money markets in the world; not many, indeed, but extremely sensitive to competing money rates. These money rates, swinging large masses of short money back and forth, would not affect the body politic or economic very much if their effects would stop there. But their effects do not stop there, because, under the gold standard which obtains throughout most of the civilised world, these oscillations entail, for the protection of the particular countries affected, certain definite acts, which very often incommode a country, or make it feel irked by something that has happened elsewhere.

The bank rate is put up in London. Some short money in New York is called back. The next thing I hear is that a New York stock broker has been shaking his fist in the face of a Britisher and telling him that all the New York trouble is due to London. Or money begins to vanish from London and go to Paris, and at once people look around for political reasons, and all kinds of allegations and recriminations are at once put forward, and very often supported, by interested parties, and they may, indeed, on occasion be true.

Here you have, indeed, new and quite fruitful sources of difficulty in international relations. They involve these questions of gold and its influence on the international situation, but all of these things, by and large, sooner or later bring with them effects upon the trade movement of the countries concerned. They all of them are interwoven and intertwined in a most inextricable way.

I do not just remember the exact allusion, but most of you who have read Darwin's *Origin of Species* will recollect his rather entertaining statement that, I think it was, the prevalence of a certain kind of clover

in a certain locality was due to the number of maiden
ladies who lived there. The proof was very obvious.
The existence of this clover depended upon the
prevalence of humble bees which depended on the
absence of field-mice, which would destroy their
combs and nests, and the prevalence of these field-
mice depended upon the presence of a larger or
smaller number of cats, and the presence of a large or
small number of cats depended upon the number of
maiden ladies that would keep them! Perhaps I have
added the last stage – I cannot remember!

I rather astonished a British audience the other day
by trying that chain of reasoning on them. I said,
"The more rich people there are in America, the
higher will your taxes in Great Britain be." They
looked at me in astonishment, and then I gave them
the *Q.E.D.* of it in this way; first, that the more rich
men there are in America, the more will be attracted
to this particular type of speculation that New York
enjoys, the holding of stocks with very low current
yields for future enhancement of value, which only
men with resources and money can do; and, secondly,
as that creates a situation which attracts a great deal
of short money, people in England see a certain
amount of profit to be made either in speculating
themselves or else in supplying the call money with
which it can be done, and that has the effect of drain-
ing London of a good deal of its liquid resources;
and, thirdly, London in self-protection, under the
gold standard, puts up the bank rate; but, fourthly,
the putting up of the bank rate, more or less according to circumstances, has a restrictive influence on
British trade. People are not as enterprising as they
might be, there is not as much extension of business,
there is more unemployment. Fifthly, when there is
more unemployment, the cost of the unemployment
insurance, or "dole," as you know it, goes up.
Finally, when that goes up, then of course taxation
goes up, and there you are ! There is probably a flaw

in my argument, but I don't see it, and I know you
can't!

The old type of politician – and, when I say
that, I include a great many men who are in power
to-day – is not in the habit of thinking of financial
transactions as having inevitable economic consequences in trade and business activity. He has no
conception of anything else but the actual figures
that are used in settlements. The fact that there are
all kinds of varying things behind those figures is
almost lost to him.

For instance, I was reading only last week, coming
over here, the final outburst of that fierce and lambent
spirit, Clemenceau – a very noble book in many ways,
but exhibiting in a very marked degree the particular
trait that I have in mind. Speaking of the damage
that was done to the treaty, Clemenceau says,
"France will only have recovered 133 milliards of
francs out of 915 milliards the war cost her. The
Young Plan gives France 18 milliard 737 million of
gold marks, which, added to the amounts received
so far, would mean total receipts for France of about
22 milliards of gold marks." Then he says, in a burst
of bitterness, "From 136 down to 22, or one-sixth of
the agreed amount!"

Clemenceau never realised, right until the day of
his death, the differences in the real values represented by these marks and francs that he is talking
about, never looked at the vast changes in what is
meant in human effort by a gold mark or by a franc,
in what is represented by that expenditure of 915
milliard francs and what is represented by the repay-
ments.

The truth of the matter is that the more you talk in
fixed terms of money, the more you are concealing
the fluctuating total of human effort that lies behind,
and these late months have shown us that, every
month, the position of debtors of all kinds has become more and more onerous, and the position of

those who have borrowed on debentures, and the like,
more difficult.

We are to some extent ruled by a measure which is
more capricious than any human mind, be it male or
female, and there is no kind of business skill which
can derive a profit from prognostication bearing
upon this subject. It is capricious beyond the mind
and the will of man.

The relations between countries now, in their
financial aspects, deal with the interest on debts;
with the surplus we have available for investment
abroad and the control of that surplus, or the leaving
of it to chance; with tariff walls and the possibilities
of recrimination and retaliation and even of suicide;
with questions of double taxation which act like a
tariff against the free flow of capital, and the elimination of double taxation which often calls for very
far-sighted and statesmanlike renunciation on the
part of individual treasuries in the budgets of debtor
and creditor countries; with the short money peril,
and all the political allegations that may attach to it.
All these things are important, and they all require
study if we are to get international relations upon the
new basis for which I ask.

Necessary for that object are, I imagine, four things.
The first is some recognised institution or clearing
house of thinking, through which these problems can
be tackled. I am, I hope, not foolish in believing – at
any rate, I think I have the support of my colleagues,
right and left, in my belief – that the Bank for International Settlements is the beginning of an institution which can develop into that kind of international
brain for a more co-ordinated and thought-out
control of these vast and hitherto capricious forces.

The second thing – and this is where this Academy
comes in – is the need for two classes of workers:
first, those who create solutions, the hard, analytical
thinkers, the economists, the men in finance and
business; and, second, the larger educated public

who will not create solutions, but will create a demand for them, together with the will to put them into force and not to obstruct them. A novel solution must not be condemned merely because it is a new thing. The public must realise the peril, and therefore, I will not say, snatch at any straw, but try any reasonable expedient and experiment that is put before them.

In this respect we want a greater harmony between the executives and the detached thinkers. I know how annoying it is to be sitting at the head of a business doing your job and realising that you cannot get straight at the goal. You have to go sometimes a step or two backwards, owing to the condition of your business or the times or the prejudices and characters of those with whom you work. The detached thinker, whether professor or not – he may be a journalist – says, "Why doesn't this executive get on with this principle? He understands it. He seems very slow about it." That kind of thinking about each other, that kind of criticism, does not make for the best, most harmonious, results.

I think it was Lord Avebury – Sir John Lubbock – a great Englishman of the Victorian era who was a very prominent banker of his day and also a great student of scientific subjects, who used to be known in banking circles as "that great scientist," but was referred to in scientific circles as "that wonderful banker." When I am sitting with my financial colleagues, they always look suspiciously at me and refer to "the academic pundits" as if I were one of them. When I am sitting with my "academic pundit" friends, they always refer to "you business men." As a result, I am, perhaps, a little sensitive on both sides.

What we want are the doers and the informers, the people who will cut coal at the face and the people who will carry it where it is wanted behind, and I appeal to this Academy to produce both kinds.

Remember that this job requires, not only self-renunciation, but great patience. In any attempt to work through men's prejudices, for the ten per cent. of the time that is needed to arrive at the right solution, ninety per cent. is required to negotiate and coax people to accept it.

The third thing that we want is to put the cost of this kind of research – which is so important to business and without which business can never be regulated on a really scientific and humane basis – upon business. It should not be supported merely by the energies and the pockets of a few theorists. It is a matter which so vitally affects business that business ought to see that the job is being properly tackled by properly accredited people, and that, for the effort put in, something is shown in the way of results. Otherwise it will drag on, and if we get a twenty-five per cent. fall in the price level in the next five years in Great Britain or elsewhere, as we have had in the past five, you can say "good-bye" to Young Plans, Dawes Plans, and anything of that kind. It will upset all the contractual relations of the whole world.

And the fourth thing is to demilitarise finance. International finance is so full of military terms of retaliation and aggression that, if we are to think of it on a scientific basis and to do justice with it in the cold light of the study, we must, at any rate, take such terms out of it, because the feelings of men are so often energised by the terms they use. They talk warlike terms and begin to feel warlike. Let us get these military terms out of the whole vocabulary, and then we can have a dispassionate study.

We have a custom in England of having a report returned each term from the school on the progress of the students in the particular subjects during the term. It is always a day of keen anticipation, for both the pupil and his parents, when this report arrives home during the holidays. Our little fellow, ten years of age, had a report from school in which a discerning teacher wrote against one of the subjects, "Does as little homework as he can, and hopes for the best!" If over the field of international finance we were to write that report, I think we should about get the truth. We expect to blunder into the truth without doing the hard apprenticeship of thinking and experimentation that it really demands. That is the task of the Academy.

My concluding word is this: One of your own wise men, Santayana, said, "Nothing requires a rarer intellectual heroism than willingness to see one's equation written out." Now, if it requires heroism on the part of an individual, it certainly requires super-courage on the part of a nation. The Anglo-Saxon nations, the English-speaking nations, have never been without that courage. May they show it in this very trying day!

INDEX